The Unique Partnership

BRITAIN AND THE UNITED STATES

The Unique Partnership

BRITAIN
AND THE
UNITED STATES

ARTHUR CAMPBELL TURNER

PEGASUS · NEW YORK

A Division of The Bobbs-Merrill Company, Inc., *Publishers*

The Unique Partnership: Britain and the United States is a part of the "America's Involvement in the World" Series, under the general editorship of Lloyd C. Gardner, Rutgers University

Author and publisher wish to thank the following for permission to reprint:
Homage to a Government, P. A. Larkin, The University, Hull, England.
To America, Concerning England by Sir William Watson. Permission granted by George G. Harrap & Company Ltd., London.
"Time, You Old Gipsy Man" from *Collected Poems* by Ralph Hodgson. Permission granted by Mrs. Ralph Hodgson; St. Martin's Press, New York; The Macmillan Company of Canada; Macmillan London and Basingstoke, England.
"The Question," copyright 1916 by Rudyard Kipling from *Rudyard Kipling's Verse, Definitive Edition* by Rudyard Kipling. Reprinted by permission of Mrs. George Bambridge; A. P. Watt & Son, London; and Doubleday & Company, Inc., New York.

DEDICATED to those three people who have meant most to me for precept, example, encouragement and much else: to the dear and kind memory of my mother, *Robina Arthur Miller Turner* (18 February 1890–21 April 1969); to my father, *Malcolm Turner* (born 29 August 1889), who has discussed the following pages with me most scrupulously and helpfully at every stage; and to my wife, *Netty,* who has contributed much, including the title, to the book.

Dr. Arthur Campbell Turner believes that he has the best possible base for writing on Anglo-American relations, in that he is strictly neither English nor American, but Scots. Born in Glasgow on 19 May 1918, he was educated at The High School of Glasgow (the school of Bryce, Campbell-Bannerman and Bonar Law), the University of Glasgow and Queen's College, Oxford. He gained his doctorate on the Berkeley campus of the University of California. In the course of a transatlantic career he has taught at Glasgow, Toronto and Berkeley. He has published extensively, mostly but not exclusively in the field of international relations. He was one of the founders of the distinguished Riverside campus of the University of California, where he is Professor of Political Science. Other publications by Professor Turner include: *The Post-War House of Commons* (Glasgow, 1942); *Free Speech and Broadcasting* (Oxford, 1944) [The Blackwell Prize for 1943]; *Mr. Buchan, Writer: A Life of the First Lord Tweedsmuir* (London, 1949); *Scottish Home Rule* (Oxford, 1952) [The Blackwell Prize for 1951]; *Bulwark of the West: Implications and Problems of NATO* (Toronto, 1953); *Toward European Integration* (Ottawa, 1953); *Control of Foreign Relations* (New York, 1957) [part-author]; *Pakistan: The Impossible Made Real* (Ottawa, 1957); *Tension Areas in World Affairs* (Belmont, California, 1964) [with L. Freedman].

Contents

Chapter One

HOW SPECIAL IS THE RELATIONSHIP?

On 5 March 1946 at Westminster College, Fulton, Missouri, Winston Churchill made a speech that was to be famous, and constitute a historic landmark. It was the speech in which he warned of the breakdown of the wartime cooperation that had subsisted with the Soviet Union, and pointed out how Eastern Europe had ceased to be an area of independent nations and had become a Soviet sphere. "From Stettin in the Baltic to Trieste in the Adriatic, an iron curtain has descended across the Continent." [1]

However, the principal theme of the speech, though this has been less noted both by contemporary journalists and by history, was a different, though related, subject: the special relationship between Britain and the United States, and advocacy of intensifying this relationship, and endowing it with continuing instruments of cooperation, as the only means whereby the safety of the parts of the world possessing free institutions could be maintained. The development of this argument fills approximately half of the whole address, and Churchill specifically identified it as "the crux of what I have travelled here to say." In these passages the phrase "special relationship" occurs again and again. Perhaps—as with the

[1] Randolph S. Churchill, ed., *The Sinews of Peace: Post-War Speeches by Winston S. Churchill* (Boston: Houghton Mifflin Company, 1949), p. 100. The speech, "The Sinews of Peace," occupies pp. 93–105. Spelling has been modified in some succeeding quotations to conform to American usage.

more vivid and famous phrase "iron curtain" itself—it is possible to show that the phrase had been used by others earlier. Nevertheless, its repeated and emphatic use by Churchill on this occasion launched it effectively on the world and from that day on secured its wide circulation.

Churchill said, "Neither the sure prevention of war, nor the continuous rise of world organization will be gained without what I have called the fraternal association of the English-speaking peoples. This means a special relationship between the British Commonwealth and Empire and the United States." Again, "Would a special relationship between the United States and the British Commonwealth be inconsistent with our overriding loyalties to the World Organization? I reply that, on the contrary, it is probably the only means by which that organization will achieve its full stature and strength."

Churchill recommended specific programs of cooperation— "the continuance of the intimate relationship between our military advisers," leading to standardization of weapons and manuals of instruction, and the interchange of officers and cadets; joint use of bases all over the world in possession of either country; and permanent defense agreements between the United States and what he (rather confusingly) called "all British Commonwealths." [2] Some of these things, it may be noted in passing, came into being after a fashion in the following years, but the fashion in which they came into being was one that Churchill did not foresee. Nor could it have been welcome to him, for it involved a downgrading, not an enhancement, of the role of the United Kingdom. The ANZUS Treaty of 1951 was a tripartite security treaty among the United States, Australia, and New Zealand. The United Kingdom was ignored. The North Atlantic Treaty of 1949 and the organization which was built upon it constituted a long-term defense structure involving the United States and Britain,

2 Churchill, *Sinews of Peace*, p. 98. The use of "Commonwealth" as a synonym for an individual "Dominion" (a term still in use in 1946), rather than as a collective expression for all British countries, appears to have been adopted here by Churchill from an American journalistic use. He employs it in this sense twice in the speech. Though it appears in the official name of Australia (*The Commonwealth of Australia*), the usage seems only to add further confusion to an area of terminology already sufficiently complex.

but only in common with other ten, later thirteen, partners; and its area of concern was limited to Europe.

Going beyond this, Churchill envisaged a day when practical cooperation would conduce to the fusion of the two communities: "Eventually there may come—I feel eventually there will come—the principle of common citizenship, but that we may be content to leave to destiny. . . ."

In his peroration he returned to the theme, beginning the final paragraph of this celebrated speech "Let no man underrate the abiding power of the British Empire and Commonwealth"—not, in fact, a very accurate piece of prophecy.[3] Despite the current difficulties, he said (in a sentence oddly full of negatives), "do not suppose that . . . half a century from now, you will not see 70 or 80 millions of Britons spread about the world and united in defense of our traditions, our way of life, and of the world causes which you and we espouse." Anglo-American cooperation was the essential guarantee of security. "If the population of the English-speaking Commonwealths be added to that of the United States with all that such cooperation implies . . . there will be no quivering, precarious balance of power to offer its temptations to ambition or adventure. On the contrary, there will be an overwhelming assurance of security."

There are a good many points of commentary suggested by the quoted passages of this speech. Some of these points and their implications will be discussed on later pages. Churchill was one of the most devoted adherents who ever lived of the thesis of the supreme desirability and importance of the cooperation of Britain and the United States—appropriately enough for the son of Lord Randolph Churchill and Jennie Jerome of New York; and in this speech he gave perhaps his

[3] It would have been difficult to underrate! Setting aside the Commonwealth, it would have been unlikely for anyone in 1946 to prophesy correctly how *short* a life the Empire had before it. With Churchill the wish was no doubt father to the thought, but many good judges made the same mistake. E.g., Professor Sir Denis Brogan told us in 1967, "I myself showed no foresight on this question, for in a book I wrote during the Second War, *The English People*, I greatly underestimated the degree to which the declining imperial structures in Asia were being shaken in ruins, and I ignored the process in Africa almost entirely." Brogan, *Worlds in Conflict* (London: Hamish Hamilton, 1967), p. 124n.

most famous and forceful, though far from his only, expression to these ideas.

His launching of the phrase "special relationship" (together with that of "fraternal association") does suggest an appropriate query with which to begin a discussion of the relations of these two countries in recent decades. Granted that Churchill on this occasion seems to have intended by the phrase chiefly a more intense relationship, which he was advocating, rather than a description of what already existed; in practice, as adopted by others and used from then onward, the "special relationship" usually refers to something taken to be inherently different, unique and distinctive in the relationship of Britain and the United States. How far is this true? The assumption, even if it turns out on examination to be valid, is at any rate worthy of examination; the more so since, in the decades since Churchill spoke, skeptics, with some justification from the course of events, have sometimes argued that there is nothing at all special, in the contemporary situation, in the relationship. It is no more and no less than the relation of any two sovereign, independent states with each other. Such an opinion has been, in some cases, advanced sincerely. On other occasions it seems to have been put forward merely in a nervous attempt to placate and erase the suspicions of other states, jealous of what, in their eyes, was manifestly an international bond unlike others. On this matter—as on many others—General de Gaulle was only the most articulate and forceful exponent of a widely held opinion.

To make a moderately obvious point first, it is naïve to suppose that there is such a thing as a standard or normal relationship between two sovereign states, to which all relationships between pairs of states more or less conform, with the sole exception of the Anglo-American relationship. To illustrate by analogy, the relationship between any two individual human beings is a unique case, whether it is casual or intimate, or anywhere on a scale in between; nor is it to be defined fully even by placing it at the proper point on such a scale.

Much the same thing must be said of the relations between states, and between the nations which they embody. Every bilateral international relationship is a special case, deriving its nature from the history and culture of the two countries and the nature of the contacts between them. Any sophisticated consideration of the relations of states must soon proceed beyond the idea that there is a standard relationship, with certain divagations from it.

The course of historical events has resulted in the world's being full of curious, interesting, particular relationships between states. Public men pay tribute to this circumstance every time when, on some occasion of international importance being celebrated that involves their country and some other one, they give voice to the cliché about "the traditional friendship between our two countries." It is a banal and oft-repeated remark; but, like many such, it also usually contains its grain of truth. There are hardly two states on the face of the earth between which there have not been, at some point in the past, some common amicable links of a noteworthy sort. Even India and Pakistan have a common past to look back upon that covers considerable stretches of their history.

Yet, just as with the relations of individuals, the necessity to classify phenomena if we are to think about them at all makes the bald statement—that each relationship is unique— unhelpful, and merely a necessary preliminary *caveat*. The fact is that these are essentially matters of more and less, with infinite gradations; and that such situations change with the passage of time.[4] But broad classifications are not only possible and helpful, but essential. And it remains broadly true, subject to this and that qualification, that certain cases of relationship between nation-states *are* exceptional and stand out from the ruck of run-of-the-mill international politics.

[4] An attempt to put actual numbers on these terms "more" and "less" has been made in recent years by members of the behavioral school of political scientists by means of analysis of transaction flows and other data. Bruce M. Russett made a study of statistical aspects of Anglo-American relations in his doctoral dissertation, published under the somewhat over-general title *Community and Contention: Britain and America in the Twentieth Century* (Cambridge, Mass.: The M.I.T. Press, 1963).

It can, however, be argued convincingly that, even if the special relationship is not quite a mid-twentieth-century invention, at any rate the number of cases of that kind has very greatly multiplied in recent decades and even in the last few years.

In the nineteenth century, international politics substantially consisted of the interrelations among half-a-dozen major European powers, all by courtesy, and to a large extent in their mutual judgment, equals. The multiplication of special cases (along with a vast increase in the actual total number of relationships) has come as a consequence of two main events: the rise to power of the United States; and the dissolution of imperial systems which embraced much of the earth.

Even the quickest glance round the contemporary world suggests the extraordinary richness and variety of possible affiliations and attitudes between nation-states resulting, in the main, from these two causes.

The breakdown of empires (great land empires at the end of the First World War, great overseas empires in the aftermath of the Second) has meant a multiplying of states, many of which are trivial, unstable, and would be, lacking international intervention or external aid, nonviable. The disintegration of empires always creates a brood of states whose relations with one another and with the former nucleus country (if it survives in some form) are in some degree out of the ordinary. This may not mean warm friendship. It may, on the contrary, mean a special touchiness, sensitivity, and rivalry. The wars of the epigoni of Alexander the Great formed the stuff of the history of the Near East for many long years, and the successors today of the great empires of the recent past seem little certain to be more pacific in their relations. But at any rate there is an inherent peculiarity in the situation.

Even more significant, perhaps, has been the effect of the United States—itself the most striking of all products of the breakup of an empire. The immense size of the United States and its geographical isolation have largely shielded it from the normal pressures of international life, and have enabled it to a quite unusual degree to conduct a foreign policy based on its own will—on actual decisions and on choices among alternatives (including isolation—the preferred alternative during most of the life of the Republic).

If the United States has an especial bond with Great Britain, it has particular affinities (or fancied affinities, and these too can affect policy—often disastrously) in a number of other directions, too.

The most obvious case of this kind is Russia. Tocqueville rightly and presciently noted that there is a strange parallelism in the situations of Russia and the United States—the two giant countries of enormous land-mass and enormous potential, each rising as it were on the periphery of Europe, from which they derive their cultures, and each developing variant versions of it. The present position of the United States and the Soviet Union is that of two states so different in degree from other states as to be really different in kind. No historical situation persists forever, but in the present and well into the future these two states exercise a uniquely dominating function, and are inevitably in some degree aware of a guarded, suspicious, and reluctant kinship, even if only based on the strange twinned roles in which fate has cast them.

Some Americans, some of the time (even if few Russians), have felt disposed to put it higher than that. Eisenhower wrote in his war memoirs, "In the past relations of America and Russia there was no cause to regard the future with pessimism. Historically, the two peoples had maintained an unbroken friendship that dated back to the birth of the United States as an independent republic. . . . Both were free from the stigma of colonial empire building by force. . . . Twice they had been allies in war. Since 1941 they had been dependent on each other for ultimate victory over the European Axis." [5] In this passage, as Reinhold Niebuhr acutely comments, Eisenhower "expressed not a unique, but a typical American viewpoint when he sought to emphasize the affinity between ourselves and the Russians with an implied barb at our British ally." [6]

[5] Dwight D. Eisenhower, *Crusade in Europe* (Garden City, N.Y.: Doubleday and Co., Inc., 1949), p. 457.

[6] Reinhold Niebuhr, *The Structure of Nations and Empires* (New York: Charles Scribner's Sons, 1959), p. 21.

But the kind of viewpoint represented in this passage, however widely held at the time, was a monster of political misjudgment, sired by geniality out of ignorance. The idea of either Tsarist or Communist Russia being free of the stigma of empire-building by force is a charming though implausible fiction.[7]

Toward China, the potential third giant power of the world, the United States has powerful and ambivalent emotions, based on the considerable size of Chinese populations in West Coast cities, and the fact that for almost a century China was the area *par excellence* of American missionary effort. The shock was correspondingly great when China became Communist in 1949. Latin America is also the beneficiary, or at any rate the focus, of a rather special set of U.S. attitudes and of U.S. interests—in both senses. Ever since the revolt of the Latin American nations against Spain and the promulgation of the Monroe Doctrine, the United States has sedulously cultivated the idea of the Western Hemisphere, including both North and South America, as a kind of world in itself, an area of happier politics, free from the vices of the Old World, from which both the United States and the Latin American nations (in flattering imitation) had broken away. The idea of common Pan-American interests was institutionalized early in this century when the Pan American Union was founded with its headquarters in Washington, D.C. However, it has always been easier for the Latin American nations to see that they have a common interest *opposed* to that of the United States, than it has been for them to perceive common interests which embrace theirs and those of the United States also. The earlier Pan-American movement was anti–United States. The idea of the solidarity of the American republics is largely a U.S. myth, or perhaps one should say an ideology as Hans Morgenthau defines it—i.e., an attractive political idea, with *some* basis in reality, propagated for political purposes neither quite hypocritically nor quite guilelessly.

Into this pattern Canada never fitted well—a Western

7 Perhaps a faint uneasiness on this point is indicated by Eisenhower's insertion before "empire building" of the word "colonial"—which presumably means, in this context, "overseas."

Hemisphere state, but not a republic, not free of European imperial bonds, not a member of the Pan American Union, or, later, the Organization of American States. Again, with Canada the relations of the United States are unique. Canada is the largest trading partner of the United States, has an enormous common border, and is forever present as a third element in any discussion of the relations of the United States with Britain. And not only with Britain—for President de Gaulle, in his 1967 visit, merely brought sharply to the forefront of attention an old fact, that Canada is a plural country, with two major European mother countries (as well as many others).

As for France, the American equivalent of Macaulay's schoolboy certainly knows of Charles E. Stanton's "Lafayette, we are here," with its implications of historic association and reciprocal obligation; he may even know that "Good Americans, when they die, go to Paris." (It has been an international economic fact of some importance in recent years that they go there in such numbers when alive.)

The "elective affinities" of the United States are not, however, confined to states with which it has genuine historic links. For a number of years, at any rate—and perhaps even now— the United States was felt (by Americans) to have a strong sympathetic bond with India, stemming from American dislike of imperialism, particularly in its most striking—i.e., the British—manifestation; and India was the most spectacular of all colonial situations.[8] Americans, unofficially, and the U.S. government, officially, had chivvied the British government for so many years about India, that there was inevitably a faint tinge of regret when, after 1947, it was demonstrated all over again by neutralist India that gratitude is not a characteristic of governments, and in particular that that old Harrovian, Mr. Nehru, could get along at least as well with that

---

[8] American liking for India was presumably the reason for American dislike of Pakistan; for Pakistanis (inexplicably) disliked and distrusted Indians, including Mr. Nehru. This aversion was no doubt accentuated by the signal incapacity of the glacial founder of Pakistan, Mr. M. A. Jinnah, to pretend that he was "just folks" for the benefit of visiting American newspapermen. (But the failure was almost equally enraging to British journalists, and to Lord Mountbatten, the last Viceroy.)

other old Harrovian, Mr. Churchill, and his colleagues in Britain, as he could with the government in Washington. Times change; and the U.S. government, in its present preoccupations, seems to make less than formerly of its supposed affinities with India.

France, itself like Britain the seat of a great world-language, has its own nexus of special relationships. It has one with Quebec, the one great French colony of settlement, and so—an uneasy one, as recent history has shown—with Canada as a whole. France has also been extraordinarily successful in maintaining close links with most of its former colonies in Africa, for which it has procured special status as "Associated States" of the European Economic Community. The six countries of the Common Market (and of the Coal and Steel Community and Euratom) clearly also constitute a group whose relations with one another are of a degree of intensity and closeness going far beyond the normal.[9]

Also within Europe one might note the association of the Scandinavian countries as constituting a sort of subsystem within the international system at large; as so also do Spain and Portugal. The Communist-bloc countries of Eastern Europe have with one another, and with Russia, a very special relationship indeed. Another closely related group is to be found in the Arab countries, held together by the common memory of a great Islamic past, by the Arabic language, by geographical propinquity, and by hatred of Israel.

Manifestly, Britain, as the former center of the largest of empires, is the focal point of a remarkably large number of international relationships of an unusual kind. All former British colonies, whatever their racial composition and wherever they are located, retain some ties with the former metropolitan power, whether of economic interest, kinship, sentiment, or culture. The proportionate importance of each of these

[9] It is relevant to point out that the Six (France, West Germany, Italy, Belgium, the Netherlands, and Luxembourg), which have found it so much easier to approach some measure of integration than have other European states, cover almost exactly the area of Charlemagne's empire. And the unity of European culture is the result of most of Europe's having earlier been within the Roman Empire.

items varies from one case to another, as does the remaining strength of the total link. In some cases these ties continue to be very strong, even in the absence or virtual absence of formal bonds. As one would naturally expect, it is where the factor of kinship, of being of common racial stock, is greatest, that the bond remains at its strongest. Thus, in the United Nations debates and votes during the Suez crisis of 1956, Australia and New Zealand were the only countries that went along with Britain all the way. Canada and South Africa, though still both members of the Commonwealth, did not.

This cursory survey of a number of unusual and anomalous international relationships has conducted us, in the end, to a reconsideration of our starting point—the relationship of Britain and the United States; for the original thirteen colonies were, after all, the greatest colonies of settlement ever peopled by the British Isles, and the relationship with them is only one particular case of the kind of thing mentioned above—that is to say, the relations between a former imperial power and an area once a colony, now independent. Viewed from the British end, in this twilight of the British imperial day, the matter of the relationship with the United States is not greatly different from the matter of relations with several other countries where also there is the common factor of blood and language. While no two of the cases are precisely alike, there is a strong family resemblance—from the British point of view—in the cases of Australia, New Zealand, Ireland, and the United States. Australia is largely (though not, since the postwar immigration from central and southern Europe, wholly) of British stock. New Zealand is wholly British in population.[10] Ireland, formerly a part of the United Kingdom, then of the British Commonwealth, now (since 1949) an independent republic, was both a colony of settlement for a comparatively small number of British people, and itself a "mother country," making a great contribution to the population and to the politics of the United States.

Of these several countries, whose relationship to the United

[10] A good deal more British than Britain, in fact.

Kingdom shows some points of similarity with that of the United States, all are certainly in a *closer* relationship to Britain than is the United States. The same formerly could have been said also of South Africa, whose white population is 40 percent British; and it might even, with some hesitancy, be said now. But closeness is not the same thing as significance, and in British eyes the relationship with the United States is overwhelmingly more important than with any of these, for the obvious reason that the United States itself overwhelmingly exceeds any of these other countries in importance. This kind of coldly realistic judgment has also been exercised at Britain's expense: to Australia and New Zealand, at any rate, the United States is obviously now more important (from the point of view of defense at least) than is the United Kingdom.

As a working hypothesis, to be qualified in detail later, the commonsense judgment must be permitted to stand. The United States and Great Britain do bear a relationship to one another that is different in kind from those between other pairs of states. This would not matter greatly if they were minor states whose mutual attitudes and policies were of very little concern to anyone except themselves. But one of the pair, the United States, though not, as it has discovered, omnipotent,[11] still "doth bestride the narrow world like a Colossus" —still, in other words, disposes of an enormous superiority in wealth and power over any other state whatever. The other, Britain, though much diminished in power from its former status of possessor of a worldwide empire based on predominance at sea, is still of importance. The two countries have a common origin and much of their history, before 1783 and in the twentieth century, has been history experienced in common. It was possible for Churchill plausibly to write a four-volume *History of the English-Speaking Peoples.* The

11 It is now almost two decades since Sir Denis Brogan, in the most famous of his articles, in 1952 warned against "The Illusion of American Omnipotence." (Reprinted in *American Aspects* [New York: Harper and Row, 1964], pp. 9–21). However, in the climate of opinion of the early 1970s, it is also perhaps worth noting that the article also said "Belief in American invincibility is, on the whole, a good thing."

extent to which they act, or fail to act, together, has determined the history of the world in the past, and may still do so in the future.

The political possibilities inherent in the relations of the two countries are well and truly grounded in racial and cultural affinity. This remains true even after nearly two centuries of American independence. Indeed, the relationship is clearly closer in the mid-twentieth century than it was in the first century of independence. Sir Denis Brogan, wisest and most knowledgeable of commentators on Anglo-American affairs, has said that "it is not only that in many fields American power has replaced British, but, despite all the nonsense talked about it, the linguistic and cultural relationship between England and America is not paralleled in any other pair of relationships." [12] H. G. Wells made an accurate point when he noted that, in British eyes and in British usage, the American is *not* just a citizen of a foreign state. "Like many Britons Mr. Britling had that touch of patriotic feeling towards America which takes the form of impatient criticism. No one in Britain ever calls an American a foreigner." [13] (American journalists work hard at maintaining the myth that Britons instead call Americans "colonials," but this extraordinary notion has, so far as the experience of the present writer goes, no basis in fact. They call them "Americans"— a class apart, neither quite British nor alien.)

Clearly, the foundation of the special relationship between Britain and the United States is demographic, the basic fact that to a considerable extent the population of the United States derives from British sources. To define with complete accuracy what that extent is, is apparently out of the question; it is undetermined, and in all probability undeterminable. Nevertheless, some general indications are possible, and the question is fundamental enough to be worth some attention.

The question bristles with difficulties, and the statistics are

12 Brogan, *American Aspects*, p. 71.
13 H. G. Wells, *Mr. Britling Sees it Through* (Atlantic Edition; New York: Charles Scribner's Sons, 1926), p. 457.

inadequate. We are looking for the kind of answers that could only be provided by the full inquisitorial panoply of the contemporary state, with regard to periods when such methods—fortunately for the citizens of both countries in those days—had not yet been invented. Thus—to mention some of the gaps in our knowledge—no immigration data for the United States was collected by government before 1820. So far as the British end is concerned, general statistical totals of immigration and emigration were published by the Board of Trade from 1873 onward, but they contain many uncertainties (e.g., how many of the passengers outward bound from Britain were really British, and how many had originated in some other country, and were merely passing through Britain?). By a peculiar irony the first complete year for which detailed particulars were recorded of each passenger embarking from Britain (including country of origin and intended destination) was 1913, which happens also to be the *last* year of large-scale emigration from Britain.

There are other large unknowns. Movement of population between the United States and Canada, especially in the prairie states and provinces, involved large numbers, running collectively into millions; yet, over much of the period, such movement was not only uncontrolled, but imperfectly recorded. Accuracy in assessment is almost as impossible as it is in estimating the flow of migration between Scotland and England, or Scotland and Ireland.

The British contribution to the population of the United States was made possible by the extraordinary fecundity of the people of the British Isles in the years between the sixteenth and the early twentieth centuries, a fertility which enabled them not only to maintain a high rate of increase of the home population, but to create through emigration whole new Britains in several distinct parts of the globe. This achievement was a very important thread in the skein of modern history, determining the destiny of lands distant from Britain in all the generations to come. Of this seeding of the world with Englishry the founding and development of the United States is the most important result. Perhaps because northwest Europe is not typically thought of as an area of "population explosion," and in fact has not been such for the past fifty years, this vast movement has not always been appreciated for what it was. The author who, perhaps, has drawn attention to it most eloquently is C. E. Carrington, in his *The British Overseas.* Carrington pointed out that "ten generations ago, in the age of Shakespeare and Ralegh," the population of England and Wales is estimated to have been about five millions, that of Ireland a little over a million, and of Scotland a little under. "These seven millions (whom we shall call for brevity the British race, without implying thereby any ethnological doctrine) have increased and multiplied, in ten generations, about eighteen or twenty times over. Their descendants now [14] number about 140,000,000 of whom rather more than half live in the United States and not much more than one-third in the British Isles. This is physically the most remarkable phenomenon in British history." [15]

Professor Carrington's book—one of the most fascinating published on its subject—is concerned with the history of the British Empire. Yet, by way of comment on the title, it is relevant to point out here that most of the English (and the other British peoples) overseas never went to British possessions overseas, contributed nothing to their strength, and do not live now in the British Empire or Commonwealth. The British Empire would no doubt have been a stronger and more durable phenomenon had they done so. In fact, they followed the path of their choice: most of them went to the United States, and they or their descendants live there now. The promise of American society, of living in a country where the standard of living for the average man was higher than it was in other countries and where the air was imbued with the suggestion of infinite possibilities—more specifically, the availability of plenty of land, the facts of low taxes and of political and social equality—these outweighed for most emigrants any considerations related to staying under the British flag. For the

---

[14] Written in 1950.
[15] C. E. Carrington, *The British Overseas: Exploits of a Nation of Shopkeepers* (Cambridge: Cambridge University Press, 1950), p. 499.

Irish, of course, who for part of the period formed the pre-dominant part of the stream of emigration, the prospect of getting away from the British flag was one of the great at-tractions of the United States.

Though the statistics lack precision, the general picture is quite clear. Between 1815 and 1940, it is estimated, approxi-mately 28 million persons left from the British Isles to settle in other English-speaking lands. Of these, about 58 percent went to the United States—by far the largest number going to one destination. About 18 percent went to British North America (the various colonies that in the course of time be-came united as Canada); about 10.5 percent to the Australian colonies and New Zealand; 7 percent to South Africa and elsewhere.[16]

The marked preference for the United States as a destina-tion does not obtain prior to 1840. Between 1815 and 1840, of the approximately one million emigrants who left the British Isles, 499,000 went to British North America, 417,000 to the United States, and 58,000 to Australia.[17] But in the period 1841–1850, 429,044 went to British North America and 127,124 to Australia, as against 1,094,556 to the United States. In every successive decade down to 1910, at least a million and a half persons emigrated from the British Isles to the United States, reaching still higher levels in the decade 1881–1890, when 2,546,018 went, and in the decade 1901–1910, which saw the record with 2,714,188.[18]

In the last few years before the outbreak of war in 1914 there was a significant shift upwards in the proportion of British emigrants electing to go to British Dominions rather than to the United States. This appears to have been due to the fact that, at the instance of Joseph Chamberlain as Colonial

16 John Bartlet Brebner, *North Atlantic Triangle: The Interplay of Canada, the United States and Great Britain* (New York: Columbia University Press, 1958), p. 109n.

17 Carrington, p. 501.

18 H. C. Allen, *Great Britain and the United States: A History of Anglo-American Relations (1783–1952)* (London: Odhams Press Limited, 1954), p. 103, citing S. C. Johnson, *Emigration from the U.K. to North America, 1763–1912* (London, 1913).

Secretary, in the first decade of the twentieth century for the first time some guidance and information services were made available to would-be emigrants by the British government. Before this time (apart from some schemes of emigration to Australia in the 1830s), emigration had been a matter of private enterprise in the most absolute sense. Whatever the causes, the shift in destinations is easily perceptible. During 1891–1900 British Dominions received only 28 percent of the total British emigration, the American magnet still being that much the strongest. However, during 1901–1910 the proportion exactly doubled, to 56 percent, and in 1911 it rose to a record 80 percent, and remained high down to 1914.[19]

The figures of emigration from Britain in the years immediately before 1914 run at such remarkably high figures—not much under three hundred thousand every year—that it is tempting to speculate how different would have been the population picture in Canada, the United States, Australia, New Zealand, and South Africa if the First World War had either never happened at all, or had broken out some years later. Another decade of such emigration would, for example, have increased significantly the size of the populations of all the Dominions, and would have had important political effects through increasing the British share of the population in Canada and South Africa, as well as in the United States. It would also have perceptibly reduced the population of the United Kingdom. (A. J. P. Taylor has pointed out as "perhaps a cynical consolation" that the number from the United Kingdom killed in the war—three-quarters of a million—was less than the loss by emigration would have been if it had continued at the same flood rate throughout the years 1914–1918.) [20]

The relative importance of the different destinations of

---

[19] R. C. K. Ensor, *England 1870–1914*, Vol. XIV, *The Oxford History of England* (Oxford: Clarendon Press, 1936), p. 500.

[20] A. J. P. Taylor, *English History 1914–1945*, Vol. XV, *The Oxford History of England* (Oxford: Clarendon Press, 1965), p. 120. The phrasing shows Mr. Taylor is aware the point is a little far-fetched: common sense suggests that being in Calgary, or California, is perceptibly different from being dead at Cambrai.

the stream of emigration varied at different times, just as did the proportionate share of the total contributed by the different peoples within the British Isles. The great period of Irish emigration begins in 1847, and is the result of the famine caused by the failure of the potato crop. Emigrants from Ireland to the United States in 1845 numbered 44,821, in 1846 they numbered 51,752, but in 1847 the figure leaped to 105,536. It stayed well above the hundred thousand mark each year for several years, reaching an extraordinary peak of 221,253 in 1851, until in 1855 it subsided to 49,627, and continued at about that level. Between 1860 and 1914, considerably more immigrants came to the United States from Great Britain (England, Wales, and Scotland) than from Ireland, though the number annually from Great Britain never passed a hundred thousand apart from three years (1870, 1882, and 1888), and never by much.[21]

The Irish emigration to the United States was different in several ways from the emigration there from other parts of the United Kingdom. It was exceptionally numerous, at any rate over a certain period of years, and it tended to create whole Irish sections of certain cities—for the Irish were seldom pioneers on the frontier of settlement. Also, unlike Scotch, Welsh, and English emigration, it was not furnished by an excess of population which still provided for an increase in the numbers remaining at home. The Irish population was permanently lowered. It never achieved again, and has not yet climbed back up to, the pre-famine, pre-emigration level. The population of Ireland was eight million in 1841, 6.5 million in 1851, 5.7 million in 1861, and slowly dwindled toward the somewhat more than four million at which it leveled off early in the twentieth century. This was (and is) all the more remarkable when one remembers that this was a time of rapid population increase throughout Europe. For the emigrants in their new land it was a different story. "Within a few years the Irish in America were far more numerous than the Irish in Ireland had ever been." [22]

21 See *The Statistical History of the United States from Colonial Times to the Present* (Stamford, Connecticut: Fairfield Publications, Inc., 1965), pp. 56–57. Tables given there are based on census reports.

22 Carrington, p. 502.

The most serious question, in the present context, posed by Irish emigration to the United States is the question whether it is to be reckoned a factor strengthening the link between Britain and the United States, or a factor militating against it. The argument that it weakened tendencies to amity and co-operation between the two countries is certainly at first sight the stronger. The Catholic Irish—and most of them were Catholic, the Ulstermen being only a small fraction of the Irish emigrants—carried with them to their new country bitter memories of hardship and oppression, and these became politically important with great rapidity in the United States, and stayed important a long time. The Irish rapidly gained control of a large number of big-city political machines, and formed a bloc of immense importance within the Democratic party. The effect was to strengthen and embitter anti-British feelings in the United States that already existed dating from the Revolutionary War and the War of 1812. Policies of an isolationist and anti-imperialist (particularly anti-*British*-imperialist) kind became the common form of American foreign policy. This bias was clearly diminishing in importance by the end of the nineteenth century, but it did not disappear; it was still significant at the time of the repudiation of the Versailles Treaty, and in the 1930s also.

By the middle of the twentieth century, the anti-British zeal of the increasingly prosperous sons of Erin had become a rather distant memory, and had ceased to be an appreciable factor in the making of policy. The grandson of "Honey Fitz" Fitzgerald, however much he enjoyed the warm welcomes on his one visit as President to the ould sod of his ancestral Ireland, was after all one of the more pro-British of Presidents.

In any case, all along there was something to be said on the other side of the ledger. The Irish spoke English, spoke and wrote it with skill and vivacity, and since they did they reinforced the English-speaking character of the United States. They had their political differences with England, but they inescapably formed part of, and contributed greatly to, its culture, which was their culture also. In politics, apart from their zeal for conspiratorial violence, chiefly to be demonstrated along the Canadian border, the Irish had learned their political methods from the English, the political structures they were familiar with were English structures, and so in a sense they underlined and strengthened the Anglo-Saxon tradition in American life. The Irish may have been unwillingly participants in the patterns of English life and culture, but the result of the centuries that had passed since the Conquest was that they had no other cultural patterns; English politics, English language, English culture, even if enrichened, modified, and in a measure changed by Irish overtones, Irish accents, were still basically English; and as time passed the differences between the Irish and the original English style diminished. John F. Kennedy resembled a good deal more closely the man who was Prime Minister during his Presidency, and his distant relative by marriage, Mr. Harold Macmillan, than Honey Fitz did Lord Salisbury or H. H. Asquith!

In the course of the nineteenth and early twentieth centuries the numerical predominance in the population of the United States of people who, or whose forbears, had come from the British Isles, was considerably diminished. At the end of the colonial period that predominance was certainly very great. Though we lack reliable statistics, estimates indicate that, at the time of the achievement of independence, the American people was composed, as to sources, of 82.1 percent English, 7 percent Scotch, and 1.9 percent Irish, making a total from the British Isles of 92 percent.[23] The next highest figure was that of people of German stock. Between 1830 and 1885, immigrants came mostly from northwestern Europe and from Germany. Then, beginning about 1880, there came the "new immigration," of people from Italy, Poland, Russia, the Baltic States—in general, from southern, southeastern, and eastern Europe. By 1900 arrivals from these sources were far surpassing the numbers from the "older" sources.[24] For

---

[23] Allen, *Great Britain*, p. 104. Other sources give somewhat lower figures for those of British stock.

[24] Donald J. Bogue, *The Population of the United States* (Glencoe, Illinois: The Free Press, 1959), pp. 350–52.

example, in 1907 (a year in which 79,037 immigrants arrived from Great Britain, and 34,530 from Ireland), the total from northwestern Europe was 190,000 and from Germany 38,000; but from the "new" sources there arrived, from Poland and other central European sources 338,000, from Italy 286,000, from Russia and the Baltic States (then part of Russia) 259,000, from other eastern and southern European sources 89,000. Thus in 1907 immigration from these new sources totaled just under a million.

During the roughly eight decades of high-level U.S. immigration, many other elements than those just mentioned also, of course, contributed: Chinese and then Japanese immigration on the West Coast, Mexican immigration across the border. None of these, however, rivaled in numbers the "new" European immigration. With the imposition of the quota system based on national origins, which prevailed from 1921 to 1967, the total flow was restricted with the objective of favoring the "old" as against the "new" sources. Depression and war in the period 1931–1945 cut down the flow to a trickle.

All these national sources have contributed over the years to the cultural diversity within the United States; and though the "melting pot" has operated to produce Americanization and to enable the United States to function as a national state, there seems good reason to believe that cultural traits, in the broadest sense, persist generation after generation.

It is difficult to find an authoritative estimate, indeed *any* estimate, of the proportionate importance, in the racial makeup of the American people at the present time, of the different sources from which it has been derived. (Statistics of the country of origin of the foreign-born are available in census reports; but, with the marked decrease in the percentage of foreign-born as part of the total population, this tells us very little in recent censuses.) Specifically, what has become, in the almost two centuries of American independence, and in the face of massive immigration from many sources, of that original Anglo-Saxon numerical predominance? Official statistics are silent on this matter; and scholars seem understandably reluctant to attempt an answer where the answer is bound to be uncertain, and the subject-matter perhaps one that would cause controversy. It can also be argued, but not altogether convincingly, that, with intermarriage between individuals belonging to different groups proceeding for many generations, such figures would be virtually meaningless.

In his systematic and immensely valuable treatise on the history of Anglo-American relations, H. C. Allen in the end on this topic concludes only that "a closer examination [of the history of immigration] demonstrates that the English-speaking contribution to the American population was by far the biggest of all the national and racial groups. The next largest groups after the British are Germany, Italy and Russia. . . . Thus the lead of the English-speaking group is proportionately greatest in the earliest years, so that, given the high rate of natural American increase, the number of Americans of British stock has always exceeded all other groups; this lead has never been lost, and, with the coming of the quota system, is unlikely ever to be lost." [25] (But, of course, the quota system has now been abandoned again. What the long-term results may be it is not possible, at this point, to predict—too little time has elapsed since the abandonment.)

We find one courageous attempted estimate in C. E. Carrington, whose calculation is based as follows. He takes 7,500,000 as a round figure of the total of emigration from the British Isles to the United States between 1830 and 1930. In the same period, as he says, we know that about 2,300,000 emigrated to Australia and New Zealand, and increased naturally to 8,000,000. (Australia and New Zealand provide such a useful basis of comparison because in their case non-British immigration was so small in this period it may be neglected statistically.) "Assuming that the 7,500,000 British emigrants to America increased at the same natural rate as those to Australasia and that the resident 'British' population of the United States increased at the same rate as the population of the British Isles, the total population of British origin in the United States in 1930 would be about 75,000,000." [26] The calculation appears grounded in reasonable assumptions. Since the population of the United States according to the 1930 census was 122.78 millions, the percentage of the population of British origin would be 61 percent.

The consideration of the importance of the British strain in the American people does not stop short, of course, with the mere question of numbers. The qualitative, or functional, aspect is also of immense importance. The British immigrants (though not the Irish in their first or second generations) tended to occupy a more than average proportion of professional and administrative posts, to fill more than their numerical share of upper-level posts in commerce, and, in short, to staff the upper rather than the lower end of the social scale. A far smaller than normal proportion of British immigrants could be classified as unskilled workers. It was a society in which the British, or British-descended, immigrant was peculiarly well qualified to flourish and, since he usually brought with him some talent, he typically did flourish. As has been frequently pointed out, it is doubtless more than mere coincidence that nearly all Presidents of the United States have been of British stock—the exceptions are Van Buren, the Roosevelts, and Eisenhower.

It is symptomatic of the dominant position which people of British stock have held in the United States that this group has never been identifiable as a group. This apparent paradox is easily explicable. The various "hyphenated" Americans—Italian-Americans, Japanese-Americans, Mexican-Americans, or whatnot—have been identifiable because they stood, in however small measure, a little apart from the mainstream of American life; the Irish-Americans, too, in respect chiefly of their religion, not of their language. But it would have savored of the absurd to speak of "Brito-Americans" or "Anglo-Americans." The Anglo-American tradition is, at any

---

[26] Carrington, *British Overseas*, p. 511. But he cautions in a footnote: "These are indications not statistics. Another estimate by Julian Huxley and A. C. Haddon (*We Europeans,* 1935) gives the percentage of persons of British origin in the population of the U.S.A. as 53.6% in 1920."

rate, if one includes within it the important Irish element, the central tradition, the central cultural pattern of American life. Its power has never been concentrated in a pressure group or at the command of one party more than the other; it has, rather, been diffused throughout America, permanent and omnipresent.

Common British and American racial origins then, can be demonstrated in large measure to exist. This has, among other things, given the two countries their greatest bonds, the common language and literature. As we move from discussing demographic questions to other matters, however, we move from an area where it is at least possible, with some caution, to speak in numbers (for the numbers, even if not wholly reliable, are available), to areas where this is not possible, and where, in consequence, the qualitative and the impressionistic necessarily hold sway.

However, the linguistic question is too important for us to allow an absence of hard statistical data to cause us to refrain from discussing the matter at all. In some sense, the common language is the basic thread of Anglo-American communion, the basis of "the Anglo-American community." Bismarck, not given to incautious and sweeping remarks, said towards the close of his life that the most important fact in the world was that the British and American peoples spoke the same language. The fact remains, however many jokes are made concerning it; and, for some reason, the subject seems to lend itself readily to jokes. Anyone who has crossed the Atlantic in either direction is familiar with the classic cases of ambiguity—the biscuits-crackers-cookies routine, the suspenders-garters-braces routine, the bonnet-hood-trunk-boot routine, not to mention the laborious scatological anecdotes which turn on the fact that some terms, innocuous on one side of the Atlantic, are conversational depth-charges on the other ("knock," "pecker," "closet," to name a few). These ambiguities are real, but not very important. They are scarcely more obtrusive than the differences in idiom, vocabulary, and usage that may be found in different regions within the same nation. It is true that linguistic variations may occasionally spell political perplexity—the two different meanings of the verb "to table" constitute the best-known example; [27] one sometimes suspects it is so well known because there are, in fact, so few examples of the kind to be cited.

One may concede the point that a common language may sometimes lead to the assumption, in some transatlantic dialogue, that there is more identity of views and purposes than really exists; this is especially true when one takes into account the subtler nuances and implications of language, rather than gross ambiguity. However, to make much of this is surely to mistake a minor matter for a major one, to regard a qualification as the same thing as a rebuttal. The plain, enormous fact is that the British and American peoples do speak and write (write more than speak, indeed, as is always true in such cases—linguistic variations are at their maximum in the spoken word) the same language, and that this tremendously underlines their sense of kinship, eases their cooperation, and reinforces the sense that their relationship is unique.

Under earlier technical conditions there might have been some question whether the two versions of English would not draw further and further apart with the passage of time, as Latin diverged, after the fall of the Western Empire, into the various Romance languages. Improbable even in the nineteenth century, this seems impossible today, in the world of radio, television, and international film. At the same time, it is worth noting two consequences of present conditions that seem inevitable. First, none of these technical instruments (radio, television, film) conduce by their nature to precision and logic in language, as the written word does. Rather they favor broad effects, slogans, vogue words, the confounding of words and phrases between which distinctions ought to be observed. This process may be observed in action every day by those who have ears to hear.

The second point is that the maintenance of a common

[27] *To table* meaning, in British usage, to put on the agenda for early action; in American usage, to postpone consideration of indefinitely.

tongue is likely to be increasingly a matter of that common tongue being dominated and shaped by those who speak it and write it in the United States. The traffic is not quite all one way; but certainly the effect of power, of numbers, of technology, tends to be in the direction of procuring British acceptance of American idioms, American names for things new and old, rather than the other way round. (It is true that many Americans find a certain snob-appeal in knowing, and using, British expressions.) This tendency frequently causes alarm and despondency, not to say, fury, in Britain. Witness the following letter to the editor of the London *Sunday Times,* which certainly does not voice only one man's view:

> I feel obliged to express my contempt for the increasing number of Americanisms which are creeping into our language.
>
> When reading a piece of good English prose one experiences an overwhelming sense of nausea at the recurrence of, for example, "Mr. So-and-so plays it cool," or at the use of that supremely undignified word, "movie," in preference to "film." While agreeing that language is constantly changing, I can find no justification for the indiscriminate substitution of legitimate English words by substandard American equivalents.
>
> This alarming trend is but a visible sign of the American influence pervading every facet of our daily lives. While we are unlikely to become the 51st state, the frightening thought persists that in a few years we will be talking about the Great British Dream, the all-British boy, holding Thanksgiving parties and eating blueberry pie.
>
> I despair that I am young enough to witness the degradation of it all.[28]

It is only fair to note that to this letter the following reply was made:

> It will be a long time before we have "The Great British Dream" or the "All British Boy" inflicted upon us, but I can assure Thomas Maxfield . . . that the language situa-

28 Letter from Thomas Maxfield, Ealing, *Sunday Times* (London), 27 April 1969.

tion is much worse than he thinks. Consider words and phrases like these:

On the level, graft, corny, beef, bellyache, pushover, phoney, deadpan, zany, date, blues, scram, wisecrack, rate (to be worth), in the doghouse.

Then there's showbiz, know-how, dog tags, through (finished). We have adopted get lost, but not take a powder, which means very much the same thing.

Mr. Maxfield is young enough to despair at the degradation of it all; I am old enough not to worry unduly and even doubt if it *is* "degradation." In these days of mass communications the greatest mass communicators on earth are bound to have some influence on our language and from my observation not all of it is bad. Some of the words we have adopted are very vivid. Think of a report of a bank robbery without getaway car, and whatever would we do without corny and deadpan and knowhow?

We absorbed blitzkrieg and flak from the Germans and camouflage, savoir faire, esprit de corps, ennui and many others from the French, and the language is none the worse for it.[29]

The natural concomitant of the common language is the common literature. The term seems fully justified, perhaps even more so than is the phrase "the common language." The great literature of the British and American peoples is genuinely a common treasure, owned and created jointly. Nearly all major books are published on both sides of the Atlantic, even though the degree of success they achieve on the two sides is often unequal, and that in curious and unpredictable ways.[30] All major authors are well known on both sides of the Atlantic. In an older generation, Kipling, Bennett, Galsworthy, Wells, and half-a-dozen others were major figures possessed of fame and readers in both countries; the same is true of O'Hara, Faulkner, and Steinbeck today. These are not exhaustive lists; the lists could indeed be extended indefinitely. There is something significant, however, in the fact that, in

[29] Letter from John Hanna, Bristol, *Sunday Times* (London), 4 May 1969.
[30] One odd example of this is the fact that *Uncle Tom's Cabin,* a book about a purely American problem, sold far more copies in Britain than it did in the United States.

thinking of names possessed of transatlantic fame, one tends
to think, in regard to the past, of British names, and of
American names in the present and the recent past. The
prestige of American literature today is infinitely higher than
in the nineteenth or early twentieth centuries, the prestige
of British literature somewhat lower. There seems no particular reason why literary distinction should flow westwards
along with world power; but power in some measure confers
prestige on everything connected with those who possess it.
There would be an interest in seeing what American authors
are saying even if American literature had not increased in
richness, variety, and competence, as in fact it has. But there
are still plenty of British authors read in the United States,
just as there were a number of American authors, such as
Emerson, Poe, and Hawthorne, familiar to the nineteenth-
century Englishman.

The author who writes in English has at his disposal the
largest potential readership in the world. It is larger by far
than the markets open to the writer in French, Spanish, or
German, though these, too, are languages possessing international literatures accessible to the publics of a number of
countries. The size of the potential audience is in itself a great
factor in creating a vigorous and significant literature.

The English language as the joint possession of the two
peoples has also furthered the interchange, with no necessity
for translating dialogue, of films and television programs. And
not merely the exchange; for a more and more common
phenomenon is the joint "Anglo-American" film, with financing, locations, and starring roles perhaps all shared. Plays,
and even whole stage productions, also cross the Atlantic,
most commonly eastwards but also sometimes westwards,
though the fate of such ventures is even more unpredictable
than it is with transplanted books.[31]

The exchanges and cooperative ventures in literature and
the arts are all part of what J. B. Brebner rightly called "the

[31] For example, the late "James Bridie" (Dr. Osborne Henry Mavor),
author of a large number of plays very successful on the London stage and
throughout Britain, never had even one Broadway success.

to-and-fro movement of people and ideas which has been a continuous process in the English-speaking world." [32]

A final and major point that must be made is the similarity of law and political institutions, stemming as they do from the same origin. The foundation of law, the Common Law, underlies the legal systems of England and Wales (though not of Scotland, a Civil Law country), as it does the legal systems of most of the fifty states (though not including Louisiana). In colonial times the British subjects in the Thirteen Colonies developed their political systems, and their political habits, on the English model. With the coming of independence the new federal government and the states created constitutions for themselves in which much was changed. The most important change was the adoption everywhere in the United States of the principle of separating executive and legislature—not so much a deliberate departure from British principles as a following of Montesquieu's misreading of the ideal principles of the British constitution, stimulated by the suspicion of the executive generated in the quarrel with the government of George III. But though much was changed, very much continued unchanged. The British and American peoples, with varying emphases, both cherish as basic principles the rule of law, the importance of the individual, the necessity of adequate discussion, the supreme importance of basing government on persuasion and consensus, and on some decent compromise between the rival disiderata of liberty and authority. Their systems of government form the two great exemplars of the two major versions—presidential government and cabinet government—of constitutional and democratic rule that have been developed in the world. Of this kind of governance, constitutional and democratic, they are the outstanding, and oldest, examples, with the greatest record in continuity and success of any major countries. Their resemblances on this point are far more significant than the differences in their versions of democracy. It is a major bond between them.

Such are some, though by no means all, of the underlying

[32] Brebner, *North Atlantic Triangle*, p. 109.

factors that justify the assertion that there is a special relationship between the United States and Britain. But the special
relationship has by no means always meant amity, or identity
of views, as we shall see as we turn to look at how it has
worked out in the past, is working out in the present, and is
likely to develop in the future.

Chapter Two

SOME TRANSATLANTIC ATTITUDES

THE BRITISH-AMERICAN relationship may be a particular one, set apart by many historical and cultural factors from the generality of international relationships. It is not, however (perhaps this is one aspect of its particularity), a symmetrical one. It has never been such, and it is not now. The mutual attitudes involved have been far from identical. Though not a symmetrical, it has been a complementary, relationship; typically it has not, apart perhaps from a somewhat limited period, been a relationship between equals. More typically it has been a relationship between a richer and a poorer partner, between a greater and a lesser, or involving other great inequalities either in characteristics or in roles. But after all this is in accordance with the family relationship to which, as has frequently been pointed out, the Anglo-American relationship bears some similarity. Family relationships are not usually relationships between equals. In the beginning, the predominance of the parent is absolute. Later, this changes, may even be reversed; but inequality persists.

In this chapter the objective is to trace some of the differences of attitudes and of policies that have marked the two nations and their governments, particularly those characteristic attitudes that have flourished over a long period.

There can be little doubt that throughout much, indeed most, of its history, the most vocal attitude in the United

States toward Britain was one of suspicion and hostility. This was combined with an unwilling respect for a power which was still richer and more important than the United States, and much more experienced in the business of international politics. This kind of attitude—hostility—was much more openly and blatantly expressed in America than anti-American sentiments ever were in Great Britain. It might be true, though it seems entirely unlikely, that anti-American sentiments were as common in Britain as the converse were in the United States; but they were never voiced by responsible (seldom, indeed, even by irresponsible) politicians, never given any stamp of official approval, never "played up" in the press. All this tends to show that there was no great market for them, that there was little advantage to be derived from being marked as the holder of anti-American opinions, no political capital to be gained thereby. On all these points there was a marked antithesis to be seen in the American situation.

The United States lacked a network of foreign policy links in the normal European sense. But so far as the young republic, in the first century and a quarter of its existence, had a traditional ally, it was France; so far as it had a traditional enemy, it was England. Independence had been won in a war with England. The same power had been the enemy in the War of 1812, the only foreign war, apart from Mexican wars and the brief Spanish-American War, in which the country was involved between the War of Independence and the First World War. Both of these wars concentrated American hostility on the former mother country.

But for England, in each of the two struggles no such concentration of hostility occurred. The war for American independence rapidly turned into a war in which Britain had to try to cope single-handedly with almost half-a-dozen European foes. There was never very much bitterness against the rebellious colonists, whose freedom from imperial rule was won, as it were, as a by-product of a vast and far-reaching struggle. The decisive battle, that of Yorktown, was lost because Britain's European enemies caused her temporarily to lose control of the sea. As for the War of 1812, it is notorious that this war, which bulks large in American history, is almost or totally unknown to the average Briton, and perhaps with good reason. To Britain it was a mere exasperating sideshow in the fight for survival with Napoleonic France.

Americans, however, cherished and sustained what Owen Wister called "the ancient grudge." The immense nineteenth-century influx of new Americans certainly was a major factor in supporting this attitude. A very numerous group among them—the Irish—brought with them a traditional dislike, or even hatred, of England well founded both in history and in their own recent experiences. Large numbers came from non-English-speaking nationalities of Continental Europe. All these groups were subject to the processes of assimilation into the traditions of their new country. But one element of that tradition was hostility to Britain. Perhaps, at this length of time, one may say that the inculcation of dislike of Britain, though it was to prove inconvenient or even pernicious in the twentieth century, had, in the operation of the nineteenth-century "melting-pot," a certain social utility. Possession of a common enemy is a great social cement between different individuals and groups. This may be a deplorable fact, but it is a fact all too firmly based on a deplorable quirk of human nature. It is generally a great deal easier to generate an enthusiasm based on dislike or hatred of something or somebody else—in general, on negative grounds—than it is to create widespread support for a policy or an idea based on liking, approval, or some positive ideal. But, of course, anti-British sentiments, ideas, prejudices, in the America of last century were not deliberately fostered by those who thought them socially useful. Rather, they were based on genuine, sincere, widespread bigotry, cynically exploited and fanned on by politicians anxious to please their constituents, by newspaper editors and journalists eager to please their readers and not go against the grain of received opinion.

At any rate, there was in nineteenth-century America, as a result of these factors, a great deal of widely voiced prejudice against Britain. Not only was it aired by politicians and in the newspapers; it was a more serious matter, and more lasting in its impact, that it was generated by the textbooks used in schools. These generally gave a very one-sided account of the issues involved in the preliminaries of the Revolutionary War, ignoring the fact that on legal grounds there was a great deal to be said for the British case. They also turned a blind eye to the very widespread support which the American view-point had had in the Britain of the 1760s and 1770s, where Burke was by no means the only, though he was the most eloquent, critic of the governmental policy which culminated in war. The false picture of a united Britain bent on suppress-ing American freedom was matched by the false picture of a united America bent on achieving it. The fact that the Tory, loyalist, cause enjoyed the support of perhaps one-third of the population of the Thirteen Colonies was as little stressed as was the harsh treatment which active loyalists received, in breach of the terms of the peace treaty, after the war.

In the last two generations scrupulous scholarship on the part of many American historians has gradually established such points with unimpeachable authority, and these newer views have gradually filtered down through the graduate schools to the colleges, to the high schools, and eventually to all levels of education. Truth has scored a modest, but real, victory. The virulence has gone out of the ancient grudge. Pro-fessional American historians had largely produced this result already before the altered state of the world and America's role in it, and the altered case of British power, came to make the ancient grudge against the hereditary foe, the loved-and-hated parent, increasingly irrelevant to contemporary reality. There is not a great deal for any lover of truth, or any Anglophile, to complain about in the version of Anglo-American relations now given in the history texts used in the schools of the republic.

It points to a distinction in national attitudes already made that there was no corresponding need for a wholesale revision of the version of these events propagated in British schools. There the American case had always been adequately, or even excessively, acknowledged. The Whig school of history-writing in England has been the dominant one to a remarkable degree, as Professor Butterfield demonstrated in a brilliant essay decades ago; [1] and the Whig tradition was anti-George III, and so pro-American. The historical revisionists in England have oddly enough, therefore, taken the same tack on this issue as those in the United States. The revisionists have tended to demonstrate that the War of Independence was *not* a conflict of heroes and saints on one side versus obscurantists and reactionaries on the other; that it was, rather, an inevitable conflict in which a vigorous nascent nation burst the not very confining bounds of imperial authority. In other words—to borrow the language of that eminent Tory and misliker of Americans (as well as of Scotchmen and sundry others), Dr. Samuel Johnson—the newer historians in Britain have tended to concentrate on seeing that "the Whig dogs should not have the best of it." [2]

Throughout most of the period since the United States became independent, however, the ancient grudge was in the ascendant. It is regrettable to note how seldom in this period did any politician or journalist try to stem the tide of anti-British demagoguery by putting, however tentatively, the other side of the case. All the evidences of life in America in the nineteenth and early twentieth centuries testify to the existence of strong, though presumably not universal, anti-British feelings. The literature, the journalism, the reports of foreign travelers in America, all demonstrate that this was the case. Sir Norman Angell, an acute observer with experience in many parts of the world, who spent a number of years in the 1890s farming in the Central Valley of California and later visited and worked in the United States many times, emphasizes in his autobiography how strong and widespread was Anglophobia, not only in the 1890s, but right on down to the 1940s. Speaking of the Central Valley farmers in the 1890s, he writes that they "were both unorganized and politically

[1] See Herbert Butterfield, *The Whig Interpretation of History* (London: G. Bell and Sons, Ltd., 1931).

[2] See George Birbeck Hill, ed., *Boswell's Life of Johnson,* Vol. 1 (Oxford: Clarendon Press, 1934), p. 502. Johnson was speaking of his methods in reporting parliamentary debates.

immature, and, like most immature folk, subject to easily
excited mass emotions. The commonest emotion was that of a
crude xenophobia, mainly Anglophobia, exploited now by a
Hearst, now by a Bryan, and all the time by Congressional
demagogues." The theme recurs in Angell's book repeatedly.
Later he compares the Anglophobia he observed, in its strength
and irrationality, to the anti-Dreyfusard movement in France,
which also he had opportunity to observe close at hand.[3]

Anglophobia was not confined to one class or one group in
the American people; indeed, it would be difficult to say
just where it found its strongest base. It was popular among
big-city populations, and among midwestern and western farmers. It was also, strange to note, true that in the Northeast,
among persons of pure English descent, suspicion of Britain,
dislike of British policies or supposed policies, was often strong.
Naturally, it was in the Northeast, among the British-descended,
that the strongest pro-British sentiments also were to be found.
Against all those who remembered too well the Revolutionary
War one has to place an Emerson, who wrote, "the American
is only a continuation of the English genius into new conditions," or a Hawthorne, with his fascinated admiration of
English scenery, English towns, English ways.

The American attitude toward Britain was a special case of
the American attitude to Europe in general. By no means all
Americans came, individually or ancestrally, from Britain, but
the overwhelming majority came from one or another part of
Europe. To Americans, Europe was the Old World, essentially
inferior, outmoded and left behind. A typical syndrome of
American behavior was the turning-away, in the second immigrant generation, from the culture and ways represented by
the old country from which the immigrants had come, in favor
of an enthusiastic embracing of the ways of the new country.
This went along with the abandonment of the old country's
language, if other than English.

The fact that Americans come from many European
sources accounts for part of the differences between American

3 Sir Norman Angell, *After All: The Autobiography of Norman Angell*
(New York: Farrar, Straus and Young, Inc., n.d. [approx. 1952]), pp. 85, 98,
and Chaps. III and IV *passim*.

attitudes toward Britain, and British attitudes toward America. When British people look westward, the United States virtually fills the whole horizon. (And, in their thoughts, they do, or they did until the 1960s, look westward oftener and more willingly than they look eastward, to Europe; the psychological distance is greater from Dover to Calais than from Southampton to New York—perhaps now one should say, from Heathrow to JFK.) Looking westward, the Englishman sees only the United States, but looking eastward, the American sees the many nations of Europe—the more westerly ones envisaged clearly, the peoples of Eastern Europe more confusedly. Of these European peoples the British, because of the ancient connection, are the most important in American eyes, but they are not the only ones. France, Germany, Scandinavia, and other places evoke claims of loyalty and affinity; and all belong, in American eyes, to the rejected past, out of which sprang America and its new, and better, order—the *Novus Ordo Seclorum* proclaimed on its Great Seal and on its currency.

American criticisms of England and of its people followed certain well-trod paths, and some points are made again and again over the whole period from independence, or earlier, to the present. Differences in manners are a potent source of irritation. Americans who have traveled in England never cease to speak of English coldness, aloofness, and reticence, as contrasted with the greater ebullience and forthcomingness typical of American manners. No doubt the contrast is overdone; but there is no doubt, either, that there is something in it, to be explained in part by the necessity, in a small and crowded land, for leaving other people alone if tolerable conditions of life are to be maintained. The hierarchical nature of English life, the persistence to the present time of a clearly observable class structure, offends American views by its antidemocratic implications. Such points as these, if aptly illustrated by well-chosen, or invented, examples, never fail to produce a pleasantly readable, mildly harmful, and eminently salable book. Margaret Halsey, whose *With Malice*

Toward Some (1938) may be taken as typical of the *genre*, was not the first or the last to provide a book of this kind that found wide acceptance. Indeed, books of this kind perhaps constitute less a *genre* than an industry. There is, of course, a corresponding industry in Britain, producing literary impressions of visits to the United States. In both cases, there would be less to say if the country under observation were a thoroughly foreign country: that would be expected to be different. The whole point of these twin schools of transatlantic commentary is perpetual amazement that a country that speaks the same language can be so disconcertingly, so quaintly, and occasionally offensively, different.

At the level of policy and diplomacy, American views of England embodied a dislike of the whole conventional apparatus, and subject matter, of international relations. There was a sincerely held belief on the part of a great majority of Americans that the people of the United States had not only removed themselves physically from Europe but had removed themselves from the routines of diplomacy, power politics, and recurrent wars, which had characterized European history for untold centuries. The United States had found a better way. Thus, what was in fact the result of a fortunate geographical situation was elevated into a proof of virtue. The Founding Fathers were not so naïve. Washington, Jefferson, Hamilton were realists with a thorough practical grounding in matters of foreign policy, power, and war. But for several generations after the War of 1812 it was believed that, for all practical purposes, it was possible to do without a foreign policy, that war and diplomacy, at any rate in the European manner, were avoidable evils, temptations to be spurned. One might have supposed that the Civil War would have provided an object lesson in the role of war in resolving conflicts otherwise not resolvable. The lesson, however, does not appear to have been applied. Indeed, the United States was in practice able to maintain its noninvolvement in European quarrels for more than half a century after the Civil War.

It is a significant illustration of the deeply ingrained American repugnance to following the behavior patterns of the European states system that the United States did not exchange diplomatic envoys of the highest rank with any government until the 1890s. (Nor would its envoys wear court dress, the accepted uniform of their profession on formal occasions. To have done so would have exposed them to ridicule and contumely at home.) [4] It is only after 1893, in President Cleveland's second administration, that some U.S. envoys with the rank of ambassador, rather than minister, were appointed. As the authorized history of the U.S. Foreign Service remarks with justified acidity, "Previously, the rank of ambassador had been regarded as too exalted for the representative of a democratic nation and was, moreover, identified with the monarchical system to whose trappings and titles the United States had no wish to defer." The policy had disadvantages. "Our envoys frequently chafed at being accorded a lower precedence in foreign courts than the representatives of many smaller states who bore the title of ambassador, and they considered that this situation detracted from the dignity and prestige of the United States." [5]

Such an attitude towards diplomacy took long to die in the United States. It lingers in the popular mind and is potent in Congress. It was only with the passing of the Rogers Act of 1924 that the U.S. Foreign Service became a professional, career service. And even now the attitude has resulted in the giving of very inadequate representation allowances (as distinct from salaries) to U.S. missions abroad. (The representation allowance of the British ambassador in Washington is approximately ten times that of the U.S. ambassador in London.) Since the exigencies of diplomatic life do not allow the American representatives to omit entertaining or fall greatly below the customary standards set in any capital by the other members of the diplomatic corps, the result is that the holders of some of the major U.S. diplomatic posts abroad are required to dip into their own pockets. Thus top diplomatic posts be-

---

[4] There is an obvious parallel to this in the attitude in the 1920s of the representatives of Soviet Russia, that other *Novus Ordo Seclorum.*

[5] William Barnes and John Heath Morgan, *The Foreign Service of the United States: Origins, Development and Functions* (Washington, D.C.: Historical Office, Department of State, 1961), p. 146.

come political plums given as rewards to those who can afford the financial strain of filling them. This is a remarkable way for the richest, as well as the most important, country in the world to behave. It cannot but be prejudicial to its interests, besides being blatantly undemocratic.[6]

Dislike of the apparatus of international relations, and of the thing itself, was naturally enough focused on a dislike of the way Britain played this particular game. This was to be expected, the more so since in the middle of the nineteenth century Britain's supremacy among the nations was at its maximum. British self-confidence was at its highest level, and so also, in consequence, was British capacity to offend American sensitivity. The vast worldwide spread of the British Empire, at that time still expanding, was a constant occasion of grievance to many Americans. The Americans had achieved their independence by breaking away from that empire. A hatred of imperialism, especially in its British version, was a central feature of their world-view. Americans little understood the vast strides toward control of their internal affairs made by the white colonies of settlement within the British Empire during the nineteenth century. In particular, the position of Canada was misunderstood. To many Americans it seemed almost as much a part of manifest destiny that Canada should some day "throw off the British yoke," and become part of the United States, as it was that the United States should expand westward to the Pacific. The reluctance of Canadians to fall in with these agreeable plans was incomprehensible.

The people of the United States thought of themselves as seceding from Europe, with the object of creating an entirely

[6] Some of these appointments would be spectacularly humorous if foreign relations were not, at the present time, a deadly serious game being played "for keeps." In June 1957 President Eisenhower nominated Maxwell Henry Gluck to be ambassador to Ceylon. Mr. Gluck's field of expertise was the running of department stores. When he was questioned before the Senate Foreign Relations Committee it was discovered that he not only did not know the name of the Prime Minister of Ceylon, he did not know the rather better-known name of the Prime Minister of India (Nehru). This did not prevent the Senate Foreign Relations Committee's approving the nomination. The bearing and language of Walter Annenberg, President Nixon's appointee as ambassador in London, was sharply criticized in the British press. (Republican administrations, however, do not have a monopoly of dubious appointments.)

improved version of its established ways. Much of European
thinking about the United States was based on a somewhat
pejorative version of the same interpretation. What Americans
regarded as a promise, Europeans might—many did—regard
as a portent. The Americans—in the view of many Europeans
—stood apart from the patterns of European history. Europeans by origin, they had ruptured tradition rather than transferred it to the New World. From the European point of view—
at least the point of view of established, aristocratic, pre-1914
Europe—there was always something anomalous, almost incomprehensible, about the United States. A people without an
aristocracy! The awkward fact of such a phenomenon was
made harder to bear by the sheer success of the United States,
made manifest as the nineteenth century wore on. Little
wonder that the United States drew such enormous numbers
of emigrants from the poor, the huddled masses, of the Old
World. Little wonder that the more comfortable classes of
Europeans, those who found not much that was wrong in the
existing system, seized every opportunity to find fault with
American manners, either as exhibited on their home ground
or as demonstrated by the ever-vulnerable American visitor
in Europe.

And, of course, there was much to find fault with. Mrs.
Trollope was a hostile witness, but the kind of crudities that
in her opinion marked *The Domestic Manners of the Americans* were for the most part merely maliciously noted, not invented, by her. Too many other observers noted the same
thing. The crudities of American politics were real crudities,
the scandals genuinely scandalous. This was particularly so in
the great age of Tammany and the city bosses; but in rural
areas the activities of the Ku Klux Klan were no symbol of
enlightenment. The Fenians who were negligently permitted
to raid across the Canadian border were not looked upon as
heroes by the Ontario farmers who suffered their depredations.
The lack of rules and regulations that in Lincoln's day permitted a horde of grubby and importunate petitioners to press
through the corridors, and even into the offices, of the White
House, did deserve the contempt of European observers.

To all these defects of the American social and political scene the English reaction was a rather special case of the general European view. The English version of aristocracy, after all, was itself a trifle *nouveau,* not to say jumped-up, by the standards of Continental aristocracy. "Gentlemen," as the Elizabethan observer said, "are made good cheap in England"; and certainly the fountain of honour poured forth an amazingly large number of new peers in the reigns of George III and Victoria. Few or no English noblemen could produce a noble genealogy to place beside that of a Radziwill or an Esterhazy. Upward social mobility was not an American invention. It was an old story in Britain, the home of the first industrial revolution. The real differences were two: that in America upward social mobility was more widespread, and the hope of it, for the average citizen, more plausible; and, secondly, that the American version lacked the satisfactory, definitive, *terminus ad quem* of the British version—that is, reception into the ranks of the landowning nobility or gentry.

As a result of this kind of consideration, the English were perhaps readier to understand and appreciate America than Continental observers. The more democratic Scots (to distinguish here between Scots and English) were, perhaps, still more ready. Of the three greatest interpretive studies of the United States that have ever appeared—de Tocqueville's *De la démocratie en Amérique,* Bryce's *The American Commonwealth,* and Brogan's *The American Political System*—two are by Scotsmen. It is, indeed, a curious point worth noting in passing, that on a whole range of matters Scotland may be found to be closer to the United States than is England. Both Scottish culture and American culture differ somewhat—not enormously—from English culture; and the differences are usually of the same kind. Both Scotland and the United States place more emphasis on democracy than England has generally done. Both, exceptions apart, lack "public schools," that immensely important private feature of the English educational system; both have always placed great emphasis on the importance of public education widely available up to the college level. The Scottish emigration to the United States was disproportionately large, and has played a role there even more important than its numbers would lead one to expect.[7]

However, if Scots often felt a little more akin to Americans and their democratic ways than Englishmen did, there was little distinction to be made between them in their condemnation of many aspects of American politics and society. The prevalence of corruption in American politics, the apparent ease with which "big money" achieves large-scale political results, was—and is—a frequent theme of condemnation. (Perhaps what is disliked is chiefly the scale and blatancy of operations. Corruption is not unknown in British politics, but it seems to flourish more in a rather petty way at the local-government level, than at the level of Westminster.) A federal system is a complicated system, and the interaction of the two layers of government, state and federal, is something the average Briton finds tedious, incomprehensible, and pointless. (It might be objected that Australia and Canada also have federal systems; but then practically no effort is ever made even to try to explain Canadian, or Australian, federalism to the British newspaper-reader.) The same British reaction is to be found to the separation of powers: to the frustration of the will of the national executive by Congress; and to the incursions into politics of the judiciary, the fact that Supreme Court decisions can be of great political importance. The British people are used to the concentration of power in the hands of the Prime Minister and Cabinet. The government of the day may not be the choice of the individual citizen, but once it is in he expects it to *govern*. Kenneth Waltz has cogently summarized this line of criticism: "By those convinced of the superiority of the British system, American parties are seen as no parties at all but rather as jumbled heaps of interest, unguided by principle and incapable of sustained or coherent activity whether in power or in opposition. The government —checked, bound and balanced—acts, when it acts at all, in

[7] On some matters of pronunciation and nomenclature, Scottish and American usage is the same, England being the odd man out. Thus, "medicine" has three syllables in America and Scotland, two in England. The article that an Englishman calls "braces" and an American "suspenders" is colloquially "galluses" in Scotland and America, but not in England. Any industrious amateur of lexicography could multiply examples.

response to pressures randomly generated and indiscriminately applied." [8]

The American legal system seems to the British observer to offer much too much in the way of possibilities of ingenious delay and nit-picking.[9] The hung jury, the endless appeals up through layer after layer of jurisdiction, the well-deserved conviction that is overturned because of some technical flaw —all this, though it derives from the same source, is alien to the British habit of fairly swift, and occasionally arbitrary, administration of justice. This kind of judicial procedure which permits a Caryl Chessman to prolong his life in the death-cell by expedient after expedient for half-a-dozen years, meanwhile writing books about his experiences, may indeed seem to the British observer preposterous. Nor is the British observer re-assured when he contemplates the criminal statistics of the society of which this is the legal system. *Any* major American city can furnish more murders in a year than the whole of the United Kingdom put together. In 1966 there were 10,918 murders in the United States. The totals that year, as it happened, were rather above average in Britain. There were all of 72 murders in England and Wales, and 23 in Scotland. The prevalence of political assassination in the United States contrasts strongly with the situation in a country where citizenship is not equated with the right to possess handguns, and where no Prime Minister has been murdered since a madman killed Mr. Spencer Perceval in the lobby of the House of Commons in 1812.

At the level of foreign-policy formulation, it has been customary for British critics of the United States to speak in terms of immaturity (the word, indeed, forms the great keynote of *all* foreign criticisms of the United States, at any level of sub-

8 Kenneth N. Waltz, *Foreign Policy and Democratic Politics* (Boston: Little, Brown and Company, 1967), p. 21. Waltz, however, does not share the view he summarizes here: the thesis of his book is that the U.S. political system is superior.

9 This view is shared by the Chief Justice of the U.S. Supreme Court, Mr. Warren Burger, who has voiced it in a whole series of speeches and lectures. E.g., on 1 July 1969 he said, "The judges, the honorable lawyers on both sides of the table, and the American people, are nearing the end of their patience with the American machinery of justice as it is now functioning."

ject-matter), uncertainty, and inconsistency. There has been some justification for this. The repudiation of President Wilson when his country refused to ratify the Versailles Treaty was a traumatic experience for Europe, and a cautionary lesson in the operations of the American system. It was regarded in Britain as an awful example of the kind of thing that is, in the British phrase, *not done;* and indeed there must be very few parallels to such a case—the repudiation by a major power of a major treaty duly concluded by its head of government, who was also its head of state. Again, the apparent necessity of American political figures to make large-scale and gratuitous statements, *pronunciamientos* often later contradicted in practice, does not inspire respect. The propensity to hand out moral lectures to foreign nations is not endearing. Too often the American maker of foreign-policy decisions (and the number of people who have a hand in doing so, and are entitled and ready to voice their views on the subject, is a wonder) seems to be engaged not in trying, in President Kennedy's fine phrase, to "shape real events in a real world," [10] but in painting a favorable picture of his own objectives for the sake of some domestic American audience.

Beyond this type of criticism, as we shall see, the kind of thing which the British observer would say about U.S. foreign policy would be different at different times. But all such criticism can be grouped under the convenient general rubric of "immaturity," as contrasted with a supposedly greater British wisdom and maturity in such matters.

It is no doubt necessary to say something, though fortunately not much, about the general habit in Britain (and elsewhere) of denigrating the quality of American life, usually in terms of "materialism" and industrialism. Materialism is one of these elusive attributes that only seem to be possessed by other people, never by the speaker. Your materialism is my legitimate desire for a higher standard of living. Very few people, very few peoples, are genuinely indifferent to questions of material well-being; of such are the saints. Until sainthood becomes more widespread, most accusations of ma-

10 Speech at Salt Lake City, 26 September 1963.

terialism amount to little more than a rationalized envy of those who have been more successful than the critic in a common pursuit. Indifference to the arts is not an American characteristic. There are undoubtedly more amateur painters, sculptors, craftsmen per thousand of population in the United States than in France, where such activity, indeed, might be regarded as exceedingly eccentric in bourgeois society. The matter of industrialization is more difficult. The technical means available to man today for altering the natural world, for subverting, disregarding, and polluting nature, are indeed appalling; and such power at its most formidable is seen in the United States. Nevertheless, it ill becomes Britain, the first great industrial power, to blame a later and more successful participant in this kind of activity. Brogan makes a valid point about this most cogently when he says that it is "a point not noted enough in the perpetual discussion of 'Anglo-American relations,' [that] a great deal of English criticism, a great many English complaints are not specifically criticisms of or complaints about America."

> They are criticisms of the modern world, complaints about modern history which are bound to use American examples simply because the modern world . . . is a world dominated, led, largely created, by America. . . . Only if you totally like the modern world (and who does?) can you escape the temptation . . . of abusing some parts of modern society, and the easiest way to do that is to take them in their most representative form, which nine times out of ten will be an American form.[11]

The abuse of the automobile, of loudspeaker systems, of industrial capacity in general, is no proof of American vulgarity. Other peoples seize on these possibilities so rapaciously, as soon as they get the chance, that it amounts, rather, to proof of the general vulgarity and bad taste of the human animal. Anyone who thinks uncontrolled industrialism is an American aberration should linger awhile in Mestre before he escapes the few miles across the causeway to Venice. Anyone who

[11] D. W. Brogan, *American Aspects* (New York: Harper and Row, 1964), pp. 70–71.

thinks smog is an American monopoly should take a good look at the Vienna basin from Wiener Neustadt on a summer's day.

To attempt to round off these brief notes on a transatlantic debate that has now been going on for some two centuries, the main point to remark is that certain themes are sounded again and again. The *leitmotif* in the American criticisms of Britain is that Britain represents *old* ways, old habits, old institutions, from which the United States has freed itself—as, in fact, the Thirteen Colonies freed themselves from their allegiance to the Crown in 1776. Britain is stuffy, fossilized, stuck-in-the-mud, lost in a dream of an archaic and irrelevant past. This is combined with a certain nostalgia for things that the United States has lost through the very fact of the breach. But with the years, the tone of the American comment has changed. Earlier, the criticism was loud to mask an inner unease, for after all Britain was still powerful; wicked, no doubt, but significant. Later, in the last two decades, the tone has modulated. It has lost its acerbity as Britain has lost its power. American comment has begun to acquire a tone of genial condescension. The enormously lengthy television coverage of the installation of Charles as Prince of Wales in July 1969 seemed to combine a reveling by the networks in such elaborate, and free, pageantry, with a kind of rueful wonder that this sort of thing is still going on.

On the British side, attitudes to the great American republic have always combined disparate and contradictory elements. On the one hand, it is regarded as an England that has gone off on strange courses, developing an ebullience, brashness, and enthusiasm for innovation that seem quite excessive to the British, and often seem combined with a demonstrable lack of judgment and—that intangible!—good taste. Nevertheless, as America marched on in its own unprecedented fashion from success to success, creating a new society unlike any that had ever been, it was a certain comfort to the older country to remember that, even if America was to be regarded as "an England gone funny," it was still England, and not some other country, that had fathered this extraordinary child.

The success of the United States could, with some minimal mental dexterity, be regarded as a kind of vicarious success for England. The failures of the United States, its inadequacies and gaucheries, were—naturally—all its own.

The literature of transatlantic criticism and of the interplay of the two cultures is by this time enormous. Even to survey it would take at least many scores of pages, and no attempt has been made here to do more than mention some of the recurring themes. Much of it is extremely readable, and, though some of it becomes obsolete with changing circumstances and mores, some of it retains astonishing appositeness even after the passage of many years or decades. This is true of the great classics of political interpretation, already mentioned.

At a more mundane level, it would be hard to better the perceptiveness of the following comment from J. B. Priestley's *Midnight on the Desert* (1937) as a statement of a characteristic difference in attitudes—and a distinction entirely favorable to the American way of doing things. Priestley is speaking of the building for him of a little working cabin at the Arizona ranch where he stayed for a time:

> This hut was a witness to the admirable spirit of Western America, and perhaps of all these states. When I had first stayed on the ranch, the winter before, I had found it hard to work in my bedroom in the patio, where people were always moving about and calling to one another. What I needed was a little place of my own to work in, well away from the main ranch buildings. So as soon as I came back, for a longer stay, up went this shack, and within a day or two it had its bookshelves, stove, and electric light. Nothing very wonderful about all this. It was easily erected, and of course I paid for it. But I feel that in any European country there would have been endless palavers and fusses, whole crops of difficulties raised, before one would have had a brand-new place to work in; if indeed one would have persisted in the face of a mountain of objections. . . .

Priestley's book is, indeed, a masterpiece of observation, full of the most acute *aperçus* in its survey of American "life, so nervous and strident, so strange a mixture of kindness and cruelty," which made Priestley, while living in the United States, feel that the English newspapers he received were "full of quaint fusses and snobberies." [12]

American comment on England, though not so large in total, is also a considerable body of literature, and its masterpieces, such as Emerson's *English Traits,* have still some relevance to the present-day scene—though they tend to be more out-of-date than English comments on America, because the British position in the world has suffered such a catastrophic change. Several admirable guides to this body of literature—or rather these two bodies, one westward-looking, the other eastward-looking—exist. The whole subject is well surveyed in H. C. Allen's *Great Britain and the United States.* Cushing Strout's *The American Image of the Old World* is outstanding of its kind. The same may be said of Allan Nevins's *America Through British Eyes,* an anthology with commentary. These twin streams of literature testify by their vast volume, and occasional high quality, to the intense and perennial, even if often critical, interest which the two peoples have in each other.

[12] J. B. Priestley, *Midnight on the Desert: Being an Excursion into Autobiography during a Winter in America 1935–36* (New York: Harper and Brothers, 1937), pp. 4–6.

Chapter Three

A NARROWING BREACH:
TURN OF THE CENTURY TO THE SECOND WORLD WAR

THE PERIOD round about the end of the nineteenth and the beginning of the twentieth centuries saw the softening of ancient grudges on both sides, and the beginnings of an Anglo-American rapprochement. "Anglo-American relations," as not just the name for a not particularly cordial diplomatic relationship, but as something to be concerned about, something subject to a hypothetical and desirable improvement, came to be a topic of discussion. It would appear, then and later, that the concern, and the associated hope, were greater for the British than for the Americans. As we shall see repeatedly, the attempt to better these relations has, on the whole, seemed more of an urgent matter to the British than to the other half of the relationship. All the same, at the turn of the century, causes and symptoms of the rapprochement were to be noted on both sides of the Atlantic.

Some dates stand out as clearly significant. In the Venezuela crisis of 1895, during which Secretary Olney lectured the government of Lord Salisbury in a singularly peremptory manner, the two countries came closer to going to war with each other than they ever had subsequent to the War of 1812. But the Venezuela crisis was the last of its kind. Both countries, having drawn back from the brink, suffered something of a change of heart, and no such occasion of tension ever occurred again. Within three years even Mr. Olney was to be found speaking well of Great Britain in the *Atlantic Monthly*. On the

British side, the Venezuela crisis seems to mark the definitive acceptance by British statesmen of the thesis that war with the United States was simply not a possible policy; though certainly something of the same tendency had been seen a quarter of a century before in the British decision to accept arbitration of the *Alabama* claims.

Various factors conduced to the pushing of American opinion, or at any rate some sectors of it, into greater friendliness toward Britain.

The nature of the American national experience was changing. In 1893, in his famous address to the American Historical Association, Frederick Jackson Turner noted that an era had ended with the passing of "the Frontier," i.e., the availability of free and desirable land for settlement in the West. Not long after, in 1898, the United States, long the denigrator of imperialism, itself became an imperial power. In that climacteric year it annexed the Hawaiian Islands, and acquired, as the result of victory in the Spanish-American War, possession of Puerto Rico, Guam, and the Philippines, and control of Cuba. In 1900 negotiations were begun with Denmark for purchase of the Danish West Indies, though the purchase was not actually concluded until 1917. There does not seem any economic or demographic relationship of cause and effect between the closing of the Frontier and the acquisition of overseas territories by the United States. There was still plenty of room for an expanding population in America, and the overseas acquisitions neither provided living space for surplus population nor affected the U.S. economy in any significant way. The relationship was rather, presumably, a psychological one. The filling-up of the interior of the country led naturally enough to a casting of eyes abroad, to an ambition for the acquisition of new territory abroad (however useless or burdensome in practice). It was an old enough story in Europe; what was new was the United States's taking European behavior as a model and exemplar, even implicitly. There were plenty of critics to point out that such a policy was a *volte-face* of no minor kind.

During the "splendid little war," as John Hay called the one-sided attack on the Spanish possessions, Britain was alone among the European powers in showing a friendly attitude toward the United States. British sea-power rendered impossible any collective anti-American intervention such as Germany would have liked to mount and which would have been a popular move on the Continent. The result was to make Britain more popular in the United States than it had hitherto been. Enthusiasm for the joint Anglo-Saxon heritage flared, and there was some talk among publicists of a possible alliance, or even of reunion. Nothing came of it, and it did not last. "The Anglo-Saxon cult, however, had to pull against the great mass of the population, whose ethnic composition and cultural background rendered them immune to its propaganda; and even among those of Anglo-Saxon lineage the dynamic appeal of the cult was confined to the years of excitement at the turn of the century." [1] Still, no doubt there was a permanent residue, of political importance and tending to make later cooperation easier. This trend of thought went along with the emergent dislike of the continuance of large-scale immigration, especially that part of it that was not only not Anglo-Saxon but not even from northwestern Europe. This sentiment was to result in the passing of legislation restricting immigration at the end of the First World War.

It was, in short, at the turn of the century that "the old sweet Anglo-Saxon spell," as Henry James named the influence that for him in particular was so potent, became an important and perceptible influence in American life. Its elitist character limited its effectiveness in politics, just as its preferential emphasis on one racial strain was basically uncongenial to American thought. Still, it existed, and in influential quarters; though British statesmen and diplomats probably exaggerated its diffusion and influence, because it was naturally strongest precisely in those parts of American society with which they had most of their encounters.

At this period similar, and more profound, influences were having a complementary effect on Britain. However, there

[1] Richard Hofstadter, *Social Darwinism in American Thought* (Rev. ed.; Boston: The Beacon Press, 1955), p. 183.

was a difference. With the United States, a feeling of kinship with Britain was emphasized by a novel strength and ebullience, an awareness of a new role as a world power and a sea power. For Britain, the turn toward the United States resulted from the perception in some quarters of a strength diminishing relatively, though not absolutely. The ritual splendors of Queen Victoria's Diamond Jubilee in 1897 were in some measure superficial and misleading. British industrial supremacy, which had been virtually absolute in the middle of the nineteenth century, was passing. At the end of that century British industrial output was being challenged by Germany's, and that of the United States was moving decisively ahead. In 1900 in steel production (a significant statistic) Germany had just edged ahead of Britain (6.7 million tons against 5); by 1910 the German figure was two-and-a-half times the British, while the American, twice the British in 1900, was between four and five times as much. Some of this was inevitable, the effect of American size, but there was no such satisfactory explanation of Britain's being surpassed in economic development by Germany. In the last decade and a half before 1914, the British economy presents a picture of virtually arrested progress. Real wages increased hardly at all. Innovation at the managerial and technical level, precisely what had given Britain its original lead, was painfully lacking. As Alfred Marshall, the great economist, observed in a memorandum written in 1903, businesses tended to be controlled by those who had inherited them, men "content to follow mechanically the lead given by their fathers. They worked shorter hours, and they exerted themselves less to obtain new practical ideas than their fathers had done, and thus a part of England's leadership was destroyed rapidly. In the 'nineties it became clear that in the future Englishmen must take business as seriously as their grandfathers had done, and as their American and German rivals were doing. . . ." [2] A. J. Balfour, the Prime Minister, in the cool, dispassionate and supremely intelligent pamphlet which he published in 1903, *Economic Notes on Insular Free*

[2] Quoted in R. C. K. Ensor, *England 1870–1914,* Vol. XIV, *The Oxford History of England* (Oxford: Clarendon Press, 1936), p. 501.

Trade, pointed to other ominous features. Britain was export-
ing ships and machinery, both of which would strengthen the
long-run competition against her. Her exports were increasingly
hampered by foreign tariffs, yet with her free-trade policy (not
given up until 1932) she lacked the means to bargain for the
reduction of such tariffs by mutual concessions.

The makers of British policy were aware (some clearly,
like Balfour, others more subconsciously) that beneath the
surface not all was well. The reaction took various forms.
Perhaps the imperial enthusiasm of the 1890s itself, the
scramble for territory, was at bottom a reaction to the sense
that the foundations of British life were insecure. In a few
years, a foreign policy of isolation was to be modified by the
Entente with France (1904) and that with Russia (1907),
agreements which already foreshadowed the line-up of 1914.

But France and Russia were not thought of at first as
potential allies. As Britain cast about for support in the playing of its world role, it was more natural to turn to where the
claims of kinship might produce a response, that is, to the
great self-governing white parts of the empire—the Dominions,
as they were to be called from 1907 onward—and to the
United States. The search for support in these quarters did not
prove vain in the long run, but it certainly was not very successful in the short run. At the Imperial Conference of 1902, the
active and able Colonial Secretary, Joseph Chamberlain, in
his famous "Weary Titan" speech, appealed for support and
tried to interest the representatives of the other parts of the
empire in imperial federation:

> Gentlemen, we do want your aid. We do require your as-
> sistance in the administration of the vast Empire which
> is yours as well as ours. The weary Titan staggers under
> the too vast orb of its fate. We have borne the burden for
> many years. We think it is time that our children should
> assist us to support it, and whenever you make the request
> to us, be very sure that we shall hasten gladly to call you
> to our Councils. If you are prepared at any time to take
> any share, any proportionate share, in the burdens of the
> Empire, we are prepared to meet you with any proposal

for giving to you a corresponding voice in the policy of the Empire.[3]

The proposal came to nothing. The Dominions over the years before 1914 made some modest voluntary contributions to the cost of imperial defense, but they were not interested in being saddled with participation in the framing of the foreign policy of the Empire.

The weary Titan, in fact, had at this point no very solid justification for feeling weary. The British had no army on the Continental scale. The British army was small and minimal in cost. British security was assumed to depend on the Royal Navy, and its cost could very easily be borne. Even in 1914 —at the climax of the naval arms race with Germany—Britain was spending only 3.4 percent of its national income on armaments, less than any other Great Power. The maintenance of that status was less of a strain on her than on any other of her competitors among the European states.[4]

The long-term hope of American support was a more subtle matter than projects of imperial federation, though it was a related idea. In Britain as in the United States, this period saw widespread advocacy of ethnic ideas exalting the role, and advocating the reunion, of "Anglo-Saxon" peoples. The limits of this group were defined with sufficient looseness not only to embrace the various strains comprising the, by this time fairly heterogeneous, people of the United States, but also the Afrikaners of South Africa, not to mention the French of Quebec. This kind of thinking is to be found in Conan Doyle, in Milner, in Kipling and many others. For some, as for Chamberlain, it was important also to extend "Anglo-Saxon" to include "Germanic"; hence his tentative approaches, viewed with little enthusiasm by his colleagues, to Germany. This extended version of the concept was also embodied in the original constitution of the Rhodes Scholarships, as set up under the will of Cecil Rhodes after his death in 1902; an aberration on

[3] Julian Amery, *The Life of Joseph Chamberlain,* Vol. IV (London: Macmillan and Co., Ltd., 1951), p. 421.
[4] Figures in A. J. P. Taylor, *The Struggle for Mastery in Europe 1848–1918* (Oxford: Clarendon Press, 1954), p. xxix.

Rhodes's part that was thoughtfully amended for him during the First World War, German candidates being thenceforth excluded.

Oddly enough, the idea of the special relationship with the United States, which might seem the most chimerical of all these related ideas that were circulating at the turn of the century, was to prove the most durable of them all, and the most potent in shaping the course of history. Of its launching in this period, Coral Bell says, "Perhaps 1896 can be regarded as the date of a firm decision by Britain that the normal sort of power competition between sovereign states must not be the mode of her relationship with the U.S." She concludes that in this period Britain intuitively assumed "that American and British interests would in the end prove complementary in the central conflicts of international politics." [5]

The same point is made by Max Beloff (but putting it "in the most brutal fashion possible") when he says that "ever since the 1890s the dominant element in the British 'establishment' has known in its heart that the world order dependent on British sea-power which was the key to the unparalleled growth of the western economy in the nineteenth century could no longer be sustained by British power alone. It was therefore the intended lot of the United States, perhaps its moral duty, to take over an increasing share of this burden and to use its new strength to further Britain's original purposes." And again: "It could thus be maintained that the 'special relationship' was something in which many British public figures felt the need to believe, so as to be able to argue that the displacement of power from Britain to the United States need not directly damage British interests." [6] This seems a very shrewd assessment. The phrases *perhaps its moral duty* and *need to believe* are particularly penetrating.

Among the concrete symptoms of implementation of the new policy were the clearing-up of all outstanding questions

[5] Coral Bell, *The Debatable Alliance: An Essay in Anglo-American Relations* (London: Oxford University Press, 1964), pp. 11, 14.

[6] In Martin Gilbert, ed., *A Century of Conflict 1850–1950: Essays for A. J. P. Taylor* (London: Hamish Hamilton, 1966), p. 154.

in Canadian-American relations, a process pushed along ener-
getically by Bryce as British ambassador in Washington, and
completed by 1911; and a British strategic abandonment of the
Western Hemisphere involving the withdrawal of remaining
garrisons from the West Indies and from Canada. On the
latter point decisions were taken and implemented in the
period 1904–1906. These decisions, precipitated by an economy drive in Whitehall, were also based on a clear-sighted
realization that the defense of British West Indian islands, or
of Canada, against the unlikely event of a U.S. attack, was
simply not practicable. Two contemporary official documents
may be quoted which point up the basis of decision with unusual sharpness. The Civil Lord of the Admiralty, A. H. Lee,
wrote in February 1905:

> I should regard a war between this country and the
> United States as the supreme limit of human folly, and I
> cannot conceive that any British statesman is willing to
> contemplate it under any circumstances, unless it were
> forced upon us beyond all possibility of avoidance.
>
> In such a war we could not possibly win—no combina-
> tion of Powers could successfully invade and conquer the
> United States—and the contest if persisted in could only
> result in the destruction of the British Empire and the
> downfall of the English speaking race.

The other comment, probably by Admiral "Jackie" Fisher, is:

> That war with the United States would be unpopular,
> and that the outcome of the struggle could only result,
> sooner or later, in the loss of Canada, are the conclusions
> difficult to avoid. It may be hoped that the policy of the
> British Government will ever be to use all possible means
> to avoid such a war.[7]

The immediate focus of the British attitude to the United
States that was emerging in this period was naturally the
Western Hemisphere and Canadian-American relations, but in
the course of time the deliberate policy of avoiding Anglo-

---

[7] Samuel F. Wells, Jr., "British Strategic Withdrawal from the Western
Hemisphere, 1904–1906," *Canadian Historical Review* XLIX (December,
1968), pp. 350–51.

American conflicts was to affect many other questions and many other areas.

Possibly the most noteworthy point about Anglo-American relations in the twentieth century is the extent to which the relationship has been a one-sided love affair, in which Britain played the role of a nervous suitor, anxious by any means or any concession to court the favor of the superbly indifferent object of his affections. Britain has generally been conscious of the need for friends. Most of its wars have been coalition wars, with Britain the leader, or at any rate member, of a group of states with common objectives. (The one war of which this is obviously not true, the War of American Independence, stands out for another obvious reason: Britain lost it.) American policy has traditionally been different. Conscious of its geographically conferred immunity, later of its overwhelming strength, the United States has not typically felt a need for allies.

The twentieth century has seen many occasions when Britain gave up a British interest, or changed a policy, in the hope of pleasing the United States. Examples of a reciprocal amiability on the part of the United States are few indeed, or nonexistent. It is hard even to think of occasions when the United States supported something *merely* because it was a *British* interest; though it is not too hard to come up with examples of policies that seem intended to sacrifice an interest merely because it was a British interest. British policy has often been thought of, especially by Americans, as Machiavellian. It would be truer to describe it, *vis-à-vis* the United States, as mildly pathetic. Perhaps there was no choice; perhaps a sedulously cultivated American friendship paid higher dividends than any alternative policy would have done. For Britain the American alliance made possible victory in the First World War; and first survival, and then victory, in the Second.

In their times of desperate struggle, the British, high and low, felt that kinship, plus the manifest justice of their cause, established a claim on the United States. Some Americans agreed with this, but it was not a general point of view, and it was one which American officeholders were very wary of indeed.

The almost three years of American neutrality, 1914–1917, in the First World War caused a puzzled resentment in Britain. British statesmen believed that more harm than good would result from expressing this feeling in public, but bitterness certainly found literary expression, nor did the poets and authors in any way misrepresent public opinion. Kipling, in a poem of 1916, called "The Question" (and meticulously footnoted in his collected edition "Attitude of the U.S. during first two years seven months and four days of the Great War") reproaches American self-interest, and hints at an analogy with Peter's denial of Christ.

> Brethren, how shall it fare with me
>   When the war is laid aside,
> If it be proven that I am he
>   For whom a world has died?
>
> If it be proven that all my good,
>   And the greater good I will make,
> Were purchased me by a multitude
>   Who suffered for my sake?
>
> That they did not ask me to draw the sword
>   When they stood to endure their lot—
> That they only looked to me for a word,
>   And I answered I knew them not? [8]

Sir William Watson's 1915 sonnet, "To America, Concerning England" shows the same astonishment and hurt:

> Art thou her child, born in the proud midday
> Of her large soul's abundance and excess,
> Her daughter and her mightiest heritress,
> Dowered with her thoughts, and lit on thy great way
> By her great lights that shine and fail not? . . .
> And at this thunderous hour of struggle and stress,
> Hither across the ocean wilderness

---

[8] *Rudyard Kipling's Verse* (Inclusive Edition; London: Hodder and Stoughton, 1933), pp. 324–25.

What word comes frozen on the frozen spray?
Neutrality! [9]

In H. G. Wells's novel *Mr Britling Sees it Through,* begun
in 1915 and published in 1916, which forms a faithful diary of
public attitudes and behavior in Britain in the early years of
the 1914 war, the anguished Mr Britling (though aware "he
was being preposterously unfair to America, and outrageously
uncivil to a trusting guest") lectures his American guest Mr.
Direck, unmercifully:

> "You think you are out of it for good and all. So did
> we think. We were as smug as you are when France went
> down in '71. . . . Yours is only one further degree of
> insularity. You think this vacuous aloofness of yours is
> some kind of moral superiority. . . .
>
> "For forty years the British fleet has guarded all Amer-
> ica from European attack. Your Monroe Doctrine skulks
> behind it now. . . .
>
> "I'm sick of all this high thin talk of yours about the
> war. . . . You are a nation of ungenerous onlookers—
> watching us throttle or be throttled. You gamble on our
> winning. And we shall win; we shall win. And you will
> profit. And when we have won a victory only one shade
> less terrible than defeat, then you think you will come in
> and tinker with our peace. . . ." [10]

(Fortunately, soon after this Mr. Direck does the decent thing
by joining the Canadian army.)

The long years of U.S. neutrality in the First World War
were followed by the appalling blow of the repudiation of the
Versailles settlement by the United States, which had had a
major share in shaping it. This included U.S. refusal of membership in the League of Nations. The effect was to reduce
sharply British hopes of active cooperation with the United
States in world tasks. Britain still thought Anglo-American

---

[9] *The Poems of Sir William Watson 1878–1935* (London: George G.
Harrap and Co., Ltd., 1936), p. 40.
[10] H. G. Wells, *Mr. Britling Sees it Through* (Atlantic Edition; New York:
Charles Scribner's Sons, 1926), p. 458.

relations enormously important, and was prepared to make considerable sacrifices with the object of maintaining them on a friendly basis; but the idea that such a policy would pay any early or substantial dividends was regretfully put aside as a very remote hope.

American voluntary withdrawal at the very moment of its highest influence over European affairs had a strange parallel in the exclusion from European affairs of Russia, newly renamed the Soviet Union. Suffering the terrible effects of revolution and civil war, and, as a revolutionary power, deliberately cold-shouldered by other states, Russia played little part in European and world politics until the mid-1930s. Thus, for a period of two decades the European states-system was abnormally concentrated upon itself. The two states, American and Russian, which were the emerging giants of world politics —each of them an equivalent in itself to several major European powers put together—played little part from 1919 until 1939 in the interactions of the European powers. Even the Munich "settlement" of September 1938—the institutionalization of surrender to Hitler on the Czech question—was strikingly anomalous in that the conference included no representatives of the Soviet Union, or of the United States (or for that matter of Czechoslovakia, whose territory was the subject-matter). It was a purely European determination of a major European question—in all probability, the last such.

To British statesmen in the 1920s and 1930s American goodwill was a lock-away security, not expected to produce any dividends or appreciation in any immediate future, but whose purchase was still worth considerable effort. To this end formidable concessions continued to be made. In the Washington conference of 1922 Britain gave up its traditional policy of maintaining the largest navy, since the U.S. Navy was not thought of seriously as a possible enemy fleet. A five-five-three ratio was accepted for the relative strengths of the British, American and Japanese navies. At the same time, as a matter of simple yielding to American pressure, seconded by Canada and to some extent by the other Dominions, Britain gave up the Anglo-Japanese alliance which had lasted for twenty years and had served Britain well. It is curious even if pointless to speculate on what the future course of events would have been if British statesmen had been tough-minded enough to stand on their own interests and their own judgment on this point. Churchill, fervent advocate of Anglo-American friendship as he was, did not think much of this particular appeasement of the United States. He wrote in the late 1940s that "the United States made it clear to Britain that the continuance of her alliance with Japan, to which the Japanese had punctiliously conformed, would constitute a barrier in Anglo-American relations. Accordingly this alliance was brought to an end. The annulment caused a profound impression in Japan, and was viewed as the spurning of an Asiatic Power by the Western World. Many links were sundered which might afterwards have proved of decisive value to peace." [11]

In 1923 Stanley Baldwin, as Chancellor of the Exchequer, went to Washington to negotiate the terms of settlement of Britain's wartime debts to the United States. He was under explicit instructions from the Prime Minister, Bonar Law, as to the basis of settlement and the maximum concessions to be made. In practice he went far beyond these, and agreed to terms which were far more onerous on Britain, amounting to a substantial acceptance of the U.S. demands. Nevertheless, on his return the British Government, instead of repudiating his concessions, confirmed them.

All three of these episodes—acceptance of U.S. naval parity, repudiation of the Anglo-Japanese alliance, agreement to the Baldwin-conceded debt repayment terms—point up vividly the fixed intention of British policy-makers to see the seeking of American goodwill as a card that trumped all other policy considerations whatsoever. The three incidents occurred in a short span of months, but under two British administrations —the Lloyd George Coalition government and the Bonar Law Conservative government. They also occurred in the very trough of disillusionment with American foreign policy, and at the end of a series of years in which the British difficulties

11 Winston S. Churchill, *The Gathering Storm*, Vol. I, *The Second World War* (Boston: Houghton Mifflin Company, 1948), p. 14.

in dealing with Ireland had been multiplied by the stream of aid, in money and in arms, given to the Irish rebels from American private sources.

As the 1920s passed into the 1930s and the world slid into the Great Depression, American isolationism became more pronounced. The United States was more interested in the Far East than it was in Europe, but had no more intention of actually doing anything in the former theatre than in the latter. There is a persistent myth (which was still being propagated by Secretary Dulles as late as the mid-1950s), that America was ready to take decisive action against Japanese aggression in Manchuria, but was frustrated by British foot-dragging. This is nonsense. To refute it one need look no further than the memoirs of the Secretary of State of that day, Henry Stimson.[12]

The egregious proceedings of the Nye Committee in 1934 conduced to the creation of the impression in the public mind that the profits which armament makers and bankers had enjoyed in the period 1914–1917 had been the primary reason for American participation in the First World War. The attitude of the public, and of the Congress, effectively narrowed the range of policy choices open to the executive. U.S. policy was hamstrung to the point where it came to consist of little but a determined isolationism. The three successive Neutrality Acts of 1935, 1936, and 1937 were an attempt to insulate the United States from foreign war, at the expense if necessary of giving up neutral rights under international law hitherto strenuously maintained by the United States. The State Department

12 See Henry L. Stimson and McGeorge Bundy, *On Active Service in Peace and War* (New York: Harper and Brothers, 1948), Chap. IX *passim* but particularly pp. 221, 230, 233, 236, and 256. The following quotations make the position particularly clear. "The treaties to which the American government was a party, unlike the Covenant of the League, were treaties without teeth. . . . Mr. Hoover was a profoundly peaceable man . . . opposed, in every fiber of his being, to any action which might lead to American participation in the struggles of the Far East. In this view he had the support of the American people. . . . The American Government would be delighted if the League would impose sanctions . . . but it would not impose sanctions of its own. This was hardly a noble position, and Stimson was not proud of his part in it." (P. 233.) "Stimson was the outstanding advocate of *collective condemnation* of Japan." (P. 236, italics added.) "In his official capacity he [Stimson] was armed with 'spears of straw and swords of ice,' and he was forced to proceed with a line of policy which seems in retrospect to have been very weak." (P. 256.)

and the administration would greatly have preferred legislation which would have enabled a discrimination to be made against the aggressor nation in the matter of arms shipments; but Congress, probably reflecting public sentiment quite accurately, decided otherwise. American public opinion in the mid and late thirties might be summarized as follows. Europe was where the wars started. If they started again, Britain would no doubt be involved; and Britain, whose power to influence U.S. policy was regarded with deep suspicion, would try to drag the United States in, as it had succeeded in doing before. To avoid the error of 1917 it was necessary to avoid all talk of rights and wrongs, and all attitudes and policies that would aid one European belligerent or disadvantage another. The United States must show its superior wisdom, even its superior morality, by refraining from participation in Old World disputes.[13]

Ernest Hemingway, that apostle of the heroic life, told his readers, in a piece that won a prize for the best article of 1935: "But of the hell broth that is brewing in Europe we have no need to drink. Europe has always fought: the intervals of peace are only armistices. We were fools to be sucked in once in a European war, and we should never be sucked in again." [14]

There is no doubt that in these years President Roosevelt soon came to possess a personal attitude that was not neutral —an attitude of hostility toward those who committed international aggression, rather than of friendship for Great Britain. But in the context of the existing attitude of public and Congress, there was little indeed that he could do. Even Roosevelt's famous "Quarantine" speech at Chicago on 5 October 1937—which did not amount, despite its picturesque phraseology, to much more than expression of the hope that *somebody*

13 As a comment published by a shrewd observer at the time of Pearl Harbor pointed out: "Americans have come to regard war as a disfiguring and rather shameful disease, like ringworm or impetigo, which nice clean nations simply don't get." See Ann Bridge [Lady O'Malley], *Facts and Fictions: Some Literary Recollections* (New York: McGraw-Hill Book Company, 1968), p. 124.

14 Quoted in Cushing Strout, *The American Image of the Old World* (New York: Harper and Row, 1963), p. 205.

would do *something* about the dictators and their aggressions —evoked much more protest than agreement at home. The United States was a giant firmly resolved only not to use its strength.

In this situation British publicists, scholars, statesmen, looked westward across the Atlantic with a mixture of longing and exasperation. If only the United States could be persuaded to get off its high moral horse and directly involve itself in what the British saw (but most Americans declined to see) as their common concerns! If only that great potential power (still, in fact, at that point underestimated) could be mobilized for the active defense of the right and the active suppression of wrong! In the late 1930s these aspirations found a singularly dusty response in the Neutrality Acts.

It happened that the Prime Minister of these years, Neville Chamberlain, was not a romantic, and was not affected, as his father had been, by the glamour of the "special relationship." His private letters showed a fixed belief that one might as well leave the United States out of British calculations. In October 1937 he commented in a letter on the "Quarantine" speech, "I read Roosevelt's speech with mixed feelings . . . seeing that patients suffering from epidemic diseases do not usually go about fully armed . . . something lacking in his analogy. . . . When I asked U.S.A. to make a joint démarche at the very beginning of the dispute, they refused. . . . It is always best and safest to count on nothing from the Americans but words." [15]

Chamberlain has been extravagantly blamed for the fact that he refused, or more strictly evaded, a suggestion by Roosevelt in January 1938 for a world conference to discuss disarmament, keeping of treaties, access to raw materials, *et quicquid agunt homines*. Allen speaks of Chamberlain's refusal as "staggering," "fantastic," "incredible," "egregious," and "appalling." [16] Churchill also condemns it eloquently. Actually, it is doubtful if the Prime Minister's coolness did any discernible harm, more than doubtful if the conference (if

[15] Keith Feiling, *The Life of Neville Chamberlain* (London: Macmillan and Co., Ltd., 1946), p. 325.
[16] H. C. Allen, *Great Britain and the United States,* pp. 729–30, 775–76.

it had ever taken place) would have achieved anything more than those dreary fizzles, the world Disarmament and Economic conferences of half-a-dozen years before. A. J. P. Taylor avoids condemning Chamberlain: "Eden was on holiday. . . . Chamberlain had more hope from direct negotiations with the dictators. . . . Chamberlain therefore replied discouragingly to the Americans, and they, who had never meant anything in particular, acquiesced gladly enough. Eden, on his return, was angry. He thought mistakenly that Chamberlain had missed a great opportunity for enlisting American support." [17] The most distinguished *American* historians of this period, Langer and Gleason, are even more explicit: "Conceivably a really strong stand by the United States Government might have changed the course of events, but . . . nothing of the kind was even remotely envisaged in Washington. Mr. Roosevelt and his advisors sympathized with the British. . . ; but there was . . . certainly no thought of assuming any political or military commitment" in connection with British policy.[18]

The conference proposal, like the "Quarantine" speech, was a gesture of goodwill without substance. The war, as far as England was concerned, was long under way, and could not be prevented, but only won, before American power began to weigh in the balance.

[17] Taylor, *English History 1914–1945,* p. 422.
[18] William L. Langer and S. Everett Gleason, *The Challenge to Isolation* (New York: Harper and Brothers for the Council on Foreign Relations, 1952), pp. 31–32.

Chapter Four

PARTNERSHIP, 1939–1945

THE SECOND WORLD WAR is the crucial turning-point in the development of relations between Britain and the United States. Two considerations stand out. First, the war marks the decisive turning-point in the transition from an American tradition of noninvolvement to a policy of active participation and continuous involvement. This is so even though it was not the beginning of U.S. intervention overseas outside the Western Hemisphere. It was important that the United States had been an "Associated Power" on the British and French side in the last year and a half of the First World War, and that her participation had tipped the scales decisively toward victory. That intervention had been short-lived, however, and it had come to be a parenthesis in policy rather than a long-term change of course. It was the Second World War that inaugurated a striking departure from American tradition in the shape of continuous involvement overseas. This was an alteration of policy that was decisive and irreversible—or, at any rate, one that has not been reversed, even after some three decades have passed.

Secondly, the Second World War is also the high-water mark of British-American cooperation. For a period of several years that cooperation was extraordinarily intense, and unprecedentedly successful. It was symbolized at the highest level by the partnership of two great men, Churchill and Roosevelt; but it

was operative at all levels in a manner virtually without precedent in the relations of sovereign states.

If cooperation did not continue with that intensity and success, one reason certainly was that the war was won in due
course, the great joint objective achieved. But the clue to
the change really was the shift in the power relationship. The
Second World War was the last period when the United States
and the United Kingdom might conceivably be regarded as
something like equals. After the war, and even towards its
end, the United Kingdom was very much the lesser partner.
The war was a crossing-point of the lines of destiny, an international chiasma. The graph line representing the power and
significance of the United States, slanting upward, irreversibly
passed that representing the United Kingdom, going down.
That this historic change was occurring was clear even at the
time; though not, perhaps, quite so manifest as it has become
in retrospect.

As we have seen, the isolationist policies of the United
States were enshrined in the three Neutrality Acts of 1935,
1936, and 1937. If faithfully adhered to, it is possible that
these would have sufficed to keep the United States out of
the war which broke out in Europe in 1939. They would also
have made German victory in that war virtually certain. The
chief contribution that the United States made to the developing crisis in the summer of 1939 was the encouragement of
Germany through the expiration in May of the provisions
permitting "cash and carry" in the 1937 Act.

The Roosevelt administration was not happy with the Neutrality Acts and worked to change them and wherever possible
to circumvent them. Roosevelt was determined that Nazi Germany should not win. There is thus some validity to the arguments of the "revisionist" school of historians when they say
that in the early years of the war Roosevelt said things he did
not mean, and that his acceptance of neutrality was not whole-
hearted. But it is absurd to say, as Tansill says, that the prime
objective of American foreign policy was the preservation of

the British Empire.[1] For Roosevelt the preservation of the British Empire was surely *le cadet de ses soucis*. His equivocations were due to his determination to pursue policies that he felt to be necessary for the security of the United States, but which were in opposition to the basically isolationist sentiments of the country. The country had to be weaned slowly from isolationism.

The war of 1939–1945 may be divided, as far as the United States is concerned, into three periods of increasing duration and intensifying involvement. The first lasts from the German, closely followed by the Russian, attack on Poland in September 1939 until the German conquest of France in June 1940. The second phase lasts from the summer of 1940 until Pearl Harbor; and the third until the complete defeat of Germany, closely followed by that of Japan, in the summer of 1945. In this third phase the United States replaced Britain as the predominant partner among the western Allies.

In the winter of 1939–1940 there was little change. The Fourth Neutrality Act, signed into law 4 November 1939, eased the situation somewhat for Britain and France by permitting them to purchase arms on a "cash and carry" basis and by legalizing short-term credits; but in some other respects it was more rigid than its predecessors. There was, in point of fact, little warlike action in western Europe that winter. Attention swiveled to a sideshow, the Russian attack on Finland which began on 30 November. The plight of Finland evoked great American sympathy, but not much more. A loan of $30 million was granted—with the proviso that it could not be used for purchasing arms. After several months of surprisingly successful defense, the Finns agreed to Russian terms and made peace on 12 March 1940. Despite the peace, Russian pressure upon Finland continued in various ways going beyond the terms of the treaty, culminating in the shutting-off of all sup-

[1] "The main objective in American foreign policy since 1900 has been the preservation of the British Empire." Charles Callin Tansill, *Back Door to War: The Roosevelt Foreign Policy 1933–1941* (Chicago: Henry Regnery Company, 1952), p. 3. If this is accepted as the case, U.S. foreign policy has been more spectacularly unsuccessful than one had hitherto supposed!

plies to Finland early in 1941. It was hardly surprising that in the aftermath of the German attack on Russia (22 June 1941) Finland reasserted its claim to Eastern Karelia and embarked on a continuation of the Winter War. Since U.S. policy is often spoken of as being less mature and less wise than British, it is appropriate to note that the differences between them on policy in regard to Finland during the war redound entirely to America's credit. Britain and France teetered in February and March 1940 on the verge of a policy of military aid to Finland (to which they had no commitment), which might well have brought them into a war with Russia; an interesting contrast to their omission in September 1939 to react in any way to the Russian attack on Poland (to which they had a commitment). Then, in December 1941, Britain allowed itself to be jostled into declaring war on Finland. This was done solely in the hope of pleasing Russia: an unnecessary and contemptible gesture without any practical effect. Even after Pearl Harbor the United States neither went to war with Finland nor even removed its minister from Helsinki, but on the contrary exerted its good offices to enable Finland to disengage, as it was able to do in the Russo-Finnish peace of September 1944.

When in the spring of 1940 the German conquest of Denmark and Norway was followed by that of the Low Countries and then, in June, by the surrender of France, it became a matter of urgency to Roosevelt's administration to do everything, in the eventual interest of U.S. security itself, to aid Britain to the extent that the existing legislation and the American supply situation permitted. Half a million rifles certified as surplus to American requirements were made available to Britain for the Home Guard. A little later (2 September) by an executive agreement (thus avoiding the necessity of Senate approval which would have attached to a treaty), fifty over-age destroyers were transferred to Britain in a complicated swap for American rights to establish bases in Newfoundland and the West Indies—"a decidedly unneutral act," as Churchill rightly called it, "an event which brought the United States definitely nearer to us and to the war," and "the first of a long succession of increasingly unneutral acts in the Atlantic which were of the utmost service to us." [2]

Churchill, in a report to the House of Commons on 20 August 1940 on this transaction, voiced one of his most famous and eloquent passages on the future of the Anglo-American relationship. "These are important steps," he said. "Undoubtedly this process means that these two great organizations of the English-speaking democracies, the British Empire and the United States, will have to be somewhat mixed up together in some of their affairs for mutual and general advantage. For my own part, looking out upon the future, I do not view the process with any misgivings. I could not stop it if I wished; no one can stop it. Like the Mississippi, it just keeps rolling along. Let it roll. Let it roll on—full flood, inexorable, irresistible, benignant, to broader lands and better days." [3]

But this was a British sentiment, not an American. No American statesman would have said this, in this or any other manner. There were significant differences in the lights in which these matters were presented by Churchill and Roosevelt to their respective constituencies. To Churchill the destroyers, the bases, and the assurance which Roosevelt had elicited that in no circumstances would the British fleet be either scuttled or surrendered to the Germans, were "parallel transactions . . . acts of good will performed on their merits and not as bargains." [4] In Roosevelt's eyes, as he presented them to the American people, they were a package deal, in which a number of obsolete vessels were exchanged for assets of incomparably greater value—rights to establish bases valuable, or essential, for American security, and an assurance that the British fleet would not in any event be added to German naval assets. The bargain was indeed as one-sided as

[2] Winston S. Churchill, *Their Finest Hour*, Vol. II, *The Second World War* (Boston: Houghton Mifflin Company, 1949), p. 404. Churchill adds, "It would, according to all the standards of history, have justified the German Government in declaring war upon them. The President judged that there was no danger, and I felt that there was no hope, of this simple solution of so many difficulties."

[3] *Ibid.*, pp. 408–9.

[4] *Ibid.*, p. 416.

could be, in a short-range sense. But perhaps Churchill was right: what mattered was the long-term implications. For the present, the transactions made very little difference. Churchill heartened his people by claiming (5 September) that "there will be no delay in bringing the American destroyers into active service." [5] In fact, only nine of the famous fifty destroyers entered British service before 1941.[6]

This was the period of unique glory when Britain, with the Dominions, stood alone against a Germany that was now dominating and organizing the European Continent against her. The British do not seem to have considered seriously any alternative policy. They were sustained by the hope, justified in the event but certainly never given any official countenance in Washington, that they would not stand alone forever.

The following period, until December 1941, saw an increasing departure by the United States from isolationism and, indeed, from neutrality. Neutrality was replaced by "non-belligerency," or the effort to give Britain all possible aid short of actually going to war with Germany. In this long series of actions, the Roosevelt administration led, with Congress and public opinion acting as a restraint. The President knew that he could not actually involve the country in war without a more substantial reason than any that had yet appeared, but he was energetic and ingenious in exploring the limits of possible action.

Many of these steps were of a naval character, taken by the President as Commander-in-Chief. They were intended to buttress U.S. security by averting British defeat in what Churchill dubbed "The Battle of the Atlantic," upon which Britain's part in the war utterly depended. Thus, in March 1941 the President authorized U.S. naval yards to repair British ships. The same month he transferred ten Coast Guard cutters to Britain to assist in antisubmarine warfare, and seized interned Axis and Danish ships in American ports.

From the spring of 1941 onward the U.S. Navy had orders to patrol the Atlantic as far east as the 25th meridian, and to radio to the Royal Navy the whereabouts of any German

[5] *Ibid.,* p. 415.
[6] Taylor, *English History,* p. 496.

vessels encountered. Greenland was taken under American control in April 1941, and in June the United States took over the garrisoning of Iceland, occupied the previous year by Britain. Both of these places were possessions of German-occupied Denmark.

In May 1941 U.S. ships were moved from the Pacific fleet to escort American merchantmen on their way to England. The *Robin Moor,* an American freighter, was torpedoed on 21 May 1941 by a German submarine. On 27 May the President proclaimed a national emergency, and said, "Our patrols are helping now to ensure deliveries of the needed supplies to England." Further steps were the freezing on 14 June of German and Italian assets in the United States and the compulsory closing of all consulates and other offices of the two countries.

After the attack on the U.S.S. *Greer* in Iceland waters on 4 September 1941, U.S. protection was extended to all merchant ships in the American patrol zone; and all German and Italian ships of war in the zone were to be fired on when sighted. On 17 October the destroyer *Kearny* was torpedoed off Iceland but reached port. Another destroyer, the *Reuben James,* was torpedoed and sunk on 31 October. Thus in the months before Pearl Harbor there was a steadily increasing U.S. commitment to the naval war in support of Britain, an undeclared war which had already led to American casualties. With dramatic irony a piquant contrast was developing between the behavior of the U.S. Atlantic fleet, already at fighting pitch and operating under battle conditions (but opposing a Germany which at this stage was being hypercautious in not provoking the United States), and the Pacific Fleet (in the theatre where the war was actually to arrive), easy-going, following the enjoyable life of subtropical service appropriate to a time of no emergency, all too successfully "trying to act and even to think in terms of peacetime routine." [7]

Concurrent with the unfolding of naval warfare in which the American navy assisted Britain in keeping the sea-lanes open, there had occurred the initiation of a vast program to

[7] Robert E. Sherwood, *Roosevelt and Hopkins: An Intimate History* (New York: Harper and Brothers, 1948), p. 365.

assist Britain, now beginning to be in desperate financial straits. The idea of Lend-Lease was propounded by President Roosevelt on 17 December 1940, and it became law on 11 March 1941. The two facets of Roosevelt's policy were complementary: it was no use Britain's buying supplies in the United States if they never reached the embattled island; but equally it was pointless to keep the sea-lanes open if British capacity to pay were to be exhausted and no other arrangements were made.

The Lend-Lease Act gave the President broad discretionary powers to authorize, when he deemed it in the interests of national defense, and to the extent to which funds were available, the production or procurement of any defense article for the use of any country whose defense was vital to the defense of the United States. The terms and conditions were merely to be such as the President deemed satisfactory. There was no condition for repayment in the normal sense.

This great measure did not end Britain's dollar problem, but it made it bearable. It was a guarantee that Britain would not fail for want of dollars. Its passing was the decisive American commitment, more significant than the eventual repeal in November 1941 of the key sections of the Neutrality Law, by which repeal the United States returned to the principle of the freedom of the seas, reclaiming the established right under international law to send its ships wherever it pleased and arm and protect them in any way possible. But if the inauguration of Lend-Lease was a godsend to Britain, surely it was also the passing-bell of British greatness. A nation that cannot conduct a war in which it is engaged without enormous subsidies from another power has in some measure lost its independence. It can hardly claim with justice any longer that it stands on an equal footing with the power whose subsidies alone make its continued existence possible; it can only pretend to that status.

The act of charity on the part of the United States was very great, but little attempt was made to spare the feelings of the recipient. It was made abundantly clear that it was charity, and charity on conditions rigidly laid down by the donor. It is grimly amusing to reflect that in the 1960s no African or Asian state, kindly condescending to accept a few hundred million dollars from the hopefully proffering United States, would put up for a moment with the kind of rigid specifications about the recipient's behavior that came along with Lend-Lease aid. (For that matter, Russia during the war did not have to put up with them either.)

> Great Britain was still a poor relation, not an equal partner. There was no pooling of resources. Instead Great Britain was ruthlessly stripped of her remaining dollars. The Americans insisted they were aiding Great Britain so that she could fight Germany and not to maintain her as an industrial power. No lend-lease goods could go into exports, and even exports not made from these had to be cut down for fear of outcry from American competitors. Thanks to lend-lease Great Britain virtually ceased to be an exporting country. She sacrificed her postwar future for the sake of the war.[8]

British exports in 1943 had shrunk to 29 percent of the 1938 level.

In the effort to demonstrate that aid was not a one-way street, Britain had considerable success. Britain instituted a program of reciprocal aid where appropriate to the United States. This was unconditional and thus was not what it was often called, "Reverse Lend-Lease." Of the total U.S. expenditure on Lend-Lease ($43.6 billion), some $27 billion went to the United Kingdom. In reciprocal aid the United Kingdom contributed about $5.7 billion. In proportion of population, resources, and industrial capacity the two streams of aid mutually exchanged may be regarded as reasonably equivalent.[9]

---

[8] Taylor, *English History*, p. 513. The "ruthlessness" is substantiated in detail in Appendix II, on Lend-Lease, in William Hardy McNeill, *America, Britain and Russia: Their Co-operation and Conflict 1941–1946* (London: Oxford University Press, 1953), especially pp. 776–77. Two small points that no historian has hitherto, I believe, pointed out: (1) The original Lend-Lease Bill, which became the statute, was appropriately numbered HR 1776. The wheel had indeed come full circle since 1776. (2) For some extraordinary reason (British inability to get American matters quite right?) Lend-Lease was invariably known colloquially in Britain as "Lease-Lend."

[9] McNeill, p. 783.

More striking, though in fact less substantial as a sign of growing Anglo-American cooperation, was the meeting at sea —in Placentia Bay, Argentia, Newfoundland—of Roosevelt and Churchill in August 1941. This was the first of the nine conferences, each a historic landmark with its own special significance, that they were to have during the war.[10] The British hoped on this occasion for solid commitments of U.S. military assistance. They did not get them. Roosevelt's chief anxiety at this point was to facilitate aid to Soviet Russia, invaded by Germany the preceding 22 June and generally (but quite wrongly) thought to be on the verge of speedy defeat. Few people followed the then Senator Harry S Truman in his argument that Soviet Russia and Nazi Germany should be left to cut each other's throats.

The curious outcome of the Placentia meeting was the "Atlantic Charter," a highfalutin declaration in eight clauses about the kind of world that the President and the Prime Minister hoped to see after the war. The document, which was issued on 14 August 1941, read as follows:

> The President of the United States of America and the Prime Minister, Mr. Churchill, representing His Majesty's Government in the United Kingdom, being met together, deem it right to make known certain common principles in the national policies of their respective countries on which they base their hopes for a better future for the world.
>
> First, their countries seek no aggrandizement, territorial or other;
>
> Second, they desire to see no territorial changes that do

[10] The list (with the code names that the military, and especially semi-military people like Churchill, love) is: (1) Newfoundland, August 1941; (2) Washington, 22 December 1941–14 January 1942, "Arcadia"; (3) Washington, 18–25 June 1942; (4) Casablanca, 14–25 January 1943; (5) Washington, 12–25 May 1943, "Trident"; (6) Quebec, 14–24 August 1943, "Quadrant"; (7) Cairo-Teheran-Cairo, 22 November–6 December 1943, "Sextant" and "Eureka"; Stalin's presence at Teheran made it the first "Big Three" conference; (8) Quebec, 11–19 September 1944, "Octagon"; (9) Yalta, Crimea, 4–11 February 1945. Before Potsdam (17 July–2 August 1945) Roosevelt was dead. Potsdam was the last "Big Three" conference at that level, no doubt because the war was at an end; but perhaps also because Stalin sensed that the possibility of playing off the United States and Britain against each other had ended too.

not accord with the freely expressed wishes of the peoples concerned;

Third, they respect the right of all peoples to choose the form of government under which they will live; and they wish to see sovereign rights and self-government restored to those who have been forcibly deprived of them.

Fourth, they will endeavor, with due respect to their existing obligations, to further the enjoyment by all States, great or small, victor or vanquished, of access, on equal terms, to the trade and to the raw materials of the world which are needed for their economic prosperity;

Fifth, they desire to bring about the closest collaboration between all nations in the economic field with the object of securing, for all, improved labor standards, economic advancement and social security;

Sixth, after the final destruction of Nazi tyranny, they hope to see established a peace which will afford to all nations the means of dwelling in safety within their own boundaries, and which will afford assurance that all the men in all the lands may live out their lives in freedom from fear and want;

Seventh, such a peace should enable all men to traverse the high seas and oceans without hindrance;

Eighth, they believe that all the nations of the world, for realistic as well as spiritual reasons, must come to the abandonment of the use of force. Since no future peace can be maintained if land, sea and air armaments continue to be employed by nations which threaten, or may threaten, aggression outside of their frontiers, they believe, pending the establishment of a wider and permanent system of general security, that the disarmament of such nations is essential. They will likewise aid and encourage all other practicable measures which will lighten for peace-loving peoples the crushing burden of armaments.[11]

The issuing of this document was an odd business on all counts. It was not the principal purpose of the meeting, though it is what it is remembered for; "the so-called Atlantic Charter was apparently a by-product of the conference rather than its

---

[11] William L. Langer and S. Everett Gleason, *The Undeclared War 1940–1941* (New York: Harper and Brothers for the Council on Foreign Relations, 1953), pp. 687–88.

primary objective." [12] It would seem that little or no preliminary work had been done by either side on preparing such a *pronunciamiento* about war aims. Churchill in general thought little of conjuring up visions of desirable postwar worlds when the immediate and still dubious issue was survival. "Ever since his advent to power Mr. Churchill had in fact refused to pronounce on the conditions of peace and the future organization of the world, fearing, as he did, that discussion of such issues would divide British opinion without serving any important or useful purpose." [13] The initiative came from Roosevelt; yet the first draft was produced by Churchill.[14] It seems to be a constant feature of the American psyche that there is a strong belief in the possibility of influencing events through the production of impressive documents showing "a decent respect to the opinions of mankind," and making fervent appeals to it in the name of first principles. The Declaration of Independence, Secretary Hay's Open Door pronouncements, the Fourteen Points, the tradition of presidential inaugural addresses—all such verbal milestones, all these missives intended also as missiles, testify to the belief.

Specifically, Roosevelt seems to have wanted to embody two things in such a document. It was to act as a guarantee that the British were not involved in making any secret treaties such as were supposed to have queered the peacemaking pitch at the end of the First World War; and it was to strike a blow for international free trade and against the British system of Imperial Preference embodied in the Ottawa Agreements of 1932. The restoration of the lost world of free trade was something of a passion with Cordell Hull (not present), the Secretary of State, and the Under-Secretary, Sumner Welles, who represented him. So one has the paradox that even on this crucial and symbolic occasion of Anglo-American cooperation part of the motivation on the American side was anti-British; or, at any rate, was the desire to force the British to change their policies.

When Welles pressed for the inclusion of the phrase "without

12 *Ibid.*, p. 677.
13 *Ibid.*, p. 678.
14 Winston S. Churchill, *The Grand Alliance*, Vol. III, *The Second World War* (Boston: Houghton Mifflin Company, 1950), pp. 433–37.

discrimination" in the clause on trade, Churchill pointed out correctly that this might be regarded as calling in question the Ottawa Agreements; when Welles said that this "was the core of the matter," Churchill gave him a broadside:

> I could not help mentioning the British experience in adhering to free trade for eighty years in the face of evermounting American tariffs. We had allowed the fullest importations into all our colonies. Even our coastwise traffic around Great Britain was open to the competition of the world. All we had got in reciprocation was successive doses of American Protection.[15]

"Mr. Welles seemed to be a little taken aback." Faces were saved all round by the insertion (in the fourth paragraph) of the phrase "with due respect to their existing obligations," an innocent-seeming loophole through which many horses and carts might be driven.

The first and second paragraphs constituted an assurance welcome to the Americans that populations and territories would not be shuffled at the end of the war in accordance with secret treaties.

On the British side, there was the hope of securing an American commitment to participation in an international organization in the postwar world. The memory of U.S. refusal to join the League was the specter to be exorcized. The last (eighth) paragraph achieved this, since it appeared to envisage a sort of Anglo-American domination of the world, pending "the establishment of a wider and permanent system of general security." This paragraph might be regarded as a triumph for Churchill, though a purely verbal one. He might not be much in favor of large-sounding plans for the postwar world, but he was very much in favor of doing *anything* that suggested that Britain and the United States would be marching down that road arm-in-arm.

Where the Soviet Union would figure in this *pas de deux* was a question not raised. The Soviet Union (unlike the United States) was already at war with Hitler's Reich, though (unlike Britain) quite involuntarily. The idea that the form

15 *Ibid.*, p. 437. Cf., Bevin's remarks quoted below, p. 165.

of the postwar world could be determined by Britain and the United States without reference to the Soviet Union (which is really the unstated major premise of the Atlantic Charter) was an odd idea. And if the question of the intentions of the Soviet Union had been looked in the eye, the whole pretty structure of velleities would have been seen for what it was, a fragile piece of tinsel. Anyone who supposed that the Soviet Union was likely to behave in accordance with the first, second, and third paragraphs of the Atlantic Charter was indeed optimistic.

Russia was, as a sort of afterthought, invited in September 1941 to express its agreement with the Atlantic Charter, and did so; but with significant reservations which ominously offset the acceptance.

The Atlantic Charter was not any sort of treaty. It had, indeed, no constitutional standing whatever. The relation between it and any actual policies followed at the end of the war is tenuous indeed. In form it was merely a press release. But it did have this much significance: it was a joint statement by the heads of government of the two states, made while one was at war, but the other as yet not. Secondly, it did indicate something that was of immense importance—the fact that the United States was already deeply concerned with the shape of the postwar world, and presumably committed to active participation in determining what it would be. This was an enormous change from the rigid, frigid isolationism of the mid-1930s. It was a great change from the situation even two years previously. Even if it did nothing else (and it did very little else) for these reasons the Atlantic Charter, and the Argentia meeting from which it emerged, gave a much-needed boost to British morale.

While Congressional debates on Lend-Lease had been proceeding, certain Anglo-American military conversations took place in Washington. While these were examples of pure contingency planning, and did not involve any commitment, they did look forward to possible participation by the United States in the war on the same side as Britain. In fact they were more important than that, for they actually determined, as it turned out, the whole shape and course of the war.

Conversations between American army and navy officers responsible for drafting war plans and their British opposite numbers began as early as August 1940 in London and Washington. The formal joint British-American staff talks, however, were begun in Washington on 29 January 1941 and concluded on 27 March. (What was going on was concealed from prying eyes—which did not mean only enemy eyes—as far as possible: the British participants wore civilian clothes and disguised themselves as "technical advisers to the British Purchasing Commission." [16]) Their conclusions were embodied in a plan known as "ABC-1." The objective was to consider what strategy ought to be "should the United States be compelled to resort to war." The ABC-1 agreement concluded that even if Japan were in the war too, the priority should be given to defeating Germany: "Since Germany is the predominant member of the Axis Powers, the Atlantic and European area is considered to be the decisive theatre. The principal United States Military effort will be exerted in that theatre, and operations of United States forces in other theatres will be conducted in such a manner as to facilitate that effort." [17] The great interest of this decision is that, despite the major changes in the war situation which occurred in 1941 (both Russia and Japan becoming belligerents, which they had not been when the document was drawn up), the major strategic principles agreed upon in ABC-1 were those which guided the actual Anglo-American conduct of the war.

When Japan attacked the United States at Pearl Harbor on 7 December 1941, the war changed its nature in several ways. It became a world war rather than a primarily European struggle. Also, though this was not immediately apparent, the role of Britain in the war slowly went into eclipse. Thenceforth the whole strength of the United States was committed to victory. The war against the Axis became a war of three allies, with two enormously more powerful than the third. The third,

16 Sherwood, p. 273.
17 McNeill, p. 8.

Britain, had, however, made a unique contribution. Her sheer survival, her lonely and unique stand, was now successfully over, with victory in the long run reasonably certain.

Victory was a long way off, however, and as it happened victory in the Far Eastern–Pacific theatre was an achievement to which Britain contributed little. The only two British capital ships in that part of the world, the *Prince of Wales* and the *Repulse,* were lost as early as 10 December; and deservedly lost, through being put into an exposed position with no air cover whatever off the coast of Malaya, where they were promptly sunk by Japanese bombers. Obviously, they should have been withdrawn to Australia. Worse was to come: the surrender on 15 February 1942 of Singapore, the great trading center which Stamford Raffles had acquired for Britain in 1819 with a prescient appreciation of its superb commercial future. A great deal of money had been spent in the 1920s and 1930s on fortifying Singapore against the threat of an attack from the sea. It was not attacked from the sea. It surrendered after a halfhearted and incompetent defense to Japanese forces that were inferior in numbers to those of the defenders in all branches except aircraft. It was three days short of nineteen months since Churchill's "finest hour" speech. The fall of Singapore was not the British Empire's finest hour. It has a claim to be regarded as its most disgraceful.

Except insofar as they had contributed to the basic research on the atomic bomb, the British played little part in the campaigns against Japan. The indecisive campaign in Burma, though it had its interesting aspects—Orde Wingate was probably the most ingenious and inventive soldier thrown up by the whole war—was regarded by the United States as unnecessary, and it was certainly inconclusive. The naval and island-hopping war in the Pacific was an American war, with some help from Australia. This crude exposure of the extent to which the British posture east of India had rested on sheer bluff was not lost on the Australians. The exposure was to have momentous consequences in the recasting of transpacific relationships in the postwar world. The then Prime Minister of Australia, John Curtin, head of the Labour party (the Aus-

tralian party always more opposed to the British connection
than are the Liberal and Country parties) declared bluntly on
27 December 1941, "Australia looks to America free from any
pangs as to traditional links or kinship with the United Kingdom. . . . We shall exert our energy toward shaping a plan
with the United States as its keystone." The ANZUS pact, to
come a decade later, was casting its shadow before. Curtin
soon secured the repatriation from the Middle East of most of
the Australian forces there, and they were put under the
command of General Douglas MacArthur when he set up
headquarters in Australia.

On 13 December 1941 Churchill and advisers left for the
United States and the series of conferences in December and
January known as "Arcadia." There was some reason on the
British part to fear that, since war had actually come to the
United States in the Pacific, the main strength of the United
States would be directed against Japan. For the British, this
was a nightmare which replaced on 7 December 1941 the
earlier one, that the Japanese might attack British but not
American territories. Churchill had given his categorical assurance that if the Japanese attacked the United States, Britain
would automatically declare war, and he was as good as his
word; Roosevelt had been unable to give any converse under-
taking. It would also have been awkward if after Pearl Harbor
Germany had refrained from declaring war on the United
States, towards which indeed Hitler's policy had been cautious
and forebearing throughout 1941. Fortunately, however, Hitler
gratuitously and egregiously demonstrated his loyalty to Japan
by declaring war on the United States; and the Japanese
averted any Anglo-American awkwardness by impartially at-
tacking both British and American possessions.

In the event, though some presidential advisers wished
otherwise, the Arcadia conference upheld the ABC-1 doctrine
of "Europe first." This was a supremely important decision.
There seems to be remarkably little evidence of the reasons
why it was made. In part, like many governmental decisions,
it amounted merely to continuing along a road already taken.

The burning problem for a long time had been a Germany actually at war; Japan had been merely a potential threat. Further, until Japan could be held in the Pacific by naval forces, Europe and the Mediterranean offered the only possibility of deploying land armies.

It seems reasonable to surmise that there were deeper motives at work. Whatever suspicions might be entertained of "British imperialism," there was a feeling of kinship toward Britain that had no parallels. More broadly, there was a feeling of cultural affinity with Europe, the home continent of the United States, that made it a matter of greater urgency to rescue the European nations suffering under German occupation than to ensure American security in the Pacific theatre.

The pragmatic decisions of the "Arcadia" conference, confirming the earlier ABC-1 contingency plans, set the scenario that was followed throughout the remaining three and one-half years of the Second World War. Nor, in the following years, despite dissident opinion in Washington, despite occasional alarms on Churchill's part, was there much real danger of Roosevelt's reneging on the determination of priority for Europe. The history of the remainder of the war to a quite remarkable extent is concerned with the execution, with a high degree of fidelity, of the lines of action decided in Washington in January and February 1942.

Another result very important for the future of Anglo-American relations was the adoption in this conference of the principle of unity of command in a particular theatre, with a supreme commander for the area of operations and mixed forces and an international staff. This concept, invented and advocated by General Marshall and adopted with some reluctance by the British, was first put into operation in the Southeast Asia theatre, and later applied in the Mediterranean and elsewhere. These combined staffs worked extraordinarily well together later in the war—not with a complete absence of friction, but with a surprisingly small amount of it. As functioning under Eisenhower in the Mediterranean and later in the invasion of Western Europe, they formed the greatest example of intimate Anglo-American cooperation in action that has so far existed. It was a degree of international cooperation without precedent in the relations of sovereign states. There is certainly no parallel to it to be found in the First World War, or, in the Second, in the relations of Russia with her allies, or in the relations of the Axis powers. Probably no two countries but the United States and the United Kingdom could have achieved such an international merger.

As a corollary to the principle of unity of command in each war theatre, but at a higher level of organization, there followed the creation of the Combined Chiefs of Staff Committee, combining the chiefs of staff of the armed services of the two countries, and, from April 1942, seized of responsibility for the entire "strategic conduct of the war." The great decisions of strategy were taken during the periodic meetings between Churchill and Roosevelt. The Combined Chiefs planned how to carry them out. They also supervised Allied supreme commanders in the field. Above all, they controlled the flow of war materials to the various theatres of action. "The Committee gave substance and continuity to Anglo-American military cooperation which could hardly have been achieved in any other way." [18]

Paradoxically enough, such intimate cooperation was achieved despite the absence of a formal alliance; as in the First World War, the United States signed none. But the U.S. commitment was much more complete than in the First World War. The period of American participation was much longer: three and a half years as against one and a half. The American contribution, and American losses, were much greater than in the first war.

The nearest to an alliance that the United States came was as a signatory of the "Declaration of the United Nations"— the phrase *United Nations* being Roosevelt's invention.[19] The

[18] McNeill p. 111.

[19] It superseded "Associated Powers." The phrase "United Nations" can, however, be found in use before. Churchill (see *Grand Alliance,* p. 683) pointed out to Roosevelt that Byron used it in *Childe Harold* ("Here, where the sword United Nations drew"). More relevantly, and surprisingly, it had been proposed at the Imperial Conference of 1917 both by Sir Robert Borden of Canada and by W. F. Massey of New Zealand as names for the group

document was signed in Washington on 1 January 1942 by Roosevelt, Churchill, Litvinov (for Russia), and Soong (for China), and later by representatives of twenty-three other states. So far as the United States was concerned, it was an executive agreement, and as such never submitted to the Senate. It was the first stage in the later creation, in 1944 and 1945, of the actual organization, the United Nations.

Nevertheless, substance is what really matters, not form. The fact that Britain signed on 23 May 1942 a treaty of alliance with Russia, and did not have a formal alliance with the United States, did not mean that relations were closer between Britain and Russia than they were between Britain and the United States.

So long as the war lasted, in substance there was, in Churchill's phrase, a "Grand Alliance" of the United States, the Soviet Union, and Great Britain, an alliance which waged war with the primary and overriding purpose of defeating Germany.

Beyond that, there was no *common* political purpose shared by the three great allies. Looking beyond the defeat of Germany, the Soviet Union indeed had purposes. Britain had purposes, or at any rate apprehensions. The United States was averse to even considering the matter. The American attitude tended to regard war and peace as discrete conditions without continuity between them. There was thought to be something almost indecent about contemplating postwar political conditions; at any rate, unless done through roseate United Nations' spectacles.

The reality of Anglo-American cooperation centered on the remarkable personal relationship of Roosevelt and Churchill. They met on nine occasions; they exchanged voluminous messages constantly; Harry Hopkins shuttled the Atlantic as a go-

Dominions fully realize the ideal of an Imperial Commonwealth of United Nations." Massey: "I have used . . . a term with the use of which I thoroughly agree, and that is the term 'United Nations'. . . . We are coming together as United Nations of the Empire and on equal terms. . . ." Arthur Berriedale Keith, *Selected Speeches and Documents on British Colonial Policy 1763–1917* (London: Oxford University Press, 1918), Vol. II, pp. 379, 390. "United Nations" like "United States" involves some grammatical and stylistic difficulties. Is it a singular or a plural? British usage avoids the question. The standard form in British newspapers is "United Nations Organization" and the standard contraction not U.N. but U.N.O.

between. There was a real, if wary, friendship between the two men: a friendship doubtless a good deal warmer on Churchill's side—he was half-American, he had bet his all on the prospect of an Anglo-American alliance—than on the side of Roosevelt. It would be sadly easy to tell, only from perusing the record of their exchanges, which was the representative of the stronger state, which was the patron and which the client. Throughout his dealings with Roosevelt, Churchill was on his very best behavior. He was exceedingly careful never to offend Roosevelt; Roosevelt for his part obviously cared very little whether he offended Churchill or not. There is a strained politeness about all Churchill's communications to Roosevelt which stops only just this side of servility.

W. H. McNeill, who wrote the first full, and still one of the best, accounts of the wartime Grand Alliance, commented (and it should be remembered he wrote while Churchill was still alive and, indeed, again Prime Minister) that "from the beginning there was an element of deference in Churchill's dealings with Roosevelt, and growing familiarity never erased it. . . . Churchill's freedom of manoeuvre was restricted: in case of serious difference of opinion he could argue against the American position, but he could never afford to risk an open break. The very phrase which Churchill chose to sign his frequent cables to Roosevelt—'Former Naval Person'—constituted a symbol of his sense of disadvantage *vis-à-vis* the President. . . ." [20]

There were, after all, profound ideological differences between the two men. Roosevelt had, as McNeill says, a "general distaste for Churchill's political views." World politics was not, or not yet, really a matter of life or death for the United States. The world was still to Roosevelt, as Europe had been to Alexander I of Russia, a moral gymnasium where timely intervention and the adroit use of power might bring about the triumph of virtue. It was the triumph of virtue and the chastising of evil that were the issues to Roosevelt, not survival. "As representative of a nation whose power was clearly on the increase, he could look to the future of the world without too

[20] McNeill, p. 18.

anxious a concern for the special interests of the United States.
American power could be trusted to look after American interests, as it were, automatically." [21] But Britain had had a
narrow squeak, Churchill dreamed more of the past than the
future, Churchill took a pessimistic view of human nature in
politics; Churchill, in short, thought, as most of the masters
from Machiavelli to Morgenthau have done, that politics is a
struggle for power.

If there were profound differences in ideology, there were
differences between the two leaders in temperament and tech-
nique too. Robert E. Sherwood perhaps described them best in
his brilliant book on the role of Hopkins, special emissary of
the President:

> It is a matter of sacred tradition that, when an American
> statesman and a British statesman meet, the former will
> be plain, blunt, down to earth, ingenuous to a fault, while
> the latter will be sly, subtle, devious and eventually tri-
> umphant. In the cases of Roosevelt and Churchill, this
> formula became somewhat confused. . . . The Prime
> Minister quickly learned that he confronted in the Presi-
> dent a man of infinite subtlety and obscurity—an artful
> dodger who could not readily be pinned down on specific
> points, nor hustled or wheedled into definite commitments
> against his judgment or his will or his instinct. And Roose-
> velt soon learned how pertinacious the Prime Minister
> could be in pursuit of a purpose.[22]

Still, up to a point they enjoyed each other's company.
Roosevelt's famous tribute had generosity in it—"It is fun to be
in the same decade with you." They were both professional
politicians who had climbed to the top of the greasy pole—to
use the phrase of Disraeli, another professional who would have
relished the company of both of them, could he have known
them. They had wide divergencies, but they had one great
overriding purpose in common.

Of the divergencies, the one that struck the British most and

21 *Ibid.,* p. 19.
22 Sherwood, p. 364. Sherwood introduces his shrewd analysis with the
cautionary words "It would be an exaggeration to say that Roosevelt and
Churchill became chums at this Conference or at any subsequent time."

which, being not lost on the Russians, surely had its share in determining the form of the postwar world, was Roosevelt's implacable hostility to the British Empire. This was to appear in some form or another during every wartime conference. It comes through very strikingly—perhaps even exaggeratedly—in Elliot Roosevelt's book about his father, *As He Saw It*. Harold Macmillan, later himself Prime Minister, and wartime Minister in North Africa, is quite blunt about it in his memoirs, written after both men were dead. "To Roosevelt, Britain owes much," says Macmillan. Churchill communicated to him his thoughts very frankly from the beginning of the war. But "Roosevelt's response was by no means as warm or as open as Churchill believed. . . . With all his apparent sincerity and charm, there lay behind the outward show of friendship a feeling of hostility—perhaps even of jealousy—of the great Imperial story of the Old Country. The British Empire was a bugbear to him. Without any precise knowledge, he would lay down the law about Indian and colonial affairs; and the liquidation of the British Empire was, whether consciously or unconsciously, one of his aims." And again, "The President was no friend of the British Empire." What disturbed Macmillan even more than the President's hostility was the President's ignorance. Roosevelt's view of the British Empire was firmly fixed in some nineteenth- or eighteenth-century stereotype. "Nor did he understand the clearly defined and steadily pursued procedures by which we had long planned to bestow, by gradual means, first political education and then political independence upon those races for whom we held responsibility." [23]

Apart from Roosevelt's personal hostility toward the British Empire, which was without much immediate practical effect, two broad themes might be said to be involved in most of the Anglo-American differences from 1942 to 1945; and the differences were, in fact, much less important than the common purposes. The first area of difference, which is important from 1942 to 1944 but becomes more or less irrelevant thereafter,

[23] Harold Macmillan, *The Blast of War* (New York: Harper and Row, 1968), pp. 120–21.

concerns questions of grand strategy. Thereafter, in 1944 and 1945, the differences of view concern attitudes to Russia.

On the first point, the British favored a strategy of avoiding an all-out land assault on Germany until Germany had been weakened by peripheral attacks on outlying parts of her power, and by blockade and bombing. Their views were determined by the comparative paucity of their resources, and by the awful memories of the trench-warfare slaughter of 1914–1918. The Americans thought little of this strategy. They wanted a direct onslaught with maximum power on the principal enemy. The second area of differences arose out of the greater British tendency to become apprehensive about postwar relations with Russia, and the prospect of Russian domination of Eastern Europe.

It is possible to argue that these differences were in fact less significant than they seemed at the time, or than they have appeared in the endless controversies of postwar historiography. They certainly figured constantly on the agenda of inter-allied conferences; they certainly disturbed the even tenor of Anglo-American cooperation. The first point led Americans to suspect their British allies of stalling and cowardice. The second point led the British to impute ignorance and naïveté to their American allies. But, in practice, that which happened happened because there were no real alternatives. A direct assault on Germany simply was not possible without immensely lengthy and complex preparations. If Anglo-American power was to be deployed in Europe at all, the Mediterranean–North African theatre, where there had never ceased to be active contact with the Axis powers, offered at first the only possibility; and that led on naturally to the conquest of Sicily and Italy. So far as Russia and Eastern Europe were concerned, if Germany was eliminated, some increase of Russian influence there was inevitable; the effect of consistently wiser and more farsighted policies on the part of the Western Allies might have produced a postwar situation there somewhat different, but hardly totally different.

Questions regarding the employment of American forces in Europe led to Churchill making his second wartime visit to Washington, 18–25 June 1942. Molotov had just concluded

visits to London and Washington during which he had im-
periously pushed the Russian demand for a "second front"
in Western Europe. (Everybody seems to have been too
polite to point out that at the time when there *had* been a front
in Western Europe, 1939–1940, the Russians had been the
allies of the Germans, and in no hurry to create any "second
front" in *Eastern* Europe. The eastern front had not been of
their making.) Roosevelt, fully sympathetic but very much the
"artful dodger" of Sherwood's phrase, consented to a public
statement on 11 June which said: "In the course of the conversations full understanding was reached with regard to the
urgent tasks of creating a Second Front in Europe in 1942."
Carefully read, this was ambiguous; but it looked like a commitment. The Americans had in mind a limited landing in
September 1942 to seize the Cotentin peninsula of France.
Churchill could not demur outright, though he had reservations. In fact the fall of Tobruk (20 June) led to a diversion
of strength to the African front that made a descent on France
impossible in 1942. The substitute was Anglo-American landings in French North Africa. Once that campaign was fully
under way, a Continental landing became impossible for 1943
also.

Churchill's June 1942 visit to Washington is significant for
another reason. In the conversations at Hyde Park on 20
June between Churchill and Roosevelt the former offered all
British assistance in the development of atomic bombs. British
scientists had already done a considerable amount of theoreti-
cal work on this. To avoid waste, it was agreed that engineering
and factory production of such a weapon should be concentrated in the United States; but one aspect of the agreement,
later not honored, was that Britain should share fully in
the information made available in the joint enterprise.[24]

After a fashion, a "second front" was established in the
Mediterranean area by the joint U.S.–British landings in French
North Africa on 8 November 1942. These brought on a
rather tangled imbroglio in U.S. relations with France, as well
as some strains in the relation with Britain.

American sympathy with France, dating back to the Revo-

[24] See Chapter VI for discussion of the development of atomic weapons.

lutionary War, was strong. The crux was the question of which
authorities, after June 1940, should be regarded as standing
for France. After the fall of France the United States was still
a neutral and, unlike Britain, maintained diplomatic relations
with Marshal Pétain's government at Vichy. Again U.S. policy
differed from British in that the United States did not regard
General Charles de Gaulle as, in effect, the head of a French
government-in-exile. The U.S. government took no very favorable view of de Gaulle, the more so after Gaullist forces took
over the St. Lawrence Gulf islands of St. Pierre and Miquelon
on 24 December 1941. When the landings in French North
Africa took place the commander on the spot, General Mark
Clark, who was supported in this by his superior, Eisenhower,
made a cease-fire agreement with Admiral Darlan, head of
the Vichy forces, who happened to be in Algeria at the time.
This policy of expediency lasted until Darlan's assassination
on 24 December 1942. The Americans thereupon switched
their bets, placing them on General Giraud, but still rebuffing
de Gaulle. Before and during the Roosevelt-Churchill conference at Casablanca (14–25 January 1943) the British, who
regarded Giraud as ineffective and quite incapable of serving
as a focus of French loyalty, tried to reconcile de Gaulle and
Giraud. Harold Macmillan, as British Minister of State in
North Africa, played a leading part in these negotiations,
and his account in his memoirs is of great interest.[25] His American colleague and opposite number was Robert Murphy. De
Gaulle and Giraud were persuaded to meet and a fragile
reconciliation and a tentative fusion of their claims to leadership was arranged.

The business of the "Anfa Memorandum" forms a curious
pendant to the Casablanca meetings. After the business was
over and "the captains and the kings" had departed, it was
discovered that Roosevelt had given his assent to a memorandum, an alleged summary of what had been agreed, that in
fact ignored the delicate compromise that had been achieved
between de Gaulle and Giraud, and spoke as though all
responsibility for French North Africa was still in Giraud's

[25] See Macmillan, *Blast of War,* Chaps. X–XIII.

hands. It is an interesting, but by no means the sole, example of the frivolous high-handedness with which Roosevelt on occasion conducted great affairs. As Macmillan comments drily, "Murphy had always been concerned with the President's rather slapdash methods of doing business." [26] Fortunately, it proved possible to render the "Anfa Memorandum" as nugatory in practice as it was inaccurate.

The question of the leadership of free France was soon settled clearly enough, though the wellsprings of later animosities between de Gaulle and the United States are to be found in this period. In June 1943 both Roosevelt and Churchill recognized a reconstructed "French Committee of National Liberation" with Giraud and de Gaulle as co-chairmen. By November, the superior political skill of de Gaulle enabled him to assume full control. The following summer, de Gaulle paid his first visit to Washington; and in October 1944, after the Allies were fighting in France and had captured Paris, the United States, Britain, and other allies recognized de Gaulle's administration as the Provisional Government of France.

The African campaigns ended triumphantly when the British-American joint forces pushing from the west met the British forces that had fought their long way from Egypt. Between them von Arnim's army was destroyed. The occasion was celebrated with a great victory parade in Tunis on 20 May 1943. (There is a fine set-piece description in Macmillan's memoirs.) [27] This, perhaps, rather than the final victory two years later, was the high point of British military achievement and prestige in the war. The forces moving from the east were almost entirely British, the forces moving from the west still contained a majority of British troops. The admiral commanding the Mediterranean forces, Admiral Cunningham, was British. Though the overall theatre commander in the last months was Eisenhower, the glory really belonged to

[26] *Ibid.*, p. 209. Murphy's memoirs, *Diplomat Among Warriors* (Garden City, N.Y.: Doubleday and Company, Inc., 1964) do not mention the Anfa Memorandum, though they are explicit enough about Roosevelt's off-handedness and frivolity. See further A. L. Funk, "The Anfa Memorandum: An Incident of the Casablanca Conference," *Journal of Modern History,* September 1954.

[27] Macmillan, pp. 259–63.

Field Marshal Alexander, the superbly competent and serene, and his field commander, Montgomery. Moreover, the desert campaign more than any other campaign of the war held the affection and interest of the British people. The annual Alamein dinner continues to be held, like the Waterloo dinner where gathered annually the dwindling survivors of the great victory of 1815. No other event of the war enjoys such a commemoration. Eighth Army, fighting its lonely war in the desert far from home, developed its own traditions and mystique, associated with fly-switches, ornate throat-scarves, and cap-visors severely remolded as Alexander did his. It was a comprehensible war, fought with numbers not overwhelmingly large in a highly suitable place, between the desert wadis and the sea, a place with something of the precision of a game board, where progress could be easily measured in terms of lateral movement in an east-west direction. Civilians and towns, these complicating factors, were mercifully few and, in any case, negligible. With the victory at Tunis which completed the expulsion of the Axis from Africa, all this was victoriously over; but it was over.

More than the African campaign was over. The year 1943 can be taken quite precisely to mark the point when world leadership moved from Great Britain to the United States. Britain, fully mobilized as no other country was (no other country conscripted women), had reached the peak of its strength, a peak which in fact could not long be maintained. The highest point of British munitions production came in 1943. To maintain the armed forces, it was necessary to withdraw men from munitions production in 1943 and 1944. The corollary was increased dependence on American production, which was amply equal to the challenge. Some of the newer weapons—landing craft, self-propelled guns, tank transporters—were hardly made in Britain at all. "In effect the British nation found itself poised like a wave on the point of breaking. The crest of military preparation . . . had to be nourished constantly from across the Atlantic; but by careful calculation, the high point of British military striking power was made to coincide with D-day in Normandy." But "the British economy no longer had any slack. Man-power, plant, materials all were fully employed, and an increase here required a decrease there." [28]

Every set of statistics told the same story. In early 1942, British munitions production was still higher than American. By the end of 1943, it was one-quarter of American, and in 1944 one-sixth.[29] American production capacity was not only supplying the United States and its allies with military equipment, it was providing for Americans a higher standard of living than before the war. In Britain the production of consumer goods had been throttled back to about one-half of prewar. In 1943 the American merchant marine surpassed the British for the first time. In the later years of the war, the British role as a Great Power was one that could be maintained only because the United States propped up Britain. A coldly rational course would have been for Britain to withdraw to a minimal role, while the United States and Russia went ahead and won the war, as they could certainly have done. Such a decision, never considered for a moment, was not in accordance with the tradition or the ethos of Churchill or those whom he represented. The British continued to bear the last extremity of strain as a price well worth paying for having a major voice, as one of the three great allies, in the shaping of the final stages of the war, and the coming peace.

In point of fact, since both the American and the Russian leaders knew well enough what the score was, Britain's weight in inter-Allied counsels in these later years was a steadily lessening one. The literary ability, the persistence in argument, the personal fire of Churchill, were only just able to maintain the pretense of equality in face of the overwhelming shift, now being made manifest, in the basic realities of power.

The tone of the later Anglo-American war conferences as it must have been has perhaps been as well suggested in an impressionistic sketch by a distinguished novelist, James Gould Cozzens, as by any historian:

> The Protagonist of the Bulldog Breed was often grumpy, half a mind on his brandy-soured stomach and throatful

28 McNeill, pp. 230–31.
29 Taylor, *English History,* p. 566.

of cigar-flavored phlegm. Grimacing, Mr. Churchill must taste, too, the gall of his situation. Fine phrases and selected words might show it almost a virtue that, far call'd our navies melt away; that, on dune and headland sinks the fire; but those circumstances also kept him from the leading position. Except as a piece of politeness, he did not even sit as an equal. His real job was to palter. His field and air marshals, on short commons of men and machines, his admirals of the outclassed fleet, all nerves bared by close to four years of war in the main unfortunate, supported him, courageous and proud, but also at the last word impotent. Across the table, . . . the Union strong and great, was in a pleasanter position; justifiably cockier. They had the ships, they had the men, they had the money, too! . . .[30]

The new shape of relations among the big three allies which was to subsist from the summer of 1943 until the summer of 1945 was exhibited clearly at the conferences, three in a row—Cairo, Teheran, Cairo—held from 22 November to 6 December 1943. Roosevelt and Churchill conferred in Cairo (on the first occasion Chiang Kai-shek was also there on Roosevelt's initiative, not Churchill's); the Teheran conference brought Roosevelt, Churchill, and Stalin together for the first time. Churchill envisaged the preliminary Cairo meeting as the opportunity to coordinate future strategy so that they could be in agreement before they faced Stalin. It did not work out that way. Roosevelt had no intention of being cajoled into forming part of a united front against Stalin. Over the next year and a half until his death, he came pretty close on a number of occasions to forming part of an American-Russian united front against Britain, or—which was only a slightly less bitter pill for Churchill to swallow—of playing the mediator between Stalin and Churchill. He enjoyed this role. Roosevelt himself had provided the classic statement of his own views, or illusions, in a letter of 18 March 1942 to Churchill in which he said, "I know you will not mind my being brutally frank when I tell you that I think I can

[30] James Gould Cozzens, *Guard of Honor* (New York: Harcourt, Brace and World, Inc., 1948), p. 394.

personally handle Stalin better than either your Foreign Office or my State Department. Stalin hates the guts of all your top people. He thinks he likes me better, and I trust he will continue to do so." [31]

At Teheran, Churchill hoped to secure the postponement of "Overlord" (the direct cross-Channel invasion) in favor of enlarged Mediterranean operations, including the possible establishment of a front in Yugoslavia or northern Greece. He had, however, to give way to Roosevelt and Stalin's united preference for Overlord. On the other hand Roosevelt, after extracting Churchill's consent to Overlord, agreed to a joint campaign against Japan in the Indian Ocean.

On the question of the direct cross-Channel invasion, Roosevelt was doubtless correct that it was the quickest way to end the war. Whether Churchill's preference for action in the Balkans was motivated by the desire to forestall the Russians there is more doubtful; this may be a reading-back into his attitudes of 1944 of his later anti-Russian stance.[32] These are matters where controversy has not yet jelled into general acceptance of a single view. Certainly it is difficult to read any outright opposition on Churchill's part to the Russians exercising a major role in the Balkans into the bizarre episode on 9 October 1944 during Churchill's visit to Moscow, when the two agreed on the share of influence each country was to have over Rumania, Greece, Yugoslavia, Hungary, and Bulgaria. The statement of the agreed position in terms of percentages was Churchill's idea.[33] It is impossible to say what on

[31] Churchill, *The Hinge of Fate,* Vol. IV, *The Second World War* (Boston: Houghton Mifflin Company, 1950), p. 201.

[32] Probably the late Chester Wilmot's very readable, vigorous, and knowledgeable work, *The Struggle for Europe* (London: Collins, 1952), which did so much to popularize the view that Eastern Europe might have been saved from being part of the Russian Empire if only Churchill's strategy had prevailed in place of Roosevelt's, exaggerates Churchill's prescience and the clarity of his thought. *If* this is what Churchill really thought, his speeches in praise of the Russians and of Stalin, which continue well into 1945, are remarkable pieces of hypocrisy. Still, it is certainly true that Churchill viewed with greater gloom than Roosevelt the fate that was in store for Poland. But, to adapt what was said of Maria Theresa, he wept, but he gave way just the same.

[33] Churchill, *Triumph and Tragedy,* Vol. VI, *The Second World War* (Boston: Houghton Mifflin Company, 1953), p. 227. The document envisaged

earth Churchill meant by all this bogus arithmetic (and his memoirs do not inform us), or for that matter what Stalin considered he was agreeing to.

Any real alignment of British and American policies regarding the postwar world in that last phase of the war was prevented by the curious and regrettable fact that there were many who filled important posts in the U.S. government who shared Roosevelt's singular world-view. With him, they thought it perfectly possible to get on with the Russians, whom they regarded more or less as simply democrats in furry hats. Like him, they greatly exaggerated the vitality and will-to-power of the British Empire, for which they had a deep dislike. The memoirs (*I Was There*) of Admiral Leahy, whose position was of great importance—he was Roosevelt's appointee as Chairman of the (U.S.) Joint Chiefs of Staff and of the (U.S.-U.K.) Combined Chiefs of Staff and had direct access to the President—are full of an embittered skepticism about Britain and British policies. (He does not seem to have acquired it in the course of these duties: when he entered upon them it was already full-blown.) By a curious policy of overcompensating for a natural cultural affinity, U.S. policy-makers during the war habitually gave Soviet Russia the benefit of the doubt, and just as habitually denied it to Britain. Suspicion was the customary attitude toward Britain; toward Russia, boundless optimism and trust. The contrast that prevailed under Lend-Lease has already been briefly alluded to: the British had to justify in detail every claim for equipment or munitions; the Russians, however, were given without scrutiny everything for which they asked, up to the limit of supplies and carrying capacity. Another example comes from the arrangements made in 1944 for the future dividing of Germany into zones of

---

a predominant Russian influence in Rumania (90 percent, "The others" 10 percent) and in Bulgaria (75–25), and a predominant British influence in Greece (90–10), "in accord with U.S.A." Influence in Yugoslavia and Hungary was to be divided "50–50." Stalin honored the agreement in regard to Greece; when British troops suppressed the Communists in Greece in 1944–45 he made no protest, though plenty of British and American newspapers did. But Stalin certainly disregarded the 50–50 sharing of influence in Hungary and Yugoslavia. Poland, a good deal more important than those cases, was not mentioned in the document.

occupation. The American authorities were scrupulously careful to obtain from Britain explicit rights of access to Bremen, which was to be a U.S. enclave in the British zone. But it was not regarded as necessary to obtain any explicit definition in regard to U.S. (and British and French) access to Berlin, an enclave in the Russian zone. This fantastic omission has had embarrassing results that continue to the present; it has already resulted in one major international crisis.

The climax, and, as it proved, virtually the end, of this period came with the three-power conference at Yalta, 4–11 February 1945. Roosevelt ran true to his previous form, and even went further in the same direction. He obviously saw little reason to conciliate Churchill, representing a nation whose power was so obviously in relative, and perhaps absolute, decline. In his first tête-à-tête with Stalin on 4 February, Roosevelt strove to create an atmosphere of kitchen-gossip intimacy by making what he called "indiscreet" comments on British policy, adding the malicious if meaningless jibe that "the British were a peculiar people and wished to have their cake and eat it too." [34] In another bilateral meeting on 8 February he said that he hoped the British would give Hong Kong back to China, although "he knew Mr. Churchill would have strong objections to this suggestion." Later in the same conversation he said that "he personally did not feel it was necessary to invite the British to participate in the trusteeship of Korea"; evoking from Stalin the near-rebuke that Stalin thought they *should* be invited. More damaging, perhaps, because of the long-term results of the misapprehensions created, was Roosevelt's opinion, expressed at the first plenary meeting of the conference, that American troops would only stay in Europe two years after the war.[35] This was a gratuitous and, as it proved, entirely mistaken pronouncement whose only effect could be to put a forced draft on Russian ambitions.

The tragedy of Yalta, and in a sense of the whole Second World War, was the sacrifice of Poland to Russian domina-

[34] *Foreign Relations of the United States: Diplomatic Papers: The Conferences at Malta and Yalta* (Washington: United States Government Printing Office, 1955), p. 572.

[35] *Ibid.*, p. 617; Churchill, *Triumph and Tragedy*, p. 353.

tion.[36] Poland, an innocent party, the victim of German and of
Russian aggression, the original cause of Britain's going to war,
was in effect handed over to Russia at Yalta by the agreement
that the Soviet puppet government, the "Lublin Committee,"
should be recognized as the provisional Polish government,
and not the Polish government-in-exile in London, which had
a direct continuity with the prewar Polish government. In this
decision Churchill at least knew what he was doing. He argued against it, got little support from Roosevelt, saw no hope
of preventing the outcome the Russians desired, and acquiesced.
As for Roosevelt and other Americans, it is doubtful if they
knew what they were doing, or greatly cared. They had no
profound or instinctive knowledge of European problems, particularly of Eastern European problems. A shallow and my-
opic optimism about Russian intentions prevailed. As the spring
of 1945 progressed, and particularly after Roosevelt's death
(12 April), Churchill sounded vigorous alarms about the
situation in Europe, but the Washington response was muted,
and in any case it was too late. The defeat of Germany had
merely laid Poland and other Eastern European countries
open to Soviet domination. Lacking the readiness on the part
of the United States and the United Kingdom for the sort of
instantaneous switch of foreign policies of which democracies
are hardly capable, perhaps no other outcome was possible.
But what was happening was concealed under a nauseating
smokescreen of illusion and pretense.

   36 This sad business has been summed up well in a few phrases by one
who was very close to it, the novelist Ann Bridge (Lady O'Malley), whose
husband, Sir Owen O'Malley, was British Ambassador to the Polish Government, in exile in London, from February 1943 until July 1945 when British
recognition was transferred to the Russian-sponsored claimants. "It was a
sad, thankless, and really hopeless assignment. If anyone cares to know, a
quarter of a century later, just how sad, thankless, and hopeless it was I
recommend them to read Chapter 21 of my husband's autobiography, *The
Phantom Caravan*. England had gone to war in 1939 for the defence of
Poland; three years and five months later the British Government, out of
deference to the ignorance of one of our two belated Allies, and the in-
temperate greed and hostility of the other, was actively engaged in selling
Poland down the river—and this while Polish men, on land and in the air,
were fighting and dying beside Englishmen for what they still, despairingly
but optimistically, believed to be our common cause, the cause of freedom.
It was a wretched, heart-sickening task. . . . In July [1945] the final sell-out
took place. . . . This bitter and cruel betrayal . . . was something that did
not bear thinking on. Alas, alas, alas!" Ann Bridge [Lady O'Malley], *Facts
and Fictions* (New York: McGraw-Hill Book Company, 1968), pp. 166, 180.

British acquiescence in the Yalta decisions was all the more necessary because Britain was looking anxiously forward to at least another year of war—"Phase II"—the contemplated interim between the defeat of Germany and that of Japan. In this period the symbol of cooperation would be British naval participation, and limited air and ground support, in the Pacific war—a proffered cooperation regarded by the U.S. Navy as superfluous and unwanted, but accepted by Roosevelt. Conversely, the British looked forward to a slow tapering-off of Lend-Lease while their reduced military role would permit them to begin an orderly restoration of their ravaged economic situation. With the use of the atomic bomb against Japan, the Far East War ended abruptly—a real disaster for Britain, whatever it might be considered on other grounds. On 2 September 1945 President Truman brought Lend-Lease to an end. The great wartime era of Anglo-American cooperation, its end already forecast by Roosevelt's death and the supersession of Churchill by Attlee, who represented Britain in the later Potsdam meetings, came to an abrupt and untimely stop. A little time was to elapse before cooperation was resumed in the changed postwar circumstances.

Chapter Five

ONE WITH NINEVEH AND TYRE

AFTER THE SECOND WORLD WAR, the story of Anglo-American relations loses its clear outlines and becomes more complex. Before that climacteric event, as has been indicated, one saw on the one side a Britain that was semi-isolationist in regard to Europe, seeing problems there but finding her primary interest in the Empire and the Commonwealth, and hoping for support, and if need arose, from America; on the other side, an America profoundly isolationist. Very soon after 1945 all this changes. The United States ceases to be isolationist, and takes over from Britain the world role and responsibilities that were formerly Britain's. Britain becomes one of America's many allies—perhaps the most important, at first certainly so: recognized as the most loyal, and in many subtle respects the closest; still, one of many.

The story becomes more complex, in short, because the policies of both Britain and the United States become more complex. As the United States assumed the burden of being a world power, indeed in some sense *the* world power, it began to have alliances, and policies, in almost all parts of the world. Meanwhile, Britain was beset by a chronic weakness that increasingly enforced withdrawals and reconsiderations of policy, first in one area and then in another. Only in one area was there an increased interest and a more positive policy —that is, Europe.

After a consideration of the dwindling and end of Britain's imperial greatness, we will proceed to survey the interaction of the two countries in the past quarter-century, particularly distinguishing where they found it possible to cooperate and agree, and where they did not.

The first of these topics—the gradual, and then hurried, dismantling of the British Empire—sets the tone for the whole period in that it is the most glaring manifestation of the general theme of British decline. When one thinks about Britain in the postwar period the loss of empire is, almost inevitably, what comes first to mind. It was a fact which indeed figured in the equations expressing the Anglo-American relationship; at the same time it also must be stated that it was only to a limited extent an area of Anglo-American interaction. American influences were present, pushing first in one direction and then —late, late in the day—in the other. But for the most part it was a matter of British policy and affecting British possessions. What was happening, however, was something that could not be ignored by the United States; nor, as it proceeded, could it possibly leave the American attitude to Britain and to British affairs unaffected.

For, certainly, the most spectacular, the most specific, change in the position of Britain in the period since the end of the Second World War has been the loss of its empire. From being the center of the largest empire that had ever been—the phrase used on the commemorative stamps issued for the Diamond Jubilee of 1897—Britain has almost, if not quite, declined to being no more than one of the more important European states, in a world in which the European powers themselves have been eclipsed by new giants wholly or partly outside Europe. Of Britain's imperial possessions and imperial posture, little enough remains: some vestigial remaining possessions; a somewhat ill-defined claim to a world role based on cultural distinction and the diffusion of the English language; worldwide trading contacts; the function of sterling as a world trading currency; and Britain's position as the center of the Commonwealth.

After a century and a quarter, the time has come when the situation approaches perilously close to that envisaged in a neglected didactic passage of Captain Marryat's neglected novel, *Masterman Ready* (1841). "Now Father," says the boy in Chapter XXVII (and in that remarkable idiom which only nineteenth-century children had the secret of), "answer me another question. You said that nations rise and fall; and you have mentioned the Portuguese as proof. Will England ever fall, and be of no more importance than Portugal is now?"

The father replies, "We can only decide that question by looking into history; and history tells us that such is the fate of all nations. We must, therefore, expect that it will one day be the fate of our dear country. . . . Did the Portuguese, in the height of their prosperity, ever think that they would be reduced to what they are now? . . . Yes, my dear boy, the English nation must in time meet with the fate of all others. There are various causes which may hasten or protract the period; but, sooner or later, England will no more be mistress of the seas, or boast of her possessions all over the world." [1] (So much for the theory that the essential hallmark of the Victorians was complacency.)

The amiable condescension shown in this passage towards Portugal, England's "oldest ally," reads all the more curiously when one remembers that, at the present time, in actual acreage of overseas possessions Britain is now far surpassed by Portugal, whose slogan appears to be that of the United States Marines—"First in, last out." Almost everyone but the Portuguese has accepted the great received truth of the moment, that the day of empire is over. On this matter the Portu-

---

[1] This passage drew my attention on my first reading of it all the more because I was at that very time, like all members of my class in school (Class 5a, The High School of Glasgow, 1929—30), involved in creating, as a year project, my "Empire Book," a kind of scrapbook with text and pictures depicting and glorifying the British Empire. This struck me at the time as a rather sinister coincidence; and I was not wrong. For my "Empire Book" I was awarded a book prize: Jules Verne's *From Earth to the Moon and a Trip Round It*, about how three men are shot from Florida to the moon, circling it and afterwards landing in the Pacific, where they are picked up by a U.S. warship. By December 1968 this fantasy had become fact. The earlier fact, of the British Empire, had become merely rather fantastic history, in retrospect almost incredible.

guese, so to speak, come from Missouri; but then, so do the Russians and the Chinese.

Whether imperial possessions are a necessary condition for Great-Power status, whether indeed they increase the strength of a power or are a drag on it, are questions on which prevailing opinion has differed from time to time, and to which the final answer is not yet clear. Manifestly they are not a *sufficient* condition—the mere fact of having colonies, even extensive colonies, does not of itself suffice to make a country one of the most important. The situation down to 1949 of the Netherlands, the situation down to 1960 of Belgium, the present situation of Portugal, all demonstrate this. At the same time, possession of Great-Power status has certainly nearly always gone along with the possession of colonies. The united Germany created by Bismarck began acquiring them in the 1880s. The United States at the very end of the nineteenth century acquired what was in effect, if not in name, an empire. The Japanese project of the 1930s and 1940s, the Greater East Asia Co-Prosperity Sphere, was in reality a nineteenth-century seaborne empire of the old familiar type. Russia has not hitherto striven for *overseas* empire, but her expansion both east and west from her original nucleus to her present position has seen the subordination to her rule of many contiguous, and frequently unwilling, peoples. It is a narrow and unrealistic definition indeed of imperialism (though it seems to have been the only meaning Roosevelt gave to the word), that restricts it to the salt-water variety.

On the other side, there is a good deal that can be said. The most striking argument is provided by twentieth-century Germany. Germany's loss of her colonies in the early days of the 1914 war, a loss which was to be permanent, did not prevent her from generating and demonstrating so much power that she twice came within an ace of conquering the whole of Europe. Also, it is clear that what might be called the imperial possessions of the United States have been rather trivial adjuncts to U.S. power, and not essential parts of it.

Another argument of a somewhat different kind (though pertaining rather to prosperity than directly to power) is provided by the present situation of major Western European countries, especially West Germany, France, and Italy. Their most impressive period of economic development and prosperity has come since the middle 1950s—that is, in a period when they had already lost, or were in the process of losing, their empires. The same point may be made in reference to Japan, whose possessions outside the home islands (and even a small portion of these) were lost as a consequence of defeat in war. The Leninist argument, that colonial possessions are essential to the prosperity of capitalist economic systems, and that capitalist countries are inescapably driven to their acquisition, has suffered the classic fate of a beautiful theory slain by some brutal facts.

The truth would appear to be that, while all states in a phase of increasing power and self-confidence will try for *some* kind of expansion, there seems to be only a more or less accidental line of causation linking, in the centuries of modern history, Great-Power status with the acquisition of colonial empires of the normal type. If the two basic attributes that earn for a state the respect or awe of other states may be said to be—assuming first a certain minimum in territory and population—the possession of empire and economic, especially industrial, strength, then certainly while the former may be the more spectacular, the latter is the more important.

In any case, there is no point in regard to Britain in delicately assessing which of the two was more important. The fact is, *both* declined, though not precisely at the same time—for economic decline preceded imperial retreat, and indeed the last phase of imperial expansion had masked economic decline. But both were symptoms and aspects of decline; both were manifest after the Second World War; together, they delineated a fact that was unmistakable. A claim to national greatness, to Great-Power status, might survive relative economic decline, if a great empire remained intact; or the claim might survive the loss of empire, if economic strength were still manifest; but no such claim could conceivably survive a *dégringolade* affecting both aspects. After all, both imperial

expansion and economic health are at bottom demonstrations
of energy, of will. One may cite here as apposite a recent
perceptive comment by an eminent literary critic: "The imaginative power of Kipling's stories . . . springs from something
more coherent than brash patriotism and unrecognized sadism.
The strange underestimate of them in the late 1940s and the
1950s may come to seem as illuminating, in retrospect, of the
retreat from empire, as the wildly hysterical overestimate of
D. H. Lawrence which accompanied it. And it may be that,
if Kipling's popularity returns in the near future, this will be
not only because the British Empire needs its imaginative
historian now it is over, but also because the values of empire
are *not so very unlike the values of economic survival:* either
one expands, says Kipling, or one dies." [2]

It is by no means easy in the British case to strike the
economic balance-sheet of empire, and conclude whether overall Britain was in measurable terms a gainer or a loser by its
possession. Most colonies cost at least as much to administer
as they yielded in increased trade. An interesting argument
that the possession of colonies was positively injurious to
Britain has been made along the following lines. Some have
held that the subtraction of talent from the service of the
metropolitan country involved in staffing the colonial services,
and above all the great Indian Civil Service, meant a loss of
talent which Britain could ill afford. It is true that entry into
the Indian Civil Service was the objective of intense examination competition for the best brains that Oxford and Cambridge could produce, over a period of many decades. The
I.C.S. offered a career of enormous interest, grueling work,
and great responsibility, appropriately rewarded by relatively
high salaries and (for the survivors) early retirement—the
ideal "career open to the talents." It is also true that the
decades when this situation prevailed were those from about
the middle of the nineteenth century until shortly after the

2 A. E. Dyson, "Literature 1895–1939," in C. L. Mowat, ed., *The New
Cambridge Modern History,* Vol. XII (2nd ed.; Cambridge: Cambridge University Press, 1968), p. 618. Italics added.

First World War—precisely the period when British industry was losing the thrust and inventiveness that it earlier displayed, and consequently losing its competitive edge over other industrial states.

It is tempting to argue that the superlative talent that went to serve India (and the not quite such glittering talent that went into other avenues of imperial service), had it been employed in Britain itself, might have maintained British industrial supremacy. Still, the relatively small numbers involved in the Indian Civil Service throw some doubt on this argument. It is likely that it was less overseas careers that did the damage to the United Kingdom than the low prestige enjoyed in English society by business, industry, and engineering as careers for the first-rate mind. This is one of the points on which the contrast between Britain and America has been most striking.

Advantages of a less easily measured sort there indeed were. Possession of its enormous empire certainly gave Britain a unique prestige in the eyes of the world, a prestige whose inevitable price was the concomitant envy which it excited. Still, *oderint dum metuant;* [3] the British Empire looked stronger than it was, and its mere existence was a potent factor in dissuading attack on any part of it. In fact, no rival power *did* attack it either in 1914 or 1939; that was left for the Japanese to do, in 1941. Also, the existence of the Empire, with all the possibilities that it conveyed of widespread travel, of careers spent in far-flung places, conduced to a certain largeness of view in the British upper classes, a certain readiness to think in world terms. This came relatively easily to generation after generation of upper-class Englishmen. It is a valuable possession in the governing class of a Great Power. Possibly the lack of any large body of persons with this kind of view has been one of the most difficult handicaps for the United States to overcome in playing its postwar, or rather post–Pearl Harbor, role. The lack of this kind of world-view

[3] "Let them hate me, so long as they fear me"; a phrase which Cicero (*Philippics,* I, 14) quoted from Accius.

was, of course, the main reason why the United States did not *have* a post-Versailles role in international politics.

As always when discussing British imperial affairs, one has to add that the case of India needs special treatment. India was the one part of the British Empire that clearly and demonstrably did make a contribution to the maintenance by Britain of Great-Power status. The solid core of this contribution was the Indian Army, which was an important factor in the politics of the entire region from the Mediterranean to Indochina and beyond. For roughly a century it was incomparably the largest and best-organized army in the whole of that area, and an eminently useful instrument of British policy. Disraeli moved Indian troops to Malta at the height of the Near East crisis of 1878. Indian troops even fought on the Western Front in the First World War. At other times, when no spectacular troop movements were in progress, and no wars, the mere existence of the Indian Army was a ponderable factor in buttressing British power all along the northern shores of the Indian Ocean.

To be precise, there were two different sets of armed forces in India under British control. First, there were whatever units of the British Army happened to be stationed in India at that time, in accordance with the long-term scheme of rotation. These usually amounted to around 50,000 men all told. Secondly, there was the Indian Army proper, officered in all its higher ranks by British officers but manned by Indian recruits. The Indian Army had a peacetime strength of somewhat under a quarter of a million, but it was capable of an almost indefinite wartime expansion; during the Second World War it comprised in all over two million men. Both the British Army in India and the Indian Army were paid for out of Indian revenues. Both, while in India or in adjacent areas, came under the orders of the Commander-in-Chief, India.

India was indeed, to a rather remarkable extent, a separate though subordinate center of power within the British scheme of things. The subcontinent constituted a subsystem within the British system, a subempire within the British Empire. It was not merely that it had its own army. It also had its own network of representatives and agents, including intelligence agents, who were responsible to the Government of India. The area where British foreign relations and military affairs were under the direction of the Government of India in Delhi (before 1912, in Calcutta), and only in an ultimate sense under the direction of the imperial government in London, extended in an arc from Aden eastwards to Singapore, including Afghanistan, Tibet, and the other smaller border states. Such a devolution of regional responsibility to the British authorities in India was perhaps inevitable in the earlier days of slow communications and travel, but it survived these conditions. The "Indian Empire"—Disraeli's splendiferous invention of 1876—came in the twentieth century in a curious, anomalous way to have an approximation to international personality. Delhi had an External Affairs Department long, long before India was a sovereign state. India was separately represented at Versailles in 1919, by Lord Sinha of Raipur (the only Indian ever to be elevated to the British House of Lords) and the Maharajah of Bikaner. India signed the Treaty of Versailles as a separate entity. India was a charter member of the League of Nations and of the United Nations.

It was in keeping with this extraordinary status that the affairs of India were not supervised, in London, either by the Colonial Office—though it was clearly the greatest and most important part of the colonial empire—nor yet by the Dominions Office, which existed after 1925 to take care of British relations with the great self-governing Dominions. India rated its own department of government in London, the India Office, and its own Cabinet member, the Secretary of State for India.

The possession of India dominated, and perhaps warped, British strategic and political thinking to an extraordinary degree. It was a genuine accession of military strength to Britain but in a very distant part of the world. Therefore, as Mr. Enoch Powell wrote in 1967, "Until twenty years ago, Britain was also India, and her military geography and location was that of India as well as of the British Isles. . . . Thus,

the British got into the habit of thinking in what are sometimes called 'global terms.' They were used to finding it as
easy, if not easier, and much more common, to apply military
power in the Persian Gulf or the Malacca Straits than in the
Skagerrak or the Straits of Gibraltar." [4] British thought on
British power, and British interests, was organized not in
terms of the normal concept of concentric circles, with the
homeland as the base, but symbolized as a kind of relatively
narrow ribbon running along the line punctuated by the stages
of British-held or dominated bases and territories: Britain,
Gibraltar, Malta, Cyprus, the Middle East (including Egypt,
Iraq, Jordan, Sudan and Aden), the Persian Gulf, India,
Burma, Malaya, Singapore and Hong Kong. The two anchors
of the concept were Britain and India. In truth there is a
certain parallel here with the "dumbbell concept" of Western
interests, which sees them as two strong centers—the United
States and Western Europe—linked by economics, alliances,
and common interests. But for a single sovereign state, the
United Kingdom, to think of its interests in terms of a "dumbbell" or "ribbon" formulation, was potentially a seedbed of
illusion. Since Britain had an auxiliary center of power in
India, thoughts of routes to India, and the defense of routes
to India, obscured the more fundamental strategic truth, that
a country can most effectively exercise power in regions
near to itself. The ability to do so diminishes with distance.
Moreover, the security of any country must depend primarily
upon its ability to act effectively, in a military sense, in areas
in its own region of the world. If that ability is not present,
military activities in distant places are no substitute.

The British concentration on, or obsession with, the high-
way to and from India, "the life-line of empire," produced
some bizarre results. It induced Churchill to move valuable
troops *into* Singapore when it was about to fall, and to sacrifice two capital ships off the coast of Malaya in a futile
prestige gesture. It prevented the British Army from developing an adequate military doctrine regarding operations with

[4] J. Enoch Powell, *Freedom and Reality* (ed. John Wood; London: B. T.
Batsford Ltd., 1969), p. 163.

large-scale armies in Europe; British professional soldiers faced such eventualities with grave reluctance. They preferred to think instead in terms of relatively small forces, of campaigns in hot climates and distant places against non-European enemies. It led to Mr. Chamberlain's curious description in 1938 of Czechoslovakia as "a small far-away country, of which we know little"—a phrase he would probably not have dreamed of applying, say, to Ceylon, which was about eight times as far away. (The airline distance from London to Prague is about 650 miles, or little further than from London north to the fleet base at Scapa Flow.) Most astonishing of all, perhaps, was the degree to which the Royal Navy was incompetently prepared to wage war in the North Atlantic, the ocean on its doorstep. Captain Russell Grenfell, R.N., the eminent naval historian, notes that the pursuit in 1941 of the *Bismarck*— an all-out and very one-sided episode—though in fact successful, very nearly came to grief on the rock of fuel shortage. "The British fleet as an integrated force was quite incapable of conducting a prolonged chase. Ships were soon dropping out by ones, twos, threes, and fours, because their fuel supplies did not enable them to follow the enemy any farther. . . . Had fast tankers formed a normal part of a seagoing 'task force,' Sir John Tovey's ships could have oiled at sea and so have pressed on after the enemy. . . ." [5]

The reason, of course, was the one-track character of British naval thought—the track in question being that by way of Malta, Alexandria, Aden, and so on. "The fact is that the Admiralty had consistently omitted, for many years, to give serious attention to the question of fuelling at sea. . . . British naval officers had become unduly 'base-minded,' the shore stocks of fuel at one of Britain's numerous naval bases being uppermost in their thoughts when any question of mobility arose." But this, incidentally, was not a mistake of which the U.S. Navy was guilty. "The American Navy, growing to maturity at a time when most of the outside fuelling bases were

[5] Russell Grenfell, *The Bismarck Episode* (New York: The Macmillan Company, 1962), p. 198.

in other hands, had long been accustomed to take its fuel and stores about with it."

The effects of thinking of the world in terms of an imperial track leading from England to India did not cease with the end of the Second World War, or with Indian independence in 1947. This pattern of thinking, if not absolutely indelible, took a little over twenty years to erase. Many years after India was independent, British statesmen continued to talk, and think, of safeguarding the sea route to an India that was not only independent, but was ostentatiously nonaligned with a nonalignment that involved being a good deal more polite and accommodating to Russia and China than to Britain or to Britain's ally, the United States. The seriousness with which Britain regarded the Suez question was not only a matter of retaining a foothold in an oil-rich region (Egypt itself has no oil); it was surely at least in part a traditional reflex, the maintaining of a route to a British India that was, in fact, no longer there. Not until January 1968 did a British government make the crucial decision to curtail, and largely eliminate, its Far Eastern role. Even then it was phrased, in words that had Kiplingesque overtones, as a withdrawal from areas "East of Suez."

If the Britain-India axis occupied a disproportionate place in British thought, the British Empire in India was something of an obsession for Americans too. There was some excuse for this. India, with its several hundred millions of population, far exceeded in population, though not in area, all the rest of the British Empire put together. The British might feel it was a place of very special commitment and responsibility and, in terms of the admirable efficiency and purity of its administration, something of a showplace; but, to Americans, it was *the* supremely odious example of imperialism, of small numbers of white men lording it over untold millions of colored men. It was the *locus classicus* of British imperialism and, in general, of European imperialism—that vice, of hostility to which the very existence of the United States was a standing affirmation. When Americans before 1947, and perhaps indeed much more recently, said "imperialism," they may have had vague thoughts of many parts of the world; but they were really thinking of India.[6]

The subject of India had certainly proved, during the war, to be the one in regard to which no meeting of minds between Roosevelt and Churchill was even remotely possible. "It was indeed one subject on which the normal, broad-minded, good-humored, give-and-take attitude which prevailed between the two statesmen was stopped cold."[7] To Roosevelt, clearly, British rule in India was anathema. Churchill, who had served in India as a young man, had views on India that were strong and, in the 1930s, more conservative than those of his party. During the war, however, he was not at odds with his colleagues. They shared his view that Indian independence could not be granted in the middle of a life-and-death struggle. Roosevelt apparently thought otherwise. The deepest trough of their differences was reached in the early months of 1942, when the Japanese had taken Burma and were supposed, generally but wrongly, to be about to launch a serious attack on India. Churchill wrote, "The President had first discussed the Indian problem with me, on the usual American lines, during my visit to Washington in December, 1941. I reacted so strongly and at such length that he never raised it verbally again."[8] However, Roosevelt raised it again through Harriman in February 1942, and on 11 March he favored Churchill with a long memorandum of advice on the subject —a proceeding of some effrontery that nicely illustrates the difference in their relative positions. (How often did Churchill give Roosevelt advice on the handling of American problems?)

Roosevelt's memorandum drew a supposed parallel between the Indian situation and the inception of the government of

[6] Perhaps the coincidence of the name *Indians* served to make Americans more interested in India than they would otherwise have been. But such an association of ideas would not be entirely favorable to the United States. After all, as the legendary visiting Englishman said to the American critic of British policy in India, "*Our* Indians are alive."

[7] Robert E. Sherwood, *Roosevelt and Hopkins: An Intimate History* (New York: Harper and Brothers, 1948), p. 512.

[8] Winston S. Churchill, *The Hinge of Fate*, Vol. IV, *The Second World War* (Boston: Houghton Mifflin Company, 1950), p. 209.

the United States. It suggested the setting up of "what might be called a temporary Government in India," "a temporary Dominion Government," which would also serve as a constituent assembly.[9] The parallel was far-fetched; Churchill drily remarks, "This document is of high interest because it illustrates the difficulties of comparing situations in various centuries and scenes where almost every material fact is totally different." There were parts of the memorandum, certainly, to which Churchill could heartily assent: "For the love of heaven don't bring me into this, though I do want to be of help. It is, strictly speaking, none of my business . . . it is a subject which of course all you good people know far more about than I do." Curiously, even on American history the document was not impeccable: Roosevelt clearly supposed that the Articles of Confederation were framed in 1783, at the end of the war, instead of the true date of 1777.[10] Robert E. Sherwood, in his *Roosevelt and Hopkins,* comments on this episode: "It may be added that, four years later, the Labor Government in Britain made a proposal to the Indian leaders which, Sumner Welles has written, was 'almost identical in principle with the suggestion made by President Roosevelt in 1942.' " [11] Sumner Welles's comment is a good deal less telling than Sherwood supposes, being in fact completely off target, for two reasons: first, by 1946 the war was over; the great objection on the part of the British Government was to fancy constitutional experimentation while the war was on. Secondly, the 1946 offer (the "Cabinet Mission Plan") *failed.* It was not acceptable to the Indian leaders. A solution was achieved only with the much more drastic plan of the following year, involving partition.

It does not appear that Churchill ever replied directly to Roosevelt's memorandum of 11 March 1942, but some months later, after the decisive victory at Alamein, he did give vent to a famous pronouncement which was, though few knew it,

9 Churchill, *Hinge,* pp. 212–13.

10 Churchill (*Hinge,* p. 213n) points out another error in American history in the message, but not this one.

11 Sherwood, p. 512.

a retort to and a dig at his great ally. In his Mansion House speech of 9 November 1942 he nailed his colors to the mast with the famous sentence, "I have not become the King's First Minister in order to preside over the liquidation of the British Empire."

Meanwhile, an initiative that Roosevelt could approve aimed at gaining the support of Indian leaders for the struggle against Japan had been attempted, and had failed. In the middle of March 1942 the insufferable Sir Stafford Cripps (whom some thought—extraordinary as it seems now—a serious contender for the premiership) had been dispatched by Churchill's government to India. As Churchill wrote to the Viceroy (Linlithgow),

> It would be impossible, owing to unfortunate rumours and publicity and the general American outlook, to stand on a purely negative attitude, and the Cripps Mission is indispensable to prove our honesty of purpose and to gain time for the necessary consultations.[12]

Cripps was armed with a draft declaration that the British government would grant India full independence if desired after the war, in return for support while the war continued. The mission was bootless, and Cripps muddied the Anglo-American waters further by concocting proposals and plans with Lewis Johnson, a special Presidential representative in India, without informing the irritated Viceroy. Cripps returned home, his fame as a left-wing hero somewhat tarnished. With the tide beginning to set toward victory later in the year, Roosevelt's specific interest in India diminished, though his implacable hostility to the British Empire of course remained.

Compared to the strong, chronic American disapproval of the British role in India, and in general of the British role in the whole colonial empire where the white Briton ruled the nonwhite native, the Dominions did not figure importantly in American thinking—perhaps because thinking about them seriously would have involved the necessity of admitting that

---

12 Churchill, *Hinge*, p. 215.

there was a great deal to be said in favor of British imperial policy, at least in some situations. American opinion, official or unofficial, in the 1920s, 1930s, or 1940s, when pushing for the disintegration of the British Empire, chose to ignore the fact that, in regard to certain large areas, *it was already in a fairly advanced state of disintegration.*

These areas were, of course, the Dominions—a list comprising, in the 1930s, Canada, Australia, New Zealand, South Africa, and the Irish Free State.[13] American opinion was not well informed about them, and in particular about the high degree of self-government they had attained. Their quasi-independence, as seen in their functioning as separate signatories of the Versailles Treaty, and as founding members of the League of Nations and later the United Nations, was generally supposed in America to be merely a device of British duplicity whereby the British voice in world affairs was multiplied by being echoed by a number of political entities still substantially under British control. The position of Canada was particularly misunderstood. There were always proposals popping up to "buy Canada from the British," or, still more attractive, to demand it as payment in lieu of unpaid war debts; in general, to make Manifest Destiny function on a North-South as well as an East-West axis.

This attitude was both confused and unjust. Any attempt at clear thinking about the evolution, and demise, of the British Empire involves accepting that, at any time down to the late 1940s, a sharp distinction was made by the British— which corresponded, in fact, to a sharp distinction in the world of external reality—between two different kinds of British imperial possessions. The colonial empire consisted of areas with no large permanent white population. These were not thought of in general as candidates for any early grant of self-government except in the most limited doses. Again, India

13 Strictly speaking, Newfoundland was also a Dominion; but in 1933 the impact of the great depression and of financial incompetence forced it to the unique regressive step of requesting Britain for a resumption of British control, and it continued under "Commission Government" until it joined the Dominion of Canada as the tenth province in 1949. Newfoundland was not a member of the League of Nations, though India was.

was an exception. As early as the early nineteenth century there were British statements looking toward a day when India would be independent. The Government of India Act of 1919 and that of 1935 afforded the educated Indian minority considerable opportunities for practice in the arts of self-government. Under the latter statute government in the various provinces was in the hands of Indian politicians; only at the center in Delhi did British control remain undivided. By the time of the Second World War the only questions—but genuinely intractable questions, all the same—were when, and how, and to what successor authority or authorities the British would hand over responsibility for the government of India. The fundamental question had been settled. But elsewhere in the colonial empire, apart from a few special cases such as Ceylon, Malta, or Cyprus, the fundamental question—of whether self-government should be granted at all—was in reality still an open question.

The overseas areas of white settlement, however, had progressed rapidly, and with little British opposition, to the running of their own affairs internally. The concept of the "Commonwealth," as distinct from "Empire," originated in the relationship of Britain with these "daughter-nations," where the settlers had, long before the end of the nineteenth century, complete control of their own domestic politics. The colony of "Canada" (actually the modern Ontario and Quebec) imposed a tariff on the importation of certain *British* goods as early as 1857. The British government did not like it, but it swallowed it.[14]

These overseas Britains attained stable political form at different times. Canada, always regarded as the senior, was created in 1867 when the British North America Act established a common federal government for Quebec, Ontario, Nova Scotia, and New Brunswick. The new Dominion of Canada was joined in the course of time by other areas of British settlement in North America north of the United States.

[14] In a way this might be regarded as the Canadian declaration of independence—a typically unstressed, commonsense, Canadian affair. If the tariff of 1857 is the Canadian 1776, the British North America Act, 1867, is the Canadian 1787.

Australia (officially known, rather confusingly, as the Commonwealth of Australia) is also a federation, created in 1900 out of six hitherto separate colonies. New Zealand, the least populous of these countries, had gained its political structure in the nineteenth century. The Union of South Africa came into being in 1910 with the union of the two old British colonies, the Cape and Natal, with the two Boer colonies, the Transvaal and the Orange Free State, which had been defeated in the South African or Boer War (1899–1902). Only a few years after their defeat, the conquered Boer colonies had been given back "responsible government"—control of their own affairs. This was thought for half a century to be a splendid, and moreover successful, liberal act of policy—until the Boer nationalist victory in the general election of 1948.

In the progress of the Dominions (the generic name adopted at the Imperial Conference of 1907 for what before that time were called "self-governing colonies") toward independence the British government seldom interposed any obstacles. Thus before 1914 all five Dominions had virtually untrammeled control of their internal policies. At the Imperial Conference of 1911—the first at which the five (Canada, Australia, New Zealand, South Africa, and Newfoundland) were all represented—domestic affairs were not an issue. The main business of the conference was rather foreign policy. This was a crucial turning-point in the process of imperial disintegration, and it may be argued that the British political genius was not very inventive in dealing with it. In general, then and later, the path of least resistance was followed. Perhaps the United States—adding piece to piece as its federal system expanded, dealing with states, territories, colonies (the Philippines), later inventing the ingenious expedient of "Commonwealth status" for Puerto Rico (definitely not the same thing as Dominion status)—in the late nineteenth and early twentieth centuries displayed more political creativeness than the United Kingdom did.

On the other hand, it is certainly true that the political pressures in the Dominions were a tide setting toward independence that it would have been difficult to make head against. But very little was attempted, and what was actually happening tended to be overlaid with a veneer of fine words. Canada, Australia, and the rest were simply going the same way that the Thirteen Colonies had gone long before, but going more gradually, and with more goodwill on both sides, and with a deceptive continuity of names and institutions. Perhaps that is the most that can be hoped for in disintegrating empires.

Some effort was made, though hardly at all by the British government, to avert such an outcome. There was a movement in favor of imperial federation at the turn of the century. A little later Lionel Curtis and the "Round Table" movement were propagandizing actively in the same cause. It was Curtis who first gave currency to the terms "Commonwealth" and "Commonwealth of Nations." It is important to realize, however, that what Curtis meant by "Commonwealth" was something different from, and really the *opposite* of, what was later called "The British Commonwealth of Nations." The matter has been put very clearly by K. C. Wheare, who comments: [15] "The use of 'Commonwealth' as a new name for the British Empire began to come into fashion after Lionel Curtis published his two books, *The Problem of the Commonwealth* and *The Commonwealth of Nations,* in 1916. It is true that Lord Rosebery, in a speech in Adelaide in 1884, had described the Empire as a 'Commonwealth of Nations,' but there can be little doubt that if Curtis had not popularized the word, Lord Rosebery's remark would not have been exhumed by research students." In 1917 and 1921 occur the first, tentative official uses of the term. "Yet, by a curious contradiction of history, as Curtis's word came into fashion, it came to mean something quite different from what he had intended it to mean. Indeed, 'Commonwealth' today stands for a situation which Curtis in his writings had deplored and which he devoted his energies to avoid and remove." Wheare continues:

> Put quite shortly, what Curtis meant by a Commonwealth of Nations was a federal union. He had a perfectly

[15] K. C. Wheare, *The Constitutional Structure of the Commonwealth* (Oxford: Clarendon Press, 1960), pp. 2–4.

logical case. . . . The characteristic of a commonwealth was the government of men by themselves. But the British Empire in 1916 was not founded on this principle. The control of defence and foreign policy rested upon the shoulders of the people of the United Kingdom alone; the peoples of the other parts of the Empire had no say in it. . . . The solution, as Curtis saw it, was to establish a parliament and government for the whole Empire to deal with defence, foreign affairs, and other important common matters, while national parliaments dealt with national matters. Through such machinery . . . the principle of the Commonwealth . . . would attain its fulfillment. If, on the other hand, each part of the Empire attained full self-government and control over defence for itself, then you would not have a commonwealth of nations.

What one would have was a collection of independent, and, at best, cooperating states. Curtis wrote, "In plain words, the issue, as seen by the writer, is whether the Dominions are to become independent republics, or whether this world-wide Commonwealth is destined to stand more closely united as the noblest of all political achievements." Wheare sums up, "The word 'Commonwealth' as it is used today, then, does not mean what Curtis meant by it."

These movements, aimed at creating central representative and executive institutions for the whole Empire, institutions that would have replaced British control, where it still existed, by a sharing of power on a federal basis between the Dominions and Britain, failed for reasons that are not too hard to seek. Apart from New Zealand, the statesmen and peoples in the Dominions gave little support to any such project. It was a United Kingdom movement, and one of rather limited vitality even there, an affair of intellectuals, publicists, and a few public servants, rather than of those who could truly either rouse public opinion or shape events. Each Dominion was primarily interested in its own affairs. As for Britain itself, interest in, and enthusiasm for, the Empire was always remarkably lukewarm. There was some general surge of imperial sentiment about the end of the nineteenth century—stimulated by the personality and interests of Joseph Chamberlain, by the Diamond Jubilee of 1897, by the Boer War—but it did not last. The sweeping Liberal election victory of 1906 was, among other things, the triumph of the Little Englanders over the imperialists.

The most significant parts of the agenda of the 1911 Imperial Conference dealt with the attempt to devise coordinated steps, chiefly military, to face the already present threat of European war. But the Dominions were cool to schemes that looked to the possibility of creating agreed policies hammered out with their participation. They feared the implications of a shared responsibility. Yet in some ways they were having the worst of both worlds. If a war came for Britain, like it or not, they would be in it too. Diplomatically the Empire was still regarded, and functioned, as one.

Already in 1911, as Curtis rightly saw, the domestic autonomy of the Dominions and their increasing importance and self-consciousness were posing the great question of which of the two foreseeable alternative courses would be followed. Either the common foreign policy of the Empire would have to be framed in a cooperative manner, or the diplomatic unity of the Empire would be replaced by a number of separate foreign policies—at which point, in substance, a Dominion would become a sovereign state.

The second development, of course, was what actually occurred. All the Dominions (as well as all of the colonial Empire, and India) automatically went to war in 1914 when Britain did. Britain at that time could still (as it could not in 1939) decree their belligerence, but it could not, even in 1914, decree how active their participation in the war would be, or what form it should take. The use of Dominion troops under British command of course occurred, but it was always a touchy subject; it was even more so in the Second World War. Dominion exertions in 1914–1918 were in fact very great. These exertions in the common cause enhanced the several national prides of the Dominions and, by something of a paradox, eroded imperial unity. Toward the end of the war a seemingly important but evanescent body, the Imperial War Cabinet, with Dominion representation, appeared. There

was some official talk of creating common organs for the
Empire as soon as the war was over. It all came to nothing.
Fissiparous political tendencies were infinitely stronger than
centripetal forces.

The Dominions, separately represented at Versailles, pushed
successfully in the 1920s for more and more autonomy, though
Australia and New Zealand were indifferent.

The movement was led by the Irish Free State. During the
war and in the early years of the peace, Anglo-Irish relations
served, as they often had done before, to bedevil Anglo-
American relations. In the Easter Rising of 1916 and the
troubles which followed in the next half-dozen years, Americans gave both sympathy and support to the Irish cause.
In the hope of gaining votes, the abortive "Resolution of
Ratification of the Versailles Treaty" which came before the
U.S. Senate, and was defeated on 19 March 1920, contained
as one of its fifteen reservations a paragraph voicing support
for the Irish cause—a matter whose connection with peacemaking with Germany was less than manifest.[16]

In 1921–1922 Ireland was partitioned and all of it, with the
exception of the Six Counties in the northeast corner with
their predominantly Protestant population, was constituted the
Irish Free State. England had always been singularly maladroit
in handling the Irish question—Ireland playing the role of
the British Balkans, and proving quite as intractable as the
real Balkans had to several other empires—and there was a
certain grim appropriateness in the fact that the decline and
fall of the British Empire, that long recessional which was to
involve, over the next half-century, the retreat from so many
pleasant places all round the world, was heralded and inaugurated by the abandonment of British power in Dublin. Giving
up Ireland was in some ways a more striking blow to British
prestige than the loss, later, of overseas pieces of the Empire,
because it was the yielding of what had hitherto been re-

---

[16] "15. In consenting to the ratification of the Treaty with Germany the
United States adheres to the principle of self-determination and to the resolution of sympathy with the aspirations of the Irish people for a government of
their own choice adopted by the Senate 6 June 1919, and declares that when
such government is attained by Ireland, a consummation it is hoped is at hand,
it should promptly be admitted as a member of the League of Nations."

garded as an integral part of the metropolitan territory, the home base.

When the Irish Free State was created in 1922 it was given Dominion status, though it was not a country of the type of Canada or the other Dominions. It was in reality a mother-country, rather than a colony of settlement. The Irish remained discontented; they wanted a republic, but the British felt, in 1922, that this was quite incompatible with membership of the Commonwealth. Twenty-seven years of fortune's battering were to follow before, in 1949, Britain was prepared to concede to a much more alien country—India—what it had not been prepared to concede to Ireland. Such is the horrendous importance of symbols in men's minds.

Restiveness on the part of the Irish Free State, of South Africa, and of Canada, led to further significant diminutions in the strength of Commonwealth links in the 1920s and 1930s. The Imperial Conference of 1926 agreed to changes in the appointment procedures and roles of governors-general which made them figureheads only, as well as other changes pointing in the same direction. The 1926 Conference also produced the classically evasive and elegant definition—in every way worthy of its author, Lord Balfour—of the mutual relationship of Britain and the Dominions:

> They are autonomous communities within the British Empire, equal in status, in no way subordinate one to another in any aspect of their domestic or external affairs, though united by a common allegiance to the Crown, and freely associated as members of the British Commonwealth of Nations.[17]

It may be noted that in this definition *Empire* is used to mean the larger entity within which the *Commonwealth* (Britain plus the Dominions) formed a special part. Later, especially in the 1950s and 1960s, as sensitivity about any use of the word *Empire* deepened from caution into sheer timidity, offi-

17 *Report of the Inter-Imperial Relations Committee,* 1926 Imperial Conference. Reprinted many places, including A. B. Keith, *Speeches and Documents on the British Dominions 1918–1931: From Self-Government to National Sovereignty* (London: Oxford University Press, 1932), p. 161. The Committee's name contains a solecism: obviously it should have been *Intra*-Imperial.

cial usage came to substitute *Commonwealth* for *Empire* as the comprehensive name for all British territories whatever their status or degree of emancipation, or lack of it. Sir Winston Churchill in his last decades usually preferred the form "Empire and Commonwealth"—by which, one suspects, he meant something like "the Empire, or, if you are squeamish enough to prefer the term, the Commonwealth." But *Commonwealth,* whatever precisely it might be taken to mean, gained ground almost exclusively in official usage. So far as the great bulk of the British people were concerned, the word emphatically did *not* come "trippingly on the tongue"; they stuck stoutly to *Empire. Commonwealth* began, and remained, a politician's word, a publicist's word, a scholar's word, for an increasingly nebulous entity.

The Statute of Westminister, 1931, responded to Dominion sentiments firmly expressed at the Imperial Conferences of 1926 and 1930, and enhanced Dominion autonomy by repealing certain laws or portions of laws, fallen into desuetude, that purported to maintain the Dominions in legal subordination to the United Kingdom. The present constitutional structure (if that is the right word) of the Commonwealth essentially rests on the Statute of Westminster.[18]

Of greater real significance were the steps which were leading to the existence of separate foreign policies, the eventually inevitable result of the failure to create common organs for policy-formation. This was the beginning of the end.[19] Canada was the first Dominion to embark on the creation of her own diplomatic system, sending a minister to Washington in 1927. Little by little embryo diplomatic services and external relations departments were built up, but no Dominion by 1939 had a full-fledged diplomatic service. The process pushed to completion only during the war and in the post-1945 years.

---

[18] See K. C. Wheare's *The Statute of Westminster and Dominion Status* (5th and last ed., 1953) as well as his *Constitutional Structure of the Commonwealth.*

[19] Nehru's remark when speaking in the Indian Constituent Assembly on 8 March 1949 is relevant: "What does independence consist of? It consists fundamentally and basically of foreign relations. That is the test of independence. All else is local autonomy." *Independence and After: Speeches of Jawaharlal Nehru (1946–49)* (Delhi: Government of India, 1949), p. 237.

Throughout the 1930s separate foreign policies were only emerging, and constitutional lawyers pondered with fascination, and a certain horror, the dawning possibility of a divisible Crown, at war in one part of its territories and at peace in another. If the Crown meant anything, the development was indeed monstrous; but the Crown, at any rate anywhere in the Commonwealth outside the United Kingdom itself, was rapidly becoming an abstraction as elusive as the Cheshire Cat's smile. These developments, little noticed by Americans, were already before 1939 seriously impairing Britain's ability to play a Great-Power role. The overseas territories of Britain, vast and impressive on the map, were not necessarily any longer accessions of strength and self-confidence to the home country. It could even work the other way; they could be a drag, a deadweight, an excuse for inaction. One reason for Britain's pusillanimous policy in the Munich crisis of 1938 was that consultation with the Dominions had shown that they were all strenuously opposed to getting involved in a war over the issue of German aggression at Czechoslovakia's expense.[20]

Events in September 1939 demonstrated vividly, by contrast with 1914, that the diplomatic unity of the Commonwealth was at an end—though the forces of loyalty were still great. Australia and New Zealand, as in 1914, regarded themselves as automatically at war when Britain was; but the Canadian declaration of war came a week later, after a parliamentary vote; in South Africa there was not only a vote in a by no means unanimous parliament, there was a preceding political crisis, and a change of prime minister. The Irish Free State remained neutral. The treaty ports, whose use had been reserved to the British armed forces under the settlement of 1922, had been surrendered to Eire in 1938 in a singularly ill-timed Chamberlainite gesture of appeasement. They were not available to the Royal Navy during the war. And, supreme anomaly, from 1939 to 1945 Dublin remained host to a German ambassador accredited to King George VI.

[20] Except for New Zealand; but the support of New Zealand, with a population of less than two millions, was not likely to tilt the scale in a European war.

The wartime neutrality of Eire was followed logically in 1949 by complete secession from the Commonwealth when Eire became the Republic of Ireland.

In 1939–1945 the other Dominions again made great exertions in the common cause, but by 1945 there could be no doubt, if there had been any before, that they had become independent nations and sovereign states. Its power manifestly weaker, Britain was ceasing to be the magnetic center that could attract and hold voluntary allegiance in any very substantive sense. The new, and more powerful, magnet was the United States. The primary commitments, and especially the primary defense arrangements, of the "Old Commonwealth" members—those who belonged to it before 1939 and still belong—are now outside the Commonwealth; they are with the United States. This is most strikingly true of Canada, but it is true not only of Canada. In the great crisis of 1940, Canada turned to the United States, and they made the Ogdensburg Agreement, setting up a permanent joint defense board with the United States. In 1951 Australia and New Zealand set up the ANZUS defense pact with the United States, and they sided with their partner in refusing to consider British membership. From 1949 onward Canadian membership in NATO emphasized the link with the United States —it was U.S. membership that created NATO, not British membership. As Professor Frank Underhill has well said, "Wherever we look today, something new has been added to the British Commonwealth, something American. All roads in the Commonwealth lead to Washington." [21]

So far as India, the great bugbear in British policy in the eyes of the United States, was concerned, the postwar years brought a speedy dissolution of the imperial connection— and, for America, a speedy disillusion. All British attempts to pass on British power in India to a single competent legatee having failed, Indian independence was accomplished under the aegis of the Labour government of Attlee when,

21 Frank H. Underhill, *The British Commonwealth: An Experiment in Cooperation among Nations* (Durham, N.C.: Duke University Press, for the Duke University Commonwealth-Studies Center, 1956), p. 99.

on 15 August 1947, the two new states of India and Pakistan were created. They were referred to as Dominions in the enacting legislation.[22]

Britain's most spectacular imperial possession was gone, and this appeared to take some of the steam out of the traditional American attitude to the British Empire. Moreover, independent India did not by any means prove so romantic and admirable an entity in American eyes as it had seemed when it was only a hypothesis, barred from reality by British intransigence. Nehru, India's virtual personification in the world's eyes and Indian Prime Minister for the first two decades of her independent existence, exhibited a neutralism that always found more excuses for Russian or (after 1949) Chinese policy than for American, and no understanding whatever for the American point of view on the Cold War. It was also observed with some bewilderment in Washington that, independence won, the relations of India with Britain were close and friendly—friendlier than with the United States. As for Pakistan, the United States had never viewed the idea of Pakistan any more kindly than Nehru and the Congress Party had. Mr. M. A. Jinnah, that austere, elegant and uncompromising champion of the idea of Pakistan, who carried it to fruition against seemingly impossible odds, had always had a bad press in America—and, in lesser measure, in Britain too, for that matter. Like de Gaulle in the 1940s and 1960s, Jinnah called forth both from Washington policy-makers and from the American press that peculiar ire they reserve for those who show no disposition to compromise on principles—especially if their principles are inconvenient to the United States—and who fail to make the required democratic obeisances. So Jinnah and his Pakistan were rather far from being Washington's darlings at Pakistan's inception. Here, however, time brought a rapid *volte-face,* for by 1953, five years after Jinnah's death, Indian neutralism and necessities of world policy led the United States to make a military agreement with Pakistan. The U.S. commitment to Pakistan was always

22 "As from the fifteenth day of August, nineteen hundred and forty-seven, two independent Dominions shall be set up in India, to be known respectively as India and Pakistan." *Indian Independence Act, 1947,* I.–(1).

qualified and limited, however; which in the long run led Pakistan to cool in its liking for the American connection.

Obviously there were other factors in the lessening U.S. resentment at the British Empire. The manifest weakening of Britain, the desperate situation she found herself in in the immediate postwar years and the consequent necessity to look for American aid; the corresponding American realization that novel world responsibilities had now descended upon the shoulders of the United States—all this made the old resentments less appropriate, and induced at least some understanding of British attitudes, an understanding previously almost wholly lacking.

W. H. McNeill, doubtless correctly, saw this new realization on the part of the United States as stemming in the first place from the professional alertness of the U.S. Navy and Air Force to the changed circumstances.[23]

> One of the most striking changes in American official and, less markedly, in American public attitudes was the new view of the British Empire which rapidly gained ground after the war had ended. . . .
>
> It was principally naval and air force circles which welcomed and moved forward into the vacuum created by Britain's weakness. The U.S. navy wished to annex strategic islands in the Pacific, and managed to restrain other elements of the American Government from making such a consummation impossible. The navy also decided to send a fleet to the Mediterranean and maintained most of the island bases in the Atlantic which had been built during the war. The U.S. air force pursued parallel policies, maintaining and even building new airfields in many far-flung corners of the earth. The two services were exactly following the policy of the Royal Navy after the Napoleonic wars, and for similar reasons.

However, this was merely the initial stage of a much broader change of attitude on the part of Americans. The traditional American, Rooseveltian attitude to the colonial question did not sit well with new U.S. world responsibilities, and traditional opinions turned out to be in some measure

[23] William Hardy McNeill, *America, Britain, and Russia: Their Co-operation and Conflict 1941–1946* (London: Oxford University Press, 1953), p. 757.

illusions when they were tested against the realities of an external world with which America was now increasingly in contact. "Events in China, India and elsewhere," says McNeill, "soon showed that liberation and the establishment of peaceable self-government were not an easy thing that could always be accomplished at will or by a simple act of abdication. As some of the complexities of the problem dawned upon the American public, a more cautious and sympathetic attitude towards British colonial policy gained ground; and when, later still, the fear of Communism and the extent of its hold upon native liberation movements became apparent, official and popular sympathy in the United States tended to come round to the side of the European colonial nations. But this reversal was not completed until after 1946."

Indeed, one may say that it was not *completed* until rather long after 1946—perhaps not until the early 1960s, if then. Such attitudes dissolve only slowly. This can be seen not only in a continuing, self-righteous opposition to British imperialism which surfaces from time to time, as we shall see, finding utterance in the 1950s in the platitudes of Eisenhower and embodiment in the policies of Dulles. It can also be seen in American attitudes to other European powers when the colonial question is raised. When that nerve was touched, there was still a tendency for the result to be an automatic, involuntary reflex. Thus during the course of the Netherlands-Indonesian question, 1946–1949, the United States bore down heavily on the Netherlands to make them give way to Sukarno, whom the United States insisted on elevating into a kind of pinchbeck Washington. The United States, in fact, never deserted Sukarno; it was the Indonesians who did. The United States persistently sympathized with the Algerian rebels rather than French authority in Algeria, although the Algerian departments of France were part of the area covered in the North Atlantic Treaty; the ultimate result of this policy may be to have the Russians rather than the Americans or the British enjoying the use of the great naval base at Mers-el-Kebir. The Portuguese policy in Africa, of attempting—so far successfully—to maintain possession of their two great colonies,

Angola and Mozambique, is the subject of chronic tut-tutting in Washington, and of implied disapproval in public statements. American official pronouncements on Africa are always directed at audiences north of the Zambezi. When India in 1961 invaded and overran Goa, a Portuguese possession, the United States refrained, like everyone else, from even attempting to reprove in the United Nations this blatant piece of aggression, so preposterously at odds with India's frequent preachings at the West about the beauties of nonviolence and of refraining from seeking the resolution of problems by force.

When, during the Kennedy Administration, Sukarno's Indonesia was hankering after possession of Western New Guinea (to which its claim was slender indeed—the inhabitants of the area bear little resemblance in race or culture to those of Indonesia), there was a moment when the Dutch seemed possibly disposed to defend it. At this juncture, the U.S. government denied to Dutch forces and officials on their way to Indonesia the rights of overflight and landing and refueling facilities normally available to aircraft of any friendly power, let alone an ally, as the Netherlands was. Throughout this minor crisis the whole interest of the United States appeared to be in seeing that Netherlands New Guinea was detached from Dutch control and safely shepherded into Sukarno's hands; as it was, under the sketchy cover of an interim U.N. regime.

McNeill thus appears to put too early, and perhaps too strongly, the American move away from the traditional attitude of anticolonialism. The Netherlands, France, and Portugal have all been given to understand in a variety of incidents— some of them of very recent vintage—that imperialist activity continues to excite American disapproval (this in the face of the obvious fact that much American activity in the last thirty years is certainly in a broad sense imperialist). These European allies were in NATO, but NATO was interpreted by the United States as having a very narrow focus.[24]

[24] In the late 1960s the United States began to be hoist with its own petard in the matter of its relations with Turkey. Turkey, responding to more friendly Soviet policies, began to insist to the United States that NATO was *solely* concerned with protecting Turkey against a direct Soviet act of aggression, and

It has been mainly in regard to Great Britain that American doubts have developed whether the disappearance of an ally's empire is really a good thing. Further, these doubts do not seem to have developed strongly before the early 1960s; they have had reference chiefly to the Far East; and they seem to have arisen because any definitive contraction of British power there threatened to leave the United States feeling a rather lonely and conspicuous figure in the East Asian region. The approaching disappearance of British influence and power in areas of the world remote from Britain was a greater matter than the ebbing of French, Dutch, or Portuguese power. It was British responsibilities, British policies, British problems that the United States thought of itself as inheriting.[25]

Since the inheritance seemed inevitable, there came a rather sudden realization—sudden and also too late—that the new American role might be less conspicuous, more defensible, if the British did *not* carry out their recessional to its ultimate conclusion. Hence the startling tendency for the reversal of the agelong pressure on Britain. Christian Herter, who was Secretary of State from 1959 to 1961, remarked on 5 May 1966, in testimony before the Senate Subcommittee on National Security and International Operations, "As you know, getting the British to hang on east of Suez was a very difficult task"[26]—a statement well calculated to make a U.S. Secretary of State of any earlier time rub his eyes in disbelief. A little later Herter said, "I am sorry that the [Atlantic] Alliance does not relate to the whole world, but I do not think that is in the cards at the present time. We are the only nation today, if you want to exclude Russia and China, that feels global responsibilities. It is a question of the extent to

that Turkey was *not* obliged to give general support to U.S. Middle East policy, to allow wide use of its territory and harbors to the United States, or to refrain from friendly relations, including economic cooperation, with the U.S.S.R. This was precisely the same "strict constructionist" view of its commitments that the United States had long been accustomed to impose upon its discomfited allies France, the Netherlands, Portugal, Pakistan, *et al.*

25 Though in Vietnam the United States is actually the heir of a *French* imperial role and problem, not a British.

26 Senator Henry M. Jackson (ed.), *The Atlantic Alliance: Jackson Subcommittee Hearings and Findings* (New York: Frederick A. Praeger, 1967), p. 119.

which we can exercise our power wherever it might be required or desirable in the world. Obviously, we cannot do everything alone. We have to have partners. We have to retain them on the European scene. If possible, we ought to keep partners on the Asian scene. . . ." There, for the United States in the 1960s, was the rub—"if possible." The sense of regrettable isolation in the exercise of supreme world power is present throughout this Jackson Subcommittee report, and many other documents of the period. The United States was, of course, suffering the anguish of a self-created dilemma (such as many dilemmas are): its loneliness was the result of having over several decades badgered, coerced, and bludgeoned the European imperial powers into yielding up their worldwide interests and territories. Regret at British withdrawal from the Far East merely constituted the dilemma in its sharpest form.

Aided by the forces of history, American policy toward the imperialisms of the European powers had indeed been successful—disconcertingly so.

> God answers sharp and sudden on some prayers,
> And thrusts the thing we have prayed for in our face,
> A gauntlet with a gift in't.[27]

By the 1960s, the gauntlet was easier to perceive than the gift.

The later stages of the disintegration of the British Empire were no doubt implied in everything that had happened before 1945, but the actual form in which the process was carried out derived from the model set in the case of India. The pattern was created by the decision in 1947 to treat the two new states of India and Pakistan as Dominions, on the same basis as Canada and the rest—and by their equally significant, and perhaps surprising, acceptance of that status. Two years later came the even more surprising mutual agreement that even when India became a republic, as it had decided to do, it would remain a member of the Commonwealth and would

[27] Elizabeth Barrett Browning, *Aurora Leigh,* bk. ii.

be accepted as such by the other members; [28] and so, at this point, the shibboleth of "common allegiance" was abandoned.

These decisions meant in the long run creating a whole series of nonwhite units of the Commonwealth to be treated exactly *as if* their relationship to Britain were the same as that of the "Old Dominions"; though in fundamental matters of culture, kinship, and their historical experience it was really quite different. It also created the possibility that some of them would choose republican forms of government in which the Crown would not figure. (The recognition of the King or Queen as "Head of the Commonwealth" is without constitutional effect.)

It is very doubtful indeed if the effect of the precedent of India and Pakistan was adequately foreseen. Again, probably the British tendency to envisage India as a special case was at work. India was manifestly a home of ancient civilizations. People had talked vaguely for more than a century of its eventual resumption of independence. The prospect of independence for the bulk of Britain's colonial possessions, however, was still no doubt thought of as being a generation or two away.

There was, indeed, a perceptible gap in time between the attainment of Indian independence and its attainment almost *en masse* by a host of other British colonies. At first there were only one or two cases. India and Pakistan became "Dominions" in August 1947; Ceylon, close to them geographically and, like them, far advanced along the path of constitutional development even before 1939, followed in February 1948. That same year, however, Burma became independent

[28] The meeting of Commonwealth Prime Ministers, in its communiqué dated 27 April 1949, noted that "under the new constitution which is about to be adopted India shall become a sovereign independent republic" and went on: "The Government of India have however declared and affirmed India's desire to continue her full membership of the Commonwealth of Nations and her acceptance of The King as the symbol of the free association of its independent member nations and as such the Head of the Commonwealth. The Governments of the other countries of the Commonwealth, the basis of whose membership of the Commonwealth is not hereby changed, accept and recognize India's continuing membership in accordance with the terms of this declaration."

and chose at the same time to leave the Commonwealth. In 1949 the Republic of Ireland also took the Burmese road.

It was in the late 1950s and early 1960s that the trickle became a torrent, as one colony after another—large and small, ready and unready—demanded its independence and was given it; in some cases it would be truer to say, was hustled into it, whether or not the demand had been made. Careful and leisurely preparation for independence, the order of the day earlier, was abandoned, and the stages of transition from less complete to full self-government were accelerated beyond what would have seemed possible earlier. The will to maintain empire evaporated within a few years. This was a movement that affected the French, the Belgian, and other empires as well as the British. There was a complete change in the climate of opinion. Most colonial powers now had as their chief purpose the early liquidation of their empires.

Ghana, the former Gold Coast, became the first black African Member of the Commonwealth in 1957.[29] Malaya followed in the same year. In 1960 came Nigeria, the most populous state in Africa, and Cyprus; in 1961 Sierra Leone, Tanganyika. . . .

However self-satisfied the British might be about the morally admirable quality of their actions in this period, there was little in this two-decades-long imperial recessional to augment the respect for Britain felt by the United States or anybody else. There was, indeed, one, perhaps too-little-noticed, item on the credit side: the complete elimination of the Communist rebellion against the government of Malaya. This movement lasted for ten years, 1948–1958, but was ground to nothing under the decisive leadership of Field-Marshal Sir Gerald Templer, his victory constituting the *only* decisive defeat of a Communist insurgency movement so far recorded. Malaya apart, it was not a dignified story. There was too much vacillation, too many policies were launched, with a flourish of

[29] After 1947, the colorless phrase "Member of the Commonwealth" gradually replaces "Dominion." It is not an exact equivalent, however, since the United Kingdom is counted a "Member of the Commonwealth" but was not a Dominion.

trumpets, that had been ill considered, and which later were abruptly abandoned; too many attitudes were struck; there was much inconsistency. There was the tedious, violent, three-cornered struggle over the future of Cyprus. There was the abandonment of the interests of white settlers in East Africa who had gone there a generation before with the express encouragement of the British government. There was the singular episode of the extrusion in 1961 from the Commonwealth of South Africa (one of Britain's major trading partners) to placate the newer members. There was the enthusiasm for endowing with federal constitutions groups of territories which turned out later to lack the common characteristics and loyalties necessary to operate them. Thus the West Indies federation was created, then abandoned (1958–1962); the Central African Federation was created, then abandoned (1953–1963), a step leading to Rhodesian independence and to Britain's inept claim to be responsible for an area where it is powerless and where no British government had ever, in fact, exercised power. The improvization of a federation in South Arabia led only to the messy withdrawal from Aden in December 1968—possibly the most undignified situation in which a British government was ever involved. In these and many other situations successive British governments exhibited neither consistency nor good judgment; nor, it is true, did they enjoy good luck. By a curious paradox many though not all phases of the great imperial withdrawal were conducted under the aegis of what was in theory the party of empire—the Conservative party—in its long tenure of power from 1951 to 1964.

It would be otiose and inappropriate here to list every historic item in the process, still more so to niggle at the technical and constitutional details, as of how Malaya became Malaysia, gained Singapore and then lost it, or how Tanganyika became Tanzania, or how some of the new Commonwealth members are republics, or how some, stranger still, are monarchies but have their own monarchs, not Queen Elizabeth II.[30] It is sufficient to say that by the end of the

---

[30] Malaysia, Lesotho, and Swaziland.

seventh decade of the century the Commonwealth had reached the fantastic total of twenty-eight members,[31] and all resemblance to the former British Empire, or even to the Smuts-Borden, pre-1947, version of the Commonwealth, was altogether lost. As for actual dependencies, Britain still had a score or so of these, but they were small, like Gibraltar and Hong Kong, and most, like the Seychelles and the Falklands, of little importance.

The statistical increase in membership of the Commonwealth, and its enormous total population (over eight hundred million), are impressive, but far from an accurate index of increasing strength in the Commonwealth association or in the British position in the world; quite the contrary. With every increase in the membership the original meaning of the Commonwealth becomes diluted to the point where it has almost become a nullity. There is, perhaps, at this point in its history not very much that needs to be said, or can be said without falling into gross distortions, about the Commonwealth. Three final points may be made.

The first is that it has changed its nature. It is simply not the same thing as it was before 1939, or rather before 1947. The "Old," or pre-1947, Commonwealth could be said with justice to be based fundamentally on racial kinship, since the peoples of the Dominions consisted wholly or largely of British settlers or their descendants, and on a consequent community of political ideas. All its members had political systems on the Westminister model. The newer members lack a British element in their populations, most are in fact nonwhite, and while some few have retained resemblances to the Westminster model in their political systems (notably India), the great majority have departed rather fast and rather far from the free institutions with which they were endowed when they became independent.

The opportunity, if it ever existed, to make something posi-

[31] In order of seniority: Britain, Canada, Australia, New Zealand, India, Pakistan, Ceylon, Ghana, Malaysia, Nigeria, Cyprus, Sierra Leone, Tanzania, Jamaica, Trinidad and Tobago, Uganda, Kenya, Malawi, Malta, Zambia, The Gambia, Singapore, Guyana, Botswana, Lesotho, Barbados, Mauritius, and Swaziland.

tive of the relationship with Canada, Australia, New Zealand, and South Africa (perhaps one should add, with Rhodesia), has gone, ousted by the arrival of the more comprehensive and thus more amorphous, predominantly nonwhite Commonwealth. The British government has passionately resisted the suggestion that there really is now an outer and an inner Commonwealth. Still, there is a reasonably clear distinction to be made between the Commonwealth members that participate in cooperating defense policies (that is, Britain, Canada, Australia and New Zealand) and those that are neutralist or hostile to the policies of the West in general. But it is because of their links to the United States, primarily, rather than to Britain, that one can make this point about the former group, Canada, Australia, and New Zealand.

The skeptic's view of the contemporary Commonwealth, which in the later 1960s became very largely the view of the British people and also, one would gather, the view of official Washington, has been superbly put by Mr. Enoch Powell, always the *enfant terrible* ready to voice what has been widely thought but not so far expressed. In a speech at Cranborne on 14 January 1966 he said:

> The great majority of people in this country see no reality or substance in the proposition that they belong to a Commonwealth comprising all that vast aggregation of territories, except for Burma and South Africa, which by colonisation, by cession, by conquest, by purchase, by a variety of other means, had come to be under the dominion or protection of the British Crown at the time of the Second World War and are now independent countries.
>
> The people of Britain observe that a number of these countries are antipathetic to one another, even to the extent of breaking off diplomatic relations and going to war. They note than an antipathy towards Britain is a marked feature of the visible, public behaviour of some of these countries, at the United Nations and elsewhere, and that none of them appears to recognise any common interest with Britain where it would override or conflict with its own. They gather that the manner in which the internal

affairs of some of these countries are conducted, though admittedly no more business of ours than ours is of theirs, are repugnant to their own basic ideas about liberty and democracy. These things the British observe in no censorious mood. . . . Only it is difficult after all this to be told that all these countries form with us a great Commonwealth which is the world's best hope and model for international and inter-racial co-operation. . . . We noted that the first steps to reconciliation between the two warring Commonwealth countries of the Indian sub-continent, steps which every person in Britain greeted with hope and relief, were achieved not in London, nor Canberra, nor Lagos, but in Tashkent.[32]

The second point is that the recent expansion and transformation of the Commonwealth did serve one arguably useful purpose. It at least assuaged the feelings of the British people. It made it easier to stomach the loss of an empire, because it adroitly concealed the fact of loss by claiming that through some conjuring trick of superb political skill nothing really was being lost: a position of political predominance was simply being transformed into a morally more acceptable position of leadership, example, and partnership. This device, of course, was already being used in regard to the pre-1939 Commonwealth. As Colin Cross bleakly says in his *Fall of the British Empire,* speaking of the 1920s and 1930s, "Flexibility in words and institutions is tolerable so long as it does not entail, also, self-deception and the use of vague words to hide reality. The 'Commonwealth' doctrine of Smuts and his fellows helped the British to embark upon an era of self-deception and self-flattery on a scale which has rarely otherwise been seen in mass psychology. Many of the British entered a kind of mirror-world in which every weakening of imperial bonds could be represented as if it were a new cord of steel." [33] How much more this has been true in the post-1945 period, when the new partners—the ex-colonies—are by their very nature less likely to follow freely Britain's lead, and when the great de-

[32] Powell, *Freedom and Reality,* pp. 188–89.
[33] Colin Cross, *The Fall of the British Empire 1918–1968* (New York: Coward-McCann, Inc., 1969), p. 174.

cline in Britain's relative position has made it impotent to provide the kind of lead that anyone would want to follow. Still,
at least the Commonwealth mythology has saved Britain from
attempts to maintain an empire by force and from vain regrets
when it has gone; and, while the operation was going on, it
had the virtues, such as they are, of a political narcotic. Here,
however, it is necessary to distinguish between different periods.
Even the best narcotic wears off in time. For many Britons,
this had happened by the middle 1960s.

A third point which must in all fairness be made is that the
twenty-seven ex-colonies who chose to remain linked to Britain
in the Commonwealth association did so voluntarily, and therefore clearly saw some merit in it. They must judge, as did
Nehru, that the relationship has "a touch of healing" in it,
or perceived with his New Zealand colleague, Peter Fraser,
that Dominion status was not "an imperfect kind of independence," but on the contrary "independence with something added." [34] For Commonwealth countries, other than
Britain, the bonuses were not entirely intangibles. They included under British law the right of their citizens to enter
Britain freely, even though *they* made no such reciprocal
concession to those who lived in the United Kingdom. This
one-sided privilege was restricted by the Commonwealth
Immigrants Act of 1962, made more stringent in 1965. Also
Commonwealth goods enjoyed a privileged position in the
British market under the various Ottawa agreements of 1932.
These have diminished in importance in the subsequent decades, but the prospect of the abolition of these advantages if
Britain joins the Common Market caused anguished protests
from Commonwealth countries from 1961 onward—this even
although these countries had, in pursuit of their own interests,
enacted many measures prejudicial to their importation of
British goods. The 1960s was the decade which exhibited
a gradual realization by Britain that it had the right and the

[34] Nehru, speech of 16 May 1949; Fraser, speech of 3 June 1947. It appears
probably significant that one cannot find equally warm and significant tributes
to the Commonwealth from non-U.K. sources of truly recent date.

necessity to protect its own interests—as the other members of the Commonwealth had long done—even if doing so endangered the Commonwealth link. There was indeed nothing startling in such behavior, yet for Britain it was a novelty.

The early 1960s were for Britain a time of harsh awakenings, in regard to its lost empire and other matters. A celebrated cold shower which contributed as much as anything to this reawakening was administered by one of Britain's most faithful friends among Americans, ex-Secretary of State Dean Acheson, in his speech at West Point on 5 December 1962, when he said:

> Great Britain has lost an empire and has not yet found a role. The attempt to play a separate power role—that is, a role apart from Europe, a role based on a "special relationship" with the United States, a role based on being the head of a "Commonwealth" which has no political structure, unity or strength . . . this role is about to be played out.

Acheson may well have felt, but he certainly did not express in this speech, one of the most natural sentiments with which the contemplation of the end of the British Empire inspires the mind—inspires, nowadays, even American minds—the sentiment of pathos, perhaps of nostalgia. Men are we, said Wordsworth, and must weep for even the shadow of what once was great. Wordsworth was speaking of Venice, and there are many parallels to Venice in the history of the British Empire. Both rested upon sea-power, both were essentially mercantile in motivation, both created a fantastically great structure of far-flung power upon an amazingly slender home base. Both in their great days exemplified the aristocratic principle at work, for both Venetians and (before the mid–twentieth century) Britons had a strong regard for hierarchy, for the notion of powers and duties as necessarily related to a certain position in society. This idea is in harmony with the idea of empire, whereas the idea of democracy is not; herein lay the root cause of the end of the British Empire. Herein, too, lay the main reason why the American democracy so misliked that empire.

There is one point on which the British Empire resembled neither Venice nor, indeed, most of those great empires whose fall has provided the raw material for historic generalization and moralizing. The British Empire did not decline gently over the centuries in the manner of Venice, or Rome, or Byzantium. From its zenith to its end was a fell lurch taking only a single lifetime, or (if defined more narrowly) one generation. If the empire's true high noon was (as Mr. James Morris maintains in his *Pax Britannica*) the Diamond Jubilee of 1897, it did not reach its greatest territorial extent until 1919, though by then, as we have seen, British control of the great Dominions was virtually nil. Between 1919 and 1939 the empire lost only Egypt, Iraq, and Weihaiwei, and of these only the last-named, a minor holding in China, was in 1939 really out of British control. On 3 September 1939 the empire was still intact; thirty years later it was substantially nonexistent. This is an imperial catastrophe without parallel, the more astonishing when it is recollected that it was not the consequence of defeat, but that on the contrary Britain was again on the victorious side in the Second World War.

What the long-run consequences for Britain are to be of her loss of her imperial role remains in doubt. So far, it does not seem to have caused any enormous psychological traumas. Even regrets appear somewhat muted in the contemporary British environment. A contemporary poet, Philip Larkin, seems to give an authentic appraisal of the national mood of weary, wry acceptance of the passing of greatness in his poem "Homage to a Government," where he says:

> Next year we are to bring the soldiers home
> For lack of money, and it is all right.
> Places they guarded, or kept orderly,
> Must guard themselves, and keep themselves orderly.
> We want the money for ourselves at home
> Instead of working. And this is all right.
>
> It's hard to say who wanted it to happen,

But now it's been decided nobody minds.
The places are a long way off, not here,
Which is all right, and from what we hear
The soldiers there only made trouble happen.
Next year we shall be easier in our minds.

Next year we shall be living in a country
That brought its soldiers home for lack of money.
The statues will be standing in the same
Tree-muffled squares, and look nearly the same.
Our children will not know it's a different country. . . .[35]

As for American opinion, it is fairly clear what has happened. That great transformation scene, the disappearance of the British Empire, has done less than nothing for Anglo-American relations, even though the former existence of the Empire was one of the great obstacles to good relations. Before, there *was* a British Empire; and on the American side there was ideological dislike, mistrust, envy—and respect. Now the Empire, along with the great navy and the position of wealth, is gone; and so is the respect. There is on the American side certainly greater friendliness, but it is a friendliness mingled with condescension. It is the kindly pity, occasionally varied by exasperation, that one shows to a relative who has come down in the world.

[35] *Sunday Times* (London), 19 January 1969.

Chapter Six

POSTWAR TO PRESENT:
AREAS OF COOPERATION, AREAS OF CONFLICT

THE QUARTER-CENTURY that followed the end of the war in 1945 formed essentially a single era in Anglo-American relations. Certainly there were seismic changes within it that suddenly drew attention to the slow subsurface shifts in relationships that underlay the surface play of events. Crucial years of this kind, worthy to be named, were 1947, 1956, 1962, 1968: occasions significant as earthquakes, which by an abrupt readjustment both reveal and relieve the slow building-up of pressures.

There are various aspects under which the developments of the period can be examined. Obviously, there are the specifics of particular events and crises as they occur. There are the fundamental, background changes in the actual facts of the position of the two countries, Britain and America, in relation to each other; as also in their attitudes to each other. There is, too, the question of the personalities of policy-makers involved, and how their clash or cooperation shaped events. The specifics of particular issues will be touched upon below as they arise. As for the background changes, inevitably one perceives the nature of the relationship as reflecting a growing asymmetry, the result of the fact that over these years the status of the United Kingdom declined; it was declining not only in relation to the staggering power and wealth of the United States, or the power of the Soviet Union, but more ominously even, in the later 1950s and the 1960s, in relation to other states such as France, West Germany, and Japan.

Something has been said on this point already, in connection with the passing of the British Empire. The passing of the Empire, involving a loss of British sovereignty over vast populations and extensive territories, was of course an absolute decline. In other respects, the British decline was a relative decline—which is, in fact, what one usually means when one refers to the decline of a state in the modern world. Britain was wealthier in 1969 than in 1939, its productive capacity very considerably enhanced. The average amount of wealth per head was higher, even though a considerable number of individuals were less wealthy, and even though the average increase of wealth was much less than it appeared to be if stated in an inflated currency. In terms of Britain's world position, however, and the regard in which Britain was held by other countries, what mattered was that while Britain had, after a halting start in the early postwar years, gone ahead, other countries had in the long run gone ahead considerably faster.

The British industrial system, the first great industrial system of the modern world, continued to be—as it had been since the later nineteenth century—an old dog that was not particularly good at learning new tricks. The brilliant inventiveness of individual Britons and the example of some progressive firms were clogged and frustrated in an industrial system whose most prominent feature was a dogged, fatigued conservatism on the part of both unions and management. If blame for the comparative sluggishness of the British economy should not be laid exclusively at the door of management or of the working man, neither could it with any apparent justice be blamed much more heavily on the policy of one party more than the other. In the twenty-five years from July 1945 to July 1970, the Labour party was in power for a total of eleven years, eleven months, and the Conservative party for a total of thirteen years, one month—a fairly close approximation to equal total periods of tenure of office.

Yet, however, one might explain it, there was a manifest weakening of industrial potency as measured against the contemporary achievement of other major states. What it came down to was that the British performance in the economic sphere in the quarter-century after the war was no better than passable; whereas to maintain anything like the former British place in the world that performance would have had to be as superlative and extraordinary as the British military effort during the war. Some U.S. Government figures showing estimated average annual growth rates of various countries in gross national product (GNP) for each lustrum since 1950 (omitting the exceptional, immediate postwar years) throw light on the bare bones of the situation: [1]

PERCENTAGE ANNUAL INCREASE IN GROSS NATIONAL PRODUCT

	1950–1955	1955–1960	1960–1965	1965–1969
United Kingdom	2.7	2.4	3.4	2.2
United States	4.3	2.2	4.8	4.2
West Germany	9.5	6.3	5.0	4.5
France	4.3	4.7	5.8	5.7
Italy	6.0	5.5	5.1	5.9
Japan	n.a.	8.9	10.0	12.6

In 1938, the total GNP of the United States was about four times that of the United Kingdom. By 1950, at which point the U.S. GNP was $434.7 billion and that of the U.K. $63.4, the ratio had become 6.85 to 1. British recovery in the subsequent two decades did not mean any narrowing of the gap, which on the contrary steadily widened. In 1960 the ratio of the two GNPs had become 7.3:1; by 1969 it had become 8.5:1. In view of the enormously larger initial base of the United States, this meant that the U.S. preponderance in wealth was becoming truly staggering, even though the U.S.

---

[1] The statistics cited here and in following passages are either directly taken from, or calculated on the basis of figures given in, a U.S. Government survey, *Gross National Product: Growth Rates and Trend Data by Region and Country*, issued 30 April 1970 by the Office of Statistics and Reports, Agency for International Development. To facilitate comparison all dollar amounts are expressed in 1968 prices.

rate of economic growth in the postwar period has not been one of the more spectacular ones, as is shown above.

It was true, of course, that the U.S. population was increasing faster than that of the U.K., so that the increased wealth was being divided among more people. In 1938, the population of the United States was only 2.25 times that of the United Kingdom—the figures were roughly 130 million to 47.5 million. In 1960 these had become respectively 179 and 52 million; by 1969, 203 million and 55.5 million. Put another way, by 1960 the U.S. population had risen to being 3.4 times that of the United Kingdom, and by 1969 the ratio had increased to 3.7 times. However, the increase in American wealth was far more than keeping pace with the population increase, and by 1969 the U.S. GNP was $890 billion, while that of the United Kingdom was $105 billion. Since the American population was not only increasing faster than the British, but the national wealth was increasing faster still, this inevitably meant that the figures that the two countries cut in the world, and the kind of roles they were qualified to play, became increasingly disparate.

Dividing total GNP figures of any given year by population for the same year gives a figure for GNP per head, and thus a rough indication of standard of living. The result of such a calculation suggests that in 1938 the American standard of living was about 1.8 times as good as the British. For 1960 the figure was 2.15, and for 1969, 2.3; i.e., the American standard of living was rather more than twice as good as the British. Personal experience suggests that, despite all the obvious *caveats,* these figures are not very wide of the mark.

Another index to the economic health and strength of countries is provided by the behavior of their currencies.[2] Here the relationship of the once omnipotent and impregnable pound sterling to the dollar suggested eloquently, and quite

2 This is, of course, not invariably true. Portugal, which has a relatively static economy, has had a very hard currency for many years, while over the same period Brazil, some parts of which have been booming, has had a chronic and disgraceful inflation. Inflation or the absence of it, a favorable or unfavorable balance of payments, also affect the strength of the currency.

accurately, the nature of the changes that were occurring
in the relations of the two countries. Prior to 1939, £1 was
equal to $4.80. At the outbreak of war, and until 1949, the
pound was maintained at a parity of just over $4. The
devaluation of September 1949 cut this drastically, so that
thenceforth the pound equaled $2.80. The second postwar
devaluation, the Wilson devaluation of 18 November 1967,
dropped the pound's equivalent value to $2.40, or precisely
half the old, prewar value.[3]

As suggested before, the fact that after 1945 the United
States continued by leaps and bounds to increase its margin
over Britain in wealth and power was less ominous than the
comparisons that might be made between Britain and other
states closer to her in size. After all, the importance of
Britain between the wars had been a resultant not only of the
existence of the British Empire, but also of the inaction in
the sphere of world politics, for various reasons, of the two
giants, the United States and Russia. Once they began to be
continuously active, Britain's role was bound to suffer at
least a partial eclipse. No such comforting reflections about
inevitability could solace the way in which other states, with
less in the way of natural advantages of size, jostled Britain
and increasingly brought in question her implicit claim to
rank third in the world in terms of significance. In 1950 the
French GNP was not quite as great as that of the United
Kingdom (84 percent of it, to be exact). In 1960, however,
France's GNP for the first time surpassed the British; by
1969 it was 130 percent of the British, or greater by about
one-third. The well-known West German "economic miracle,"
of course, provided a more spectacular transformation. In
1950 the GNP of West Germany was only 70 percent of
the British. In 1956 the GNP of West Germany accelerated
past the British GNP, and by 1960 amounted to 116 percent
of it; by 1969 this figure had become 136 percent. The economic development of Japan in the postwar period provides the

[3] The new parity, like the historic one, was quite convenient, for a British
penny, formerly precisely equal to two American cents, was now precisely
equal to one—a convenient equivalency that was to be completely destroyed
by the British decimalization of currency in February 1971.

greatest contemporary example of economic expansion. In 1952, the first postwar year for which figures are available, the GNP of Japan was 51 percent of that of Britain. In 1960 it was 76 percent. In 1964 for the first time the Japanese GNP surpassed the British. By 1969 the GNP of Japan was 161 percent of that of the U.K.

The British performance was not satisfactory. Many ingenious efforts were made to explain and palliate it; unfortunately, they were inconsistent. Britain was being outdistanced in the economic race by countries whose factories had been devastated and which had therefore had to start afresh (an alleged advantage), but also by countries whose factories had not been touched; by countries at the beginning of their industrial development, but also by highly industrialized countries such as Britain itself is; by countries rich in natural resources, but also by at least one country (Japan) with practically none; by countries which had been on the winning side, by countries that had been on the losing side, and by at least one country (France) that had been defeated and had then been on the winning side. Economic development is not an end in itself, of course, and no sane man regards it as such, nor is it an index of the happiness of a populace; it is perfectly possible that Portugal is the happiest country in Europe. But it *is* an index of the significance of a country. It happens to be the foundation on which wealth, strength, and the esteem of other states rest. It endows a state with freedom of choice as to its policy.

In what ways, if any, did the attitudes of the two peoples, British and American, towards each other change in the quarter-century after the Second World War? Of course there was some change, in response to the changes in background reality; but the changes were slow and subtle, and perhaps easier to trace on the British than on the American side. On the American side, the old wariness about Britain died hard. Illusions about the United Nations made it assume a slightly new form—instead of keeping the British at a distance merely on general principles, because they were wicked, they were to be kept at a distance because being too friendly toward them might endanger the beautiful prospects of the United Nations. This attitude was strong for the first two or three years after the war, and lingered on in an attenuated form afterwards. It can be found stated with some emphasis in a book, on topics similar to the present one, that was published in 1945 and republished in 1948. Both Crane Brinton, the author of the book, and Sumner Welles, who wrote an Introduction to it, were so far from sharing the vision of Churchill's Fulton speech that they positively go out of their way to show they regard close Anglo-American cooperation not so much as a consummation devoutly to be wished for, as a danger to be guarded against. Cold blew the west wind indeed. Sumner Welles pontificated in his Introduction:

> Nothing would prove to be more destructive of our present hopes for world peace than for the Anglo-Saxon powers to create an Anglo-Saxon bloc for the purpose of dominating or "ganging up" on other nations.[4]

Crane Brinton if possible outdoes him by making the same point three times over in his concluding pages, resorting even to italics:

> It is in this task of building up international government by discussion and compromise, *and only in this task,* that Anglo-American cooperation can usefully continue the work it began during the war.
> We and the British . . . had better not develop a *joint* sense of virtue, a combined holier-than-thou attitude towards the rest of the world. Of all forms of Anglo-American collaboration, this would certainly be one of the worst. . . . In . . . the United Nations, it is to be hoped

---

[4] The fear of seeming to "gang up" with the British is an ingenious American semantic device frequently used (e.g., later by Dulles and Eisenhower) to give cooperation with them a pejorative cast. As with many slangy or idiomatic phrases that tend to compel instant assent from the unthinking, the logic of the phrase is not at all clear. If there are causes that ought to be upheld, does not common sense and interest dictate that good men had better "gang up" in defense of them? Benjamin Franklin, it will be remembered, thought it better to hang together than to hang separately. The United States has never been heard to express dislike of the idea of ganging up on Communist China, and was mightily offended when others were less keen.

that the United States and Britain will not in fact form an Anglo-Saxon bloc. . . . They should work together, *but not as one.* . . .

We and the British shall have to steer, not in the same boat but in the same fleet, through dangerous and largely uncharted waters. . . . One [danger] is an Anglo-American collaboration so close as to seem to the rest of the world an Anglo-American bloc against the rest of the world.[5]

Within a few years of the time when these passages were written—that is, by the late 1940s—the hope of remaining on good terms with Russia, and of making the United Nations work as intended, had been abandoned by American policy-makers and the American public. But America was still chary of the British embrace, America preferred to think in generic terms about "the European allies," even if in practice cooperation with Britain was closer, and more continuous and more effective, than with anyone else. It is also interesting to observe that American spokesmen remained reluctant to voice—perhaps even to face in their own minds—the proposition that the United States was stepping into Britain's place, was assuming an imperial or at any rate quasi-imperial role as the chief upholder of the Western way of life—with all that that implied in the way of long-term effort, necessity for consistent policy, and readiness to face international unpopularity if necessary.

A rather special degree of collaboration with Britain on the part of the United States was, however, a fact of life throughout the late 1940s, the 1950s, and the early 1960s, and was accepted as such by American public opinion. Then the status of the special relationship becomes more questionable for various reasons. The death of Kennedy and increasing American involvement in East Asia leading to a recrudescence of isolationism; on the other hand the relative decline in Britain's importance, quite clearly visible by the mid-1960s—all these factors modulated American attitudes. Policy toward Britain,

[5] Crane Brinton, *The United States and Britain* (Cambridge, Mass.: Harvard University Press, rev. ed., 1948), pp. viii, 269–73.

or toward Europe as a whole, became a proportionately less part of the total concerns of Washington policy-makers, and of the public.

On the British side in the postwar years, there was a much more clear-sighted recognition of what was basically happening. It was welcomed both in Whitehall and by the British public. What was feared above all was an American withdrawal from European responsibilities such as had followed the First World War. When, after a couple of years, it became clear that this was not going to happen, there was only pleasure and relief in Britain. It is, indeed, remarkable that this great readjustment in power politics, the supersession of the British role by the United States, occasioned so little bitterness in Britain. As one observer said in 1949, "On the British side the change is being faced with more grace and resolution than might, perhaps, have been expected. It is not easy to accept second place when one is accustomed to first place. It is not easy to accept charity when one is accustomed to give it." [6] Such was the fact; explanation is more difficult. Perhaps the basic explanation is that these changes came as no surprise to the rulers of Britain. The more intelligent among them had been well aware for forty or fifty years that this was how the world was going. Macmillan's wartime remark about the British being cast as the Greeks of the new Roman Empire is well known. A second point is that the easy British acceptance of the changed situation in the early postwar period may have been intellectual, rather than visceral. Later, after Suez, after the Empire had gone, after it had become clear that Britain was in danger of ranking far lower than merely second in the Free World, some bitterness did emerge, at least among those Britons who still cared about questions of world politics—a diminishing minority.

One would also have to make a distinction between the attitudes in Britain of those on the Left and those on the Right of the political spectrum. Here a paradoxical shift had taken place. In the nineteenth century, the British upper classes

[6] Arthur Campbell Turner, address to the Rotary Club of Berkeley, California, December 1949, printed in *California Monthly,* January 1950.

were supposed, with some justice, to have an anti-American bias. The friends of America were to be found among people like Cobbett, Cobden, Bright—opponents of aristocracy at home, who hailed a society that was free of aristocracy and in which the working man had come into his own. To them, America was a model of what society should be, the hope of the future. By the mid–twentieth century, attitudes had changed indeed. It was the upper classes who regarded with approval the great exemplar of a successful capitalist society, the apostles of the Left who viewed it with dour suspicion for the same reason, impugning its motives, rejoicing in its every difficulty, exaggerating its internal problems. This ideological cleavage in attitudes to the United States was, of course, observable in all European countries and, indeed, within the United States itself.

But, in general terms, all sections of the British public increasingly as the postwar years wore on acknowledged that leadership had passed elsewhere. Decades earlier the Anglo-American poet Ralph Hodgson, brooding on the course of empire taking its way westward, had apostrophized the old gypsy man, Time:

> Last week in Babylon,
> Last night in Rome,
> Morning, and in the crush
> Under Paul's dome;
> Under Paul's dial
> You tighten your rein—
> Only a moment,
> And off once again. . . .
> Time, you old gipsy man,
>   Will you not stay,
> Put up your caravan
>   Just for one day? [7]

Time had not stayed, and the British people knew it. It is in

[7] Ralph Hodgson (1871–1962), lived in Ohio in the latter decades of his life. The poem, first published in 1917—an appropriate year for this sentiment, the year of the Bolshevik Revolution and of America's entry into the war—is republished in his *Collected Poems* (London: Macmillan and Co. Ltd., 1961), p. 62.

these years that one begins to read the poetic and significant phrase, "America is where our weather comes from." [8]

Power was not the only long-term variable; personalities mattered too. There is, of course, a school of historical thought which decries the influence of personalities—chiefly because of the fear of exaggerating the role of "great men"—and places all stress instead on the play of impersonal, broad historical forces. Still, it would appear to be an error to write the former off entirely. Perhaps it is particularly an error in the sphere of Anglo-American relations, because in that relationship communication is especially facile, and both accord and dislike can be evoked, and perceived, more easily than in most international relationships. The wartime cooperation of Britain and the United States would certainly have been significantly different, might very easily have been much less, if the great instruments of that cooperation had not been Roosevelt and Churchill. In the postwar epoch, it would certainly seem that substantial historical results flowed from the personal relationships created by the accidents of who held this or that office on one or the other side of the Atlantic at particular times. That Acheson liked and respected Bevin; that Acheson and Franks had the very highest mutual respect and liking; that Dulles and Eden cordially detested each other; that Kennedy and Macmillan had a warm mutual regard: such personal attitudes were real factors that weighed in the balance, and played important parts in determining the course of events.

In assessing the interplay of personalities, it is not always, or solely, the relationship between President and Prime Minister that matters, though that was what mattered most during the war. Some Secretaries of State, like Acheson, who are men of strong character and are trusted by their chiefs so that they exercise a real, though delegated, authority are historic factors in their own right; others, like Rusk, are not. Much the same might be said of British Foreign Secretaries. Some British am-

---

[8] I have been unable to find a source for this fine phrase, accurate both meteorologically and metaphorically.

bassadors in Washington carry great weight and influence and
for a time are significant links in the relationship; this, however,
is rarely the case with American ambassadors in London (who
are often able, but who *must* be rich).

At the level of Presidents and Prime Ministers, the accidents of history had the result that there have been ten different sets or "pairs" during the period in question (excluding
the Kennedy-Home combination, which lasted only one
month). Truman and Attlee held their high offices contem-
poraneously for six years, three months (July 1945–October
1951)—the longest-lasting of any of these combinations.
Truman-Churchill had a span of one year, three months
(October 1951–January 1953); Eisenhower-Churchill, two
years, three months (January 1953–April 1955); Eisen-
hower-Eden, one year, nine months (April 1955–January
1957); Eisenhower-Macmillan, four years (January 1957–
January 1961); Kennedy-Macmillan, two years, nine months
(January 1961–October 1963); Johnson-Home, eleven months
(November 1963–October 1964); Johnson-Wilson, four years,
three months (October 1964–January 1969); Nixon-Wilson,
one year, five months (January 1969–June 1970); Nixon-
Heath, since June 1970. Manifestly, some of these pairings
possessed much more historical significance than others, de-
pending on their duration, on personalities, on the events of
the period—and on the personalities of others holding British
or American offices at the same time as the principals.

Personalities seem to have been more important than party
affiliations in making cooperation easy or difficult. With two
major parties alternating in power in both Britain and the
United States, there are four possible combinations in terms
of the parties filling the chief executive posts in the two countries at any given moment. From July 1945 to July 1970, a
Democratic President in the White House found himself
dealing with a Labour Prime Minister in Downing Street during ten years, six months of the period; a Democratic President
with a Conservative Prime Minister, during five years. The
combination of a Republican President and a Labour Prime
Minister prevailed during one year, five months (that

is, only while Nixon and Wilson held office concurrently);
the combination of a Republican President and a Conservative Prime Minister during eight years, one month. There
does not seem to be much correlation between ideological
affinity and ease of communication and cooperation, or the
reverse; which is not very surprising. After all, in this period
all British administrations were to the political left of *all* U.S.
administrations. There is the further point that Congress
may or may not be dominated by the same party as holds the
Presidency, and may or may not be prepared to go along with
what the President proposes.

If the Truman-Attlee period, covering the first six postwar years—and about one-quarter of the whole postwar era
down to the present—was on the whole a time of successful
American-British cooperation, as it was, this could hardly be
attributed either to ideological affinity in the two administrations, or to any great cordiality or fellow-feeling between
the President and the Prime Minister themselves. Most Americans were profoundly out of sympathy with the domestic aims
of the Attlee government, the first Labour government of Britain
which had ever enjoyed a clear majority. Most Americans were
astonished by the results of the British general election of July
1945, for American opinion always found it difficult to understand how anyone could vote against Churchill—just as British
opinion always found it difficult to understand why anyone
should vote against Franklin D. Roosevelt. In both cases, there
was a failure to comprehend, or even to be aware of, the distrust and dislike with which each man was viewed by very large
segments of opinion in his own country. Though there were
several very successful personal relationships at somewhat lower
levels during this period, Truman and most of his colleagues
over the years seem to have found Attlee rather trying, officious,
and lacking in charm. In his memoirs, published while Attlee was still alive, Truman says, apropos of Attlee's first ap-
pearance at the Potsdam Conference in the capacity of head
of the British delegation, "The new Prime Minister had
been present at the conference from the beginning and I had
come to know him well. Attlee had a deep understanding of

the world's problems, and I knew there would be no interruption in our common efforts." [9] This seems a little perfunctory; nor is it possible to find in Truman's memoirs any references to Attlee expressive of greater warmth.

The new Prime Minister, for his part, had little reason to feel cordiality toward the new President for his first significant decision *vis-à-vis* Britain. This was the abrupt ending of Lend-Lease, announced on 21 August 1945. Truman dismisses it rather casually in his memoirs, as he did in a press conference at the time, as being strictly in accordance with the legislation authorizing Lend-Lease.[10] Acheson, however, records that "in later years President Truman said to me that he had come to think of this action as a grave mistake." [11] Acheson himself condemns it roundly as "unnecessary," "wrong," and "disastrous," with "the most far-reaching and harmful consequences," and holds that such a decision might well not have been taken but for the accidental absence from Washington of William L. Clayton and himself. At any rate, it certainly placed Britain, which was in no shape to switch instantly from total concentration on the war to peacetime economic activity, and which had been forced during the war to sell off the larger part of its foreign investments, in an impossibly difficult position.

The only recourse seemed to be a large loan from the United States, and this was negotiated in the next few months, Keynes being the chief British negotiator. The British asked for five billion dollars; they got $3,750,000,000. They hoped for at least two billion dollars of it to be interest-free; none of it was interest-free, and the rate was fixed at two percent; but since a five-year grace period was permitted at the beginning the true rate was 1.63 percent. Britain perforce accepted a general commitment in favor of multilateral trade programs and against discriminatory agreements (such

[9] Harry S. Truman, *Year of Decisions,* Vol. I, *Memoirs* (New York: Doubleday and Company, Inc., 1955), p. 395.

[10] *Ibid.,* pp. 475–76.

[11] Dean Acheson, *Present at the Creation: My Years in the State Department* (New York: Norton and Company, Inc., 1969), pp. 28, 122.

as the Ottawa agreements); more serious was the commitment to reintroduce convertibility of the pound (that is, for foreign holders of sterling—no one was worrying about domestic holders) one year after the loan came into effect. On these bases the loan bill was framed, and was signed into law by the President on 15 July 1946. The U.S. loan was helpful but not adequate, precisely as Keynes had predicted. It did, however, avert the feeling of virtual desperation which had seized the British when the termination of Lend-Lease was announced, though the "business as usual" atmosphere which underlay that announcement and permeated the loan negotiations caused apprehensions for the future which were, in fact, not to be justified in the event. Convertibility, when it was restored in July 1947, proved hemorrhagic in effect, and was abandoned after five weeks. By that time, however, international relations, including Anglo-American relations, had entered a quite new phase.

The beginning of 1947 sees the inauguration of a positive and creative period of U.S. foreign policy which is really without parallel either earlier or later. The actions taken within the next six months constituted a real climacteric in world politics; together with various related actions extending over the next two and a half years, they shaped the main aspects of the relations of the major powers into the form which they still essentially retain, after a quarter of a century. The main themes were the interpreting of Russian foreign policy as resting on an aggressive Communism which was a danger to the rest of the world; and the demonstration of a qualified readiness to resist such aggression. Other countries were to be assisted to resist Communism by massive economic aid. There also emerged a readiness to undertake defense commitments, and, indeed, to fight at least limited wars in circumstances thought to be convenient—not for the lands already lost to Communism and apparently written off; and not for Czechoslovakia, either in 1948 or 1968; nor for Hungary in 1956; but for Korea and for South Vietnam. In general terms, the new policy meant the end of American isolationism. It implied a novel readiness to assume long-term responsibilities outside the United States and outside the Western Hemisphere. Perhaps the most interesting aspect of it was the extent to which it meant taking over the kind of responsibilities, duties, and policies that had hitherto been borne or pursued by Britain.

The bold decisions of this period have not escaped criticism. A revisionist school of historians has arisen, as was almost inevitable, which claims that the threat from Russian Communism was either exaggerated or nonexistent; that Russian policy was defensive.[12] Some would go so far as to argue that the United States provoked the Soviet Union by an implacable hostility demonstrated since 1917 (the gospel according to D. F. Fleming), or since 1945 (according to Alperovitz). But a defensive policy which is pursued by means of subverting the independence of formerly sovereign states beyond one's frontiers (as the U.S.S.R. did in the period 1944–1948 to half-a-dozen states of Eastern Europe), and turning them for one's own purposes into a glacis of compulsorily "friendly" states—i.e., into parts of a hegemonial or imperial system—is a policy bound to be obnoxious to other states: not only the states whose independence is subverted, but very naturally to others beyond them. In such circumstances, those who direct the policy of other states have to be criminally negligent if they make the optimistic assumption that no threat exists to their own security. From the beginning of 1947, the United States abandoned this optimistic assumption.

12 Revisionists are not always correct. Sometimes they are themselves subject to revision, and the previous view is reestablished. Thus in recent years the German historian Fritz Fischer has evoked great hostility in his own country by scrupulously proving with chapter and verse that German ambitions in the First World War were indeed inordinate and intolerable to other states. This is what everyone thought in England in 1914–18, but all good liberal historians in Britain and America in the 1920s and 1930s decried any such belief as hysterical war propaganda. See his *Griff nach der Weltmacht* (Düsseldorf: Droste Verlag, 1961); English translation, *Germany's Aims in the First World War*, with introduction by Hajo Holborn (New York: Norton and Company, Inc., 1967), 644 pp. The even more eminent Gerhard Ritter has said the same thing in the fourth volume of his monumental, unfinished work on the problem of militarism in Germany, *Staatskunst und Kriegshandwerk*, published in Munich in 1968. An English translation of Ritter's work by Heinz Norden is to be published by the University of Miami Press.

Criticism of a more valid kind can be made from another side. If the United States wished to restrain Communist aggression, it was unconscionably slow in facing up to the problem. It only did so after Eastern Europe had been swept into the silence and uniformity of the Communist maw. The United States was also naïve in being so astonished by the events of 1945–1947. They were entirely foreseeable. No one in Eastern Europe but realized with sad heart, when the Yalta decisions were announced, that for them the end of the war would merely mean the substitution of Russian for German domination. Yet in the winter of 1944–1945 there had been, in fact, absolutely no need for the United States to make concessions to a Russia that was totally exhausted.

The "New Course" of American policy in the postwar years is rightly and indelibly associated with the name of Dean Acheson, a man of incomparable energy, wit, and capacity for business, one not afraid either of making decisions or of making enemies in the pursuing of what he considered the right cause. Acheson already had vast experience in public affairs behind him when he became Undersecretary of State on 27 August 1945, a post he held until 1 July 1947, under two Secretaries of State, Byrnes and Marshall. During a little more than one-third of that time he acted as Secretary of State because of the absence of his chief.[13] He was Secretary of State from January 1949 to January 1953.

Acheson's posture in foreign-policy matters was basically the firm American patriotism of a highly cultivated man. He was not, as some of his critics said, unduly under British influence. He was not, in fact, a man very easily subject to *any* influence outside his own conscience and judgment. But he was, in the main, a good friend to Britain. He says of himself (speaking of 1950), "My own attitude had long been, and was known to have been, pro-British." [14] He found cooperation with most of his British confreres exceptionally easy and productive.

This was not, indeed, true of Sir Archibald Clark Kerr,

[13] Acheson, *Present at the Creation,* p. 122.
[14] *Ibid.,* p. 387.

Lord Inverchapel, who was British Ambassador in Washington for two years from June 1946. "Lord Inverchapel . . . was an agreeable companion but unsatisfactory as a diplomatic colleague. Unquestionably eccentric, he liked to appear even more eccentric than he was, producing an ultimate impression odd enough to be puzzling." There was "the conversational puzzle of knowing what he meant, whose views he was representing, and how what one said in reply appeared in his telegrams to London." [15] Relations with Inverchapel's chief, Ernest Bevin, who was British Foreign Secretary from July 1945 to March 1951—that is, during the whole of this seminal period—were a happier story. Bevin, whom Acheson calls in his memoirs "my trusted and admired friend," [16] was, as Pepys said of General Monck, a plain, blunt man; but, as with Monck, he had the capacity to evoke affection even in the most unexpected quarters. It will always be one of the minor mysteries of history how the shambling, uncouth Bevin, with a purely working-class background, with syntax as disorganized as Eisenhower's, got on so extraordinarily well not only with the permanent officials of his own Foreign Office, but also with the urbane, point-device Acheson; but it was so. Doubtless Bevin's utter honesty and sincerity were the answer. In 1946 Bevin, more than any American, was the West's spokesman against Russia. He, the lifelong trade-union official, repelled with scorn and contempt the presumption of the U.S.S.R. in claiming to be the authentic champion of the laboring masses.

Even more noteworthy than the Acheson-Bevin relationship, however, was the exceedingly cordial relationship between Acheson and Sir Oliver (later Lord) Franks [17] when

---

15 *Ibid.,* p. 178.

16 *Ibid.,* p. 504.

17 Franks (born 1905) is an extraordinarily brilliant administrator, whose career is unique in British history for the number of quite different top posts he has held. Professor of Moral Philosophy at the University of Glasgow at the outbreak of war, he subsequently became, in chronological order: the highest civil servant in the Ministry of Supply; Provost of Queen's College, Oxford; British ambassador in Washington; Chairman of Lloyds Bank; and Provost of Worcester College, Oxford. His Reith Lectures of 1954, *Britain and the Tide of World Affairs* (London: Oxford University Press, 1955), though

the latter was British ambassador in Washington, which led
to truly remarkable arrangements for informal consultation.
Franks, whom Acheson calls "one of the most able—and
also most delightful—men it has ever been my good fortune
to know and work with," was *en poste* in Washington from
June 1948 until January 1953—an unusually long tenure of
the position. Acheson records that not long after becoming
Secretary of State (January 1949) he made the ambassador an
"unorthodox proposal." [18] The proposal was that they should
meet and talk regularly, and in total confidentiality, about
any international problems they saw arising. "Neither would
report or quote the other unless, thinking that it would be
useful in promoting action, he got the other's consent and
agreement on the terms of a reporting cable or memorandum."
The two men met at one or the other's residence, usually at
the end of the day, before or after dinner. Each kept the
meetings secret not only from the press—astonishing triumph in Washington—but also from the bureaucracies
of which each man formed a part. State Department and
Foreign Office knew nothing of it; consequently, the clamor-
ous diverse opinions of Commonwealth or Congress had no
opportunity to intervene. The arrangement was wholly successful. "Later, comparing the relations between our governments during our time with those under our successors, we
concluded that whereas we had thought of these relations
and their management as a part of domestic affairs, they had
regarded them as foreign affairs." This was indeed a very
rare, perhaps unique, episode in the history of diplomacy.
Only in the context of Anglo-American relations could
such an arrangement have occurred. Only in that context
could the representatives of two sovereign states conceivably
have regarded their common concerns as *"a part of domestic affairs."*

---

largely outdated now, were very perceptive and contained some shrewd thrusts
on the present topic, e.g. (p. 35): "The American tradition has little knowledge
of glorious failures. In the Anglo-American relationship British policy has to
pass the test: can the British deliver?"

[18] Acheson, *Present at the Creation*, pp. 323–24.

The handing-over of supreme responsibility for leadership of the West from Britain to the United States occurred in the spring of 1947 with a clarity, definitiveness, and brevity that are exceptional in history. Indeed, without being impossibly far-fetched, it may be said to have happened on the afternoon of Friday, 21 February 1947, in a room in the old State Department building in Washington, when Mr. Sichel, First Secretary at the British Embassy, handed over to Mr. Loy Henderson of the State Department carbon copies of two notes from the British Government.[19] There was not much diplomatic ambiguity about the notes; as Acheson says, "They were shockers." One dealt with Greece, the other with Turkey. They reviewed the needs of Greece for extensive financial aid to ward off internal collapse and guerrilla subversion, and of both countries for extensive economic and military support to resist continuing heavy pressure from the Soviet Union. Britain had hitherto been providing both countries with assistance. The British government, however, would be unable to do so beyond the end of March, and therefore hoped that as of the first of April the United States would assume the burden. The beginning of April was six weeks away.

This was a crossroads of history; what Joseph M. Jones, who wrote the classic history of the crisis, *The Fifteen Weeks,* aptly called "that *carrefour* of time." As he says,

> For decades massive historical caravans had been observed moving slowly toward predictable destinations: Great Britain toward loss of Empire and inability to maintain the balance of power in Europe and order in Asia; Western continental Europe toward instability and weakness; the United States toward economic and military pre-eminence in political isolation; and the Soviet Union toward a fundamental challenge of Western civilization.[20]

19 Carbon copies because Inverchapel was not able on Friday to deliver the ribbon copy to the Secretary, as he had wanted to do, the Secretary being out of Washington. Acheson suggested this procedure so that preliminary work could be begun in the State Department over the weekend. Formal presentation of the notes took place on the Monday. Acheson, p. 217.

20 Joseph M. Jones, *The Fifteen Weeks* (New York: The Viking Press, 1955), pp. vii, 9.

By bold action the challenge was met. The next weeks of intense activity displayed the not too common spectacle of "the government of the United States operating at its very finest, efficiently and effectively, and of the American people responding to leadership in a manner equally splendid." The threat of isolationism was ended; the dangers were deflected. In his message to a joint session of Congress on 12 March, President Truman proposed the assumption of support for Greece and Turkey, and more broadly enunciated the declaration (to which the name the "Truman Doctrine" came to be given) that it would thenceforth be the policy of the United States "to support free peoples who are resisting attempted subjugation by armed minorities or by outside pressures."

The month of June saw the birth of a still broader economic initiative by the United States when General Marshall, Secretary of State, suggested in his Harvard Commencement address that the United States might provide financial assistance to put the European countries back on their feet. Ernest Bevin took up the suggestion enthusiastically and the next few months saw the launching of the European Recovery Program—that great enterprise which in the course of a few years did actually succeed in its objective. Later programs of economic aid to other parts of the world were largely unsuccessful, but Europe *was* enabled by timely American assistance to attain the road to recovery; the process of regaining high productivity and prosperity went in fact much faster than had been anticipated.

Britain benefited from "Marshall Aid" to the total extent of about two billion dollars. The beginning of aid, however, did not prevent Britain's having a serious balance-of-payments problems in 1949,[21] worsened by a slight American recession,

[21] Britain's balance-of-payments problems have been recurrent ever since the war. There is a cyclical pattern. They tend to occur in odd-numbered years (1947, 1949, 1957, 1961, 1967 . . .). In the 1960s the United States ceased to be able to look down its nose at this sort of thing, since it too began to run a very heavy balance-of-payments deficit; but the United States, as de Gaulle bitterly and accurately pointed out, was enabled by the Bretton Woods agreements to ignore this kind of situation in a more high-handed manner than any other country.

which led to the sterling devaluation of September, 1949. Typically, the decision to devalue was made known in advance to Acheson and to a few other U.S. officials, as well as to the Canadian government, but not to the French or anyone else.[22]

There was a telling little episode during the discussions in Washington that preceded devaluation. Paul Hoffman saw fit to exhort Bevin to try harder to export to the American market. Bevin rounded vehemently on Hoffman in precisely the same fashion that Churchill had done to Sumner Welles at Placentia Bay in 1941,[23] making exactly the same point:

> Bevin . . . had been interested, he said, for many years in British industry and several times he had heard free traders urge the British workers to make the sacrifices necessary to compete in the great American market. Every time, as soon as they had made a little progress, the Congress set up a howl about cheap foreign labor and raised the tariff to new heights. . . . Would we guarantee that if Europe sought to balance its payments by exports to the United States, Congress would let them come in? [24]

The tendency of Congress, under pressure from its constituencies, to react to foreign competition by raising tariffs indeed touches an extremely raw nerve for Britons and other Europeans. In 1970 there were clear and ominous possibilities that Congress might do the same again. The point made so forcefully by Bevin (and earlier by Churchill) had not ceased to be relevant. (There is always a latent tendency abroad, easily awakened, to regard the U.S. government— so democratic and therefore so apt to act in foreign policy matters on domestic grounds—as fundamentally untrustworthy; as, so to speak, a kind of *perfide Albion* writ large. But the criticism is a matter less of imputing Machiavellian cunning than total unreliability and irresponsibility.) [25]

22 Acheson, *Present at the Creation*, p. 325.

23 See above, p. 79.

24 Acheson, *Present at the Creation*, pp. 324–25.

25 Two illuminating items from one day's newspaper (*Los Angeles Times*, 16 July 1970): (1) "The House Ways and Means Committee has unceremoniously dumped further efforts to repeal the much-debated 'American selling

Concurrently with inaugurating economic aid, the United States was embarking on a course directly contrary to the whole previous tradition of its foreign policy, in assuming long-term alliance commitments. The spur to do so was felt in two alarming events of the spring of 1948: the Communist *coup d'état* in Prague, and the interdict by the Russians on Western land transportation to Berlin. The path of alliance had been exemplified by the Brussels Treaty of March 1948 among Britain, France, and the Benelux trio; an example which Bevin undoubtedly hoped would lead to the inclusion of the United States in such a system. This end was facilitated by the passage of the Vandenberg Resolution of 11 June 1948 in the U.S. Senate. The North Atlantic Treaty of 4 April 1949 linked the United States and Britain with ten other countries in mutual defense commitments extending for at least twenty years. To the original twelve were added Greece and Turkey in 1951 and West Germany four years later.

For the United States, the North Atlantic Treaty was an arrangement uniting it with a number of other countries in order to resist Communist aggression, and with that sole purpose. To Britain, it was the nearest thing available to the real desideratum—an exclusive, all-purpose Anglo-American alliance. Britain's eagerness for the latter on any terms (or on no stated terms at all) was demonstrated a year before the signature of the North Atlantic Treaty by the curiously informal and even offhand manner in which, during the tense spring of 1948, the British government accepted

---

price' system over certain benzoid chemicals—thereby reneging on a key element in the 'Kennedy Round' world trade agreement which was laboriously negotiated in Geneva from 1961 to 1966. A variety of trade concessions on American exports to GATT countries were obtained only on condition that the protectionist ASP legislation which dates back to the early 1920s would be repealed. . . ." (2) The Foreign Minister of Thailand, speaking in Bangkok at an American Chamber of Commerce luncheon, said that the United States appeared to be on the verge of a national mental breakdown that has affected its reliability as an ally. He said it was "difficult for those working closely and loyally with the United States to expect a well-reasoned and balanced reaction from their disturbed partner." He said that Thailand was continually subject to criticism in the American press and from American politicians not for *opposing* the United States but for *supporting* it . . .

the tentative U.S. suggestion of stationing American bombers in East Anglia. The U.S. government had expected to encounter misgivings, haggling, apprehension at the supposed risks; there was none of this. The British accepted with relief, not qualms, the return of this symbol of the tacit Anglo-American alliance. The U.S. bombers had only been away from England for three years.

A little later the British government made a crucial decision in a matter which did not directly involve the United States. This was the decision of June 1950 not to become a party to the Schuman Plan—the proposal for a European Coal and Steel Community. The Coal and Steel Community, formally inaugurated in 1952 with France, West Germany, Italy, and the Benelux countries as members, was to prove the nucleus and model for the European Economic Community (the "Common Market"), launched in 1958, and so of the whole drive toward Western European economic, and perhaps political, integration. There was very little debate about the Labour Government's decision; it seems to have been almost automatic. It was also, most commentators would think now, a wrong decision. By July 1961 the Conservative Government of that day had come to that conclusion. By 1967 the Labour Government of the day had done likewise. Yet in the context of 1950 the reasons for rejection of the proposal are not hard to seek.

The rejection was hardly a decision; it was more like a reflex, the inevitable outcome of certain deeply held attitudes. Both British parties agreed on the rejection, and there was little perceptible dissent from public opinion. The Labour Party was thoroughly averse to linking the nationalized coal and steel industries of the United Kingdom to the free-enterprise industries of the Continent. It could hardly be expected to muster up enthusiasm for a plan whose objective was to make private enterprise work better under the stimulus of competition. Bevin, also, correctly perceived from the first that the plan had long-range implications that were hostile to national sovereignty. As the foreign editor of *Figaro* comments, "Ernest Bevin was, without a doubt, the first Brit-

ish statesman to gauge the true scope of the French proposal
and to grasp that it was intended to introduce a new factor
into the problem of Europe's development towards unity." [26]

Churchill had become a great champion of European
unity in his frustrating years as Leader of the Opposition since
1945, but there was something slightly bogus about this. It
was the enthusiasm of a statesman in opposition who has to
find a great cause with which to keep himself in the lime-
light; he sought a European role because he was out of
power at home. He thought European unity was a very good
thing—for other countries than Britain. In the same way, the
United States has usually favored international integration,
provided it does not involve the United States. Churchill—and
Attlee, and Bevin—were all determined that British involvement
in the European Continent should not go substantially beyond
that of the United States. It was British influence that had
watered down the proposed powers of the Council of Europe,
and made it almost a nullity.

Britain, in 1950, saw chiefly the fact that a European
federation, or any substantial steps in that direction, would
manifestly exclude the United States, which might thus have a
good excuse for reducing or ending its participation in European defense. Even if Europe genuinely became strong
enough in itself not to need American participation, such a
development would not be welcomed to Britain. Secondly,
membership in a European federation would deprive Britain
of her freedom of action in relations with the United States,
thus making it impossible for Britain to maintain her position
as America's privileged partner. There was also the threat
to the Commonwealth relationship. However, in this period it
is always difficult to know whether in the minds of British
statesmen the Commonwealth connection was a factor
truly weighing in the decision-making process (if it was,
British policies were being shaped not so much at Westminster as in the land of Cockaigne); or, as one rather suspects,

[26] Roger Massip, foreign editor of *Figaro*, in *European Community*, May
1970, p. 6.

it was a consideration dragged in to justify decisions that had already been made on other grounds.

Underlying all this were more fundamental unstated major premises. The Continental nations had recent experiences of defeat, of being overrun and occupied by the Germans. The tenuous thread of their independent existence had been maintained by the device of governments-in-exile, mostly in exile in London. All this had created a mood of skepticism about the adequacy and viability of the nation-state which encouraged international experimentation. There was none of this in recent British experience. The British state had maintained itself, Britain had not been invaded. The state had coped with magnificent vigor and flexibility with the appalling strains of war—had done so, indeed, far better than in 1914–1918. England had, as usual, saved herself by her exertions, and Europe by her example. There was some excuse for the British to feel that their Britain was a cut above the mere foreigners of the Continent; on the recent showing, it was. There was less excuse, but there was some, for feeling essentially that Britain, if not quite the equal of America or Russia, resembled them more than it did France or Italy.

All this was thoroughly understandable. Still, it was a wrong decision, and this became clear in due course. There was not much point in opting for the oceanic policy as against the Continental—for the Commonwealth and the United States as against participation in European integration—unless something could be made of the former policy; and, perhaps inevitably, very little was made of it. Britain made the same mistake again in the period of 1955–1957, when the Common Market was in process of gestation. The offer of the Sybilline books was declined a second time.

Thus 1950 saw the United Kingdom poised on the horns of a dilemma on which it was, essentially, still poised twenty years later. In 1950 it was still *trying* to foster the North American, oceanic relationship. In 1970 it was *trying,* in the face of formidable obstacles, to "join Europe."

In the 1950 British decision the United States played

no part. Acheson, who was in Paris and then in London during precisely those days—discussing the readmittance of West Germany to the West European comity, and the necessity for German rearmament—had to fend off the unjustified suspicions of Bevin that the Schuman Plan was something he had cooked up with the French. During the negotiations that followed he insisted that there should be no U.S. pressure on Britain to join or not to join.[27] There was some slight American pressure in favor of the plan as a whole, and in favor of making the proposed organization stronger rather than weaker. That was all. There was something of a paradox here. The question of British membership in the Coal and Steel Community, and all that it implied, in fact underlay the whole question of future Anglo-American relations and would determine their character, and yet it was not discussed directly, and remained formally a marginal issue, in regard to which the only U.S. policy was "hands off." But for America, of course, this was a correct attitude, in every sense. The decision to be made was a British decision, and right or wrong they would have to live with it.

Agreeing with the United States, or at any rate avoiding disagreement, on European policy was easy for Britain. Agreeing with American policy on the Far East, or the Middle East, was, as the British say, a different kettle of fish. Alliances, whether formal or implicit, are after all devices of convenience. They are at their most real—perhaps they only truly exist—in relations to areas, or topics, where there is a firm common interest perceived as such by the two or more states who are parties to the alliance. Friendly attitudes and habits of cooperation may or may not be carried

---

[27] Acheson sent a circular instruction to all U.S. missions in western Europe, "The U.S. is not to be a party to negotiations and is to have no official association or observers. . . . We are to take no position concerning UK-French issues on the Plan. . . ." (Acheson, p. 388.) It was also at this moment that Acheson was disconcerted to find that some of his subordinates had been concocting with British confreres a paper on the special nature of Anglo-American relations. Acheson felt that such a document was highly inexpedient and dangerous, and had all copies suppressed. It would have been interesting to read it. (Acheson, p. 387.)

over into areas where there is an unequal, or no, perception of a common interest.

In regard to the latter, one ally may regard with an easy (and infuriating) calm damage to interests of the other ally which the latter regards as important or even vital, i.e., worth fighting for. In regard to Europe, policy agreement between Britain and the United States was relatively easy, because both parties believed in similar, great, simple objectives: the achievement of Western European economic recovery, readiness to defend Western Europe against a threat from the east.

Elsewhere, no such clear consensus existed. The bare bones of British foreign policy in the postwar years have been set forth with a certain stark elegance by Grant Hugo, who has pointed out that, in a world whose politics are dominated by two superpowers, Britain has felt it essential to seek the protection of the one whose price is the more likely to be compatible with British national interests, aspirations, and policies. This is, of course, the United States, and the price paid by Britain for American protection has been a general readiness to go along with American policy. "The working formula for British foreign policy thus becomes to obtain the maximum protection at the minimum price or, in other words, to endeavour to increase the credibility of the American nuclear deterrent in so far as this serves to protect Britain, while simultaneously opposing any tendency towards the use or threat of nuclear warfare in disputes irrelevant to vital British interests." [28]

The United States, a Pacific power, was very much more interested in the Far East than was Britain. Britain hoped to hang on to Hong Kong, but considered her ability to do so was much more dependent on the goodwill of China than on any British capacity to defend it. Apart from that, on the

---

[28] Grant Hugo, *Britain in Tomorrow's World* (New York: Columbia University Press, 1969) p. 212. This is a very intelligent, sparkling, and iconoclastic work. Much the same point is made in a somewhat similar book equally deserving of praise, Anthony Hartley, *A State of England* (New York: Harcourt, Brace and World, Inc., 1963), p. 60.

periphery of the Far East there was Malaya, where Britain fought a lonely and successful war without American aid. In the Middle East both powers had interests, but rarely coordinated the defense of them. The gravest disagreement on the Middle East came later, in Eden's time as Prime Minister; but disagreement on the Far East was obtrusive, and did some damage to Anglo-American relations, in the Truman-Attlee period.

The most obvious point of difference was the British recognition of Communist China in January 1950, very soon after the Communists gained control of all mainland China. This contrasted with the continuing U.S. recognition and support of Chiang Kai-shek. British policy on the question of recognition has on the whole been more consistent than that of the United States. As befits a country whose very life depends on commerce, it has tended to treat recognition as a mere coming to terms with a situation that actually exists, rather than the granting of a seal of approval. (Only occasionally, as in regard to the Spanish government in 1946, or Rhodesia in 1965, has it wandered from this path.) The United States has more frequently (though not with complete consistency) followed the seal-of-approval interpretation of recognition, regarding it as a mild sanction.

However, it would be idle to pretend that in 1950 the U.S. government had a completely free hand to choose. For the previous half-dozen years it had been considerably involved in the civil struggle in China, as Britain had not. It would have been very difficult, in domestic terms impossible, suddenly to ditch Chiang and recognize the Communists. Also, it would have produced no advantages. Britain, France, and other countries that recognized China did not succeed in establishing any real contact with the Chinese government, did not prevent their commercial interests being destroyed or their subjects being treated with indignity. It can be argued that the United States, by means of the talks with Chinese representatives held intermittently in Warsaw over a long period of years, has had more real diplomatic contact with that unique phenomenon in international politics, the present government of China, than states that followed the traditional course of recognition and the establishment of permanent missions in Peking.

When the Korean War broke out in June 1950, Britain supported the United States. The Commonwealth Division, consisting of some 12,000 troops (mostly British but with Canadian and Australian contingents) was the largest contribution to the allied army under American command (and American forces were, of course, well over nine-tenths of the total). This was something; but in the opinion of many Americans it was not enough. A little under a thousand British were killed in the Korean War; a little over thirty thousand Americans.

The British were nervous all during the Korean War that the United States might become involved through it in a larger war. They did not like the U.S. "neutralization" of Formosa proclaimed at the start of the Korean War, as it implied that American power would be used to prevent Chiang's government there being overthrown. There were disputes over trade policy too; the British went along with a limited embargo on the shipment of strategic goods to China, but would not imitate the U.S. total embargo.

Attlee was sufficiently worried by the statement of President Truman at a press conference (30 November 1950) that the use of atomic weapons would not *necessarily* be ruled out in Korea [29] that he made a hurried visit to Washington. British opinion was inclined to regard this visit as a crucial intervention that injected some sense and moderation into American policy. There is not much in this self-flattering interpretation. Acheson and other members of the administration clearly regarded it as a tedious and officious piece of butting-in which was without any substantial results whatever. The U.S. government was also exasperated during the Korean conflict by the British government's penchant for acting as a pipeline to Washington for advice from

[29] No summary in a phrase of what Truman said can avoid being misleading. As the full text shows, he was merely avoiding in a perfectly proper fashion the efforts of the press to harry and badger him into making an express commitment which would have implied a major policy decision, of a negative kind, that had never been made. See Acheson, p. 479.

Nehru's India. The advice was usually pessimistic and assumed that American forces were on the verge of a disastrous rout only to be averted by humiliating concessions which Nehru's government recommended to the United States.

The whole question of the development of atomic weapons, and their possible use, had been a sore point between Britain and America for many years past. In the early years of the war, British atomic research was ahead of American. When the United States became a belligerent, it appeared to make sense that British research should be thrown into a common pool, and that the vast process of manufacturing the bomb should be done physically in the ample spaces of the United States and utilizing its enormous resources. The terms of continuing British-American cooperation in atomic matters were spelled out in the Quebec Agreement of August 1943, which was known to very few people indeed (Attlee, though an important member of the British War Cabinet, heard of it first when he became Prime Minister), and in the even more obscure Roosevelt-Churchill Hyde Park memorandum of September 1944.

The latter document promised "full cooperation" not only during but *after the war*. There was, in fact, a good deal of foot-dragging on the American side in carrying out these agreements. General Groves, director of "Manhattan District" (U.S. code name for the atomic bomb project; the British name was "Tube Alloys") from 1942, made a boast of it later: "I was not responsible for our close cooperation with the British. I did everything to hold back on it. . . . I did not carry out the wishes of our Government with respect to cooperation with the British. . . ." [30] Acheson, who as Undersecretary first became acquainted with these matters in 1945–1946, had a more scrupulous conscience:

> . . . for with knowledge came the belief that our Government, having made an agreement from which it had gained immeasurably, was not keeping its word and performing its obligations. Like all great issues it was not simple.

[30] U.S. Atomic Energy Commission, *In the Matter of J. Robert Oppenheimer: Transcript of Hearing. . . .* (Washington, D.C., 1954), p. 175.

> Grave consequences might follow upon keeping our word, but the idea of not keeping it was repulsive to me. . . .

And again:

> The honeymoon of Anglo-American relations existing during the war was clearly coming to an end, and some of the commitments of the marriage seemed to be causing pain to one of the spouses.[31]

Repeated attempts by the British, beginning with a visit to Washington by Attlee in November 1945, to obtain the continuance of wartime cooperation failed in the face of the unholy alliance in American policy-making between the internationalists (who thought the whole thing should be under U.N. control) and the nationalists (who thought no one should have access to the "secret" but America); to both groups, an exclusive Anglo-American cooperation was anathema. This constellation of forces on the question of atomic energy was in fact a grouping that had been seen before—on many questions in many decades—and had always served to defeat (and perhaps always will) those who would like to see a strengthening and institutionalization of the special relationship between Britain and the United States.

At the November meeting Attlee found Truman personally sympathetic and cooperative; "when he left Washington both he and Mackenzie King thought that the memorandum the three of them had signed had removed all difficulties in the way of peacetime cooperation. They were soon disabused." [32] In April 1946 Attlee informed Harriman in London that if the proposed McMahon Act was passed Britain would be forced to build her own plants for atomic energy production for both civil and military purposes. He requested from Washington detailed information on the construction and operation of atomic energy plants. This request met with a blank refusal on 15 April 1946. A final plea was made by Attlee in an extremely long telegram

---

31 Acheson, *Present at the Creation*, pp. 164, 166.

32 Francis Williams, *A Prime Minister Remembers: The War and Post-War Memoirs of the Right Hon. Earl Attlee. . . . Based on his Private Papers and on a Series of Recorded Conversations* (London: Heinemann, 1961), p. 109.

sent to Truman on 6 June 1946 which rehearsed quite accurately the whole history of Anglo-American cooperation on the project and summarized the existing agreements, concluding with a request for "that full information to which we believe that we are entitled, both by the documents and by the history of our common efforts in the past." [33]

Any reasonably impartial reader is bound to find this document unanswerable. Truman must have found it so. He did not answer it.

The McMahon Act (properly the Atomic Energy Act) became law on 1 August 1946, and placed an interdict on the conveyance of information about atomic matters. However, as relations with the Soviet Union became more tense a revision of the situation seemed desirable even to the United States, and this came about in the *modus vivendi* of January 1948. The British had at least a couple of high cards: their control of the Congo uranium ore supplies, and the existence (at least on paper, in the Quebec Agreement) of a British veto on the actual use of the bomb—it was to be used only by "mutual consent." As usual, thoughts about the general indispensability of American goodwill prevented the British from using their advantages *à outrance*. Vandenberg had warned that "failure to revamp the agreements would have a disastrous effect on Congressional consideration of the Marshall Plan." The result was the *modus vivendi,* which left decision as to use of the weapons entirely in American hands, ended U.S. anxieties about raw material supplies, but on the other hand authorized a limited exchange of information between Britain and the United States. According to Acheson, this "relieved the extreme apprehensions of the senators but left the British with a sense of having been ungenerously, if not unfairly, treated." [34] There, essentially, the matter remained for a decade. Negotiations in 1949 for a revision of the *modus vivendi* which might have led to a revival of the essential features of wartime cooperation—joint research, and manufacture solely in the United States—looked for a time to be going well, and their

[33] *Ibid.,* pp. 112–17.
[34] Acheson, *Present at the Creation,* p. 168. Cf. also Chaps. 19 and 35, *passim.*

prospects were enhanced by the Russian test explosion of an atomic weapon in August 1949, which demonstrated that the American "secret" was mythological; but the pitch was queered —and for a long time—by the arrest in February 1950 of the naturalized British scientist Klaus Fuchs on charges of passing information to the Russians.

Meanwhile, the British had gone ahead successfully, *faute de mieux,* on their own atomic weapons program. As Attlee said in retrospect, "Once Congress proceeded to pass the McMahon Bill we had to go ahead on our own. . . . We had to hold up our position *vis-à-vis* the Americans. We couldn't allow ourselves to be wholly in their hands. . . ." [35] The first British atomic weapon was tested in Australia in October 1952.

The outbreak of the Korean War led Attlee's government, in an access of loyalty to its American ally, to accept American urging to embark on a large rearmament program. By January 1951 the British government had agreed to embark on a program that was to cost £4.7 billion ($13.16 billion) over three years, and the United States, obsessed by Korea, had been prodded by Britain into appointing Eisenhower to the allied command in Europe, thus beginning to clothe the bare bones of the North Atlantic Treaty with the institutional and command structure of the North Atlantic Treaty Organization. The British rearmament program was so ambitious as to be seriously out of line with British economic capacity; embarked upon by the prickly Attlee, it was later considerably cut back by the pro-American Churchill.

When Churchill returned to power as a result of the general election of October 1951 (initiating a period of Conservative governments, confirmed in office by the general elections of 1945 and 1959, that was to last for thirteen years), he was only one month short of his seventy-seventh birthday. Though still capable of making extraordinary returns to his best form for short periods, he was physically running down, easily fatigued, and with a short attention span —or, for things he was not interested in, no attention at all.

35 Williams, *Prime Minister,* p. 118.

He had already had one stroke, in 1949. He was, of course, anxious to restore Anglo-American cooperation to the high level it had had during his previous tenure of the premiership, but his hardest attempts to do so came after Eisenhower had succeeded to the presidency in January 1953.

Churchill paid a visit to Washington in January 1952, but not very much came of it. "Little was accomplished by way of final agreement beyond ending our differences over the Atlantic Command." [36] Churchill paid strangely little heed to the question of European integration, which had been his great theme during his late-1940s period in opposition. He was contemptuous of the European Defense Community project, which Dulles supported but which finally foundered in the summer of 1954 on the rock of French rejection. When a substitute for it was found in the devices of admitting a rearmed Germany into the Brussels Pact group, enlarged and renamed Western European Union, and then into NATO, this was Eden's achievement as Foreign Secretary, not Churchill's (nor Dulles's either). In Far Eastern matters, the more-or-less successful outcome of the Geneva Conference of 1954 was also to Eden's credit. It followed on the British refusal to have anything to do with Dulles's rather ill-defined proposals for giving the French aid at Dienbienphu or in Indochina generally.

In the area of strategic weapons policy, Churchill was responsible for the decision, taken in 1952, to build a new fleet of bombers, which were to form the backbone of the British deterrent force for the next decade and a half. This step was not taken with the intention of following a course of action separate from the United States, but was rather "a logical, sequential step in U.S.–British joint military planning." [37]

[36] Acheson, *Present at the Creation*, p. 596. Cf. also on this visit Chap. 62, *passim*. There is a charming exchange of very cordial letters with Eden on pp. 605–6 puffing away an imaginary storm that the press had dreamed up between Eden and Acheson.

[37] Raymond Dawson and Richard Rosecrance, "Theory and Reality in the Anglo-American Alliance," *World Politics,* October 1966, p. 34. The new bomber fleet was known as the V-bombers because their class names were Valiant, Victor, and Vulcan.

Apart from these matters just mentioned, there were two main themes of this period. One was Churchill's desperate eagerness to play the role of world peacemaker, and the other was the tendency of events in the Middle East to exacerbate Anglo-American relations.

During his last administration Churchill became more and more impressed by the appalling prospect of world war with the kind of weapons science was developing. In the mid-1940s, when there was an American nuclear monopoly, an American hegemony of the world seemed physically a possibility, and Churchill and most Britons would have happily settled for that. (Among those who concurred in this view was Bertrand Russell, as doubtless some of his admirers would prefer to forget.[38] Later Russell changed his views on the benevolence of American domination.) With the Russian attainment of a nuclear bomb, the case was altered. Then in November 1952 the United States attained the still more horrible thermonuclear bomb, and the Soviet Union, closing the gap, followed in August 1953. Britain was to acquire a similar weapon in 1957.

Thus during the Churchill-Eisenhower period (January 1953–April 1955), nothing interested the failing Churchill very much except the attempt, entirely abortive in the event, to exploit his personal influence with Eisenhower and the tradition of Anglo-American cooperation in order to make a supreme effort, at a summit meeting or meetings of the leaders of the three countries, to arrive at some accommodation with Russia that would avert the threat of world war. "He was obsessed," says Macmillan, "by his hopes of going down to history not only as the greatest War Minister but as the greatest peacemaker in the world." [39] He was, as Mac-

[38] See his article in *Horizon*, no. 100, 1948. On 29 November 1948 Harold Nicolson noted in his diary: "Viti and I discuss after dinner whether Bertie Russell was right in stating that we should make war on Russia while we have the atomic bomb and they have not." Nigel Nicolson, ed., *Diaries and Letters of Harold Nicolson*, Vol. III, *The Later Years 1945–1962* (New York: Atheneum, 1968), p. 155. Russell explained later he had *only* meant to force a settlement on Russia by the threat of war.

[39] Harold Macmillan, *Tides of Fortune: 1945–1955* (New York: Harper and Row, 1969), p. 533.

millan says (adopting the phrase which Churchill's father had
applied to Gladstone), "an old man in a hurry." But no one
else quite saw things at that point in the light he did. "Eden
had little hopes of much fruitful business with the Russians
at this time. Although willing to go along with Churchill up
to a point, in his heart he preferred the policy of first building
up our strength." As for the Americans, and particularly for
Eisenhower, the whole idea was quite distasteful to them, for
a whole string of reasons. Eisenhower did not like, or trust
himself at, summit meetings. He believed in organization, staff
work, and leaving things to his subordinates as far as possible.
(To some extent his distrust of the summit conference as a
diplomatic method was quite justified. Acheson did not think
much of them either.) The Americans in general might justly
reproach Churchill with some inconsistency. It was, after all,
he who in the Fulton speech had urged them to be up and
doing in opposing the spread of Communism. They could
hardly be blamed for looking askance at advice from him,
only a few years later, to moderate their zeal, just at the
time when (it seemed to them) they were beginning to get
Western defense reasonably organized.[40]

Churchill was now aspiring to play the role of the reasonable middleman who could moderate between the two hostile
parties—precisely the role that Roosevelt had enjoyed playing (to Churchill's suppressed fury) between Churchill and
Stalin in the later years of the war. But there is always something officious, smug, and offensive in this role: there is such
an implication that the mediator alone is reasonable, and is
possessed of a superior wisdom. The implication is particularly

[40] This was far indeed from being the only inconsistency in Churchill's
record. The Fulton "iron curtain" speech itself is open to the charge that it
expressed horror at conditions that Churchill himself had in part brought
about. The extraordinary "percentage" deal with Stalin on 9 October 1944
(see p. 97, above), could have no other meaning than that certain countries
were being handed over to Communism whether they liked it or not; and the
plain meaning of Yalta, in which Churchill participated, was that Poland was
being handed over to the Russians. Why all the surprise on his part a year
later when these things had happened? Again, the champion of British rearmament in the 1930s was protesting a weakness that he himself had helped to
bring about, when as Chancellor of the Exchequer (1924–1929) he ruthlessly
cut back appropriations for the armed forces.

galling to the one of the two parties who has previously looked upon the middleman as something of a friend, whose lofty impartiality is therefore all the more resented. Also, America's power had enabled Roosevelt to give a real significance to the role. Churchill had felt he had to be very careful indeed not to offend him—Stalin cared less. In the 1950s Churchill (and Macmillan, who essayed the role later with some success) had no such advantage. Neither the United States nor Russia need concern themselves, *au fond,* with what Britain wanted.

Another point was that the supposition that the inauguration of Eisenhower made the moment particularly auspicious for the revival of Anglo-American wartime intimacy was entirely fallacious. Many entertained this fallacy. H. C. Allen wrote at the end of his monumental historical study of the Anglo-American relationship, published in 1954,

> With the election of Eisenhower and the prospect of possibly four years or more of power or influence wielded by these two men . . . it is hard to believe that all will not be well.[41]

But there is, of course, no real evidence that Eisenhower had any particular fondness for the British. He was not of British descent. What he really thought about them remained impenetrably locked in his heart, but it probably did not differ very greatly from what most small-town Middle Westerners thought of them.

What *is* absolutely clear and explicit is that Eisenhower had not the slightest intention in the world of permitting anything like the old exclusive wartime Anglo-American intimacy to be resurrected. He rebuffed every single tentative that Churchill made in this direction with a certain dexterity, but with a clarity in which the courtesy only just concealed the sharpness of the intention. The note of difference was unmistakable even in the first messages they exchanged in the aftermath of Eisenhower's election. In congratulating him, Churchill pledged

[41] H. C. Allen, *Great Britain and the United States: A History of Anglo-American Relations (1783–1952)* (London: Odhams Press, 1954), p. 983.

> our assurance that, to the utmost limits of our strength, we will work with him for those great causes which we have guarded and cherished in ever greater unity as the generations have rolled by.

Eisenhower responded:

> I, too, look forward to a renewal of our cooperative work in the interests of a free world.[42]

Churchill met Eisenhower in New York in December 1952, in the month before his inauguration. Eisenhower recalled the meeting thus:

> The Prime Minister voiced the hope that the United States and Britain would be able to build and sustain a special closeness in international relationships; in effect he hoped that we could so well coordinate our views and decisions that we could resume our wartime closeness and act jointly in the affairs of the family of nations.
>
> I told him that the United States always put an unusual value on her relationship to Britain and that the history of World War II was in itself sufficient to assure particularly strong ties not only between us personally but between our two nations. On the other hand, I warned against the dangers of any concern in world opinion that we meant to form a two-power "coalition." To do so would create jealousies and suspicions that would be harmful in our work toward a world of justice.[43]

A dusty answer indeed; to form a two-power coalition was precisely what Churchill dreamed of doing.

In August 1953 Winthrop Aldrich, U.S. ambassador in London, told his friend Harold Macmillan that "Eisenhower was embarrassed by Churchill's attempt to revive, by personal correspondence, the old Churchill-Roosevelt relationship." [44] When Churchill and Eisenhower met again, in December 1953, Eisenhower recounts,

---

[42] *Daily Telegraph* (London), 8 and 11 November 1952.
[43] Dwight D. Eisenhower, *Mandate for Change 1953–1956* (Garden City, N.Y.: Doubleday and Company, Inc., 1963), p. 97.
[44] Macmillan, *Tides of Fortune*, p. 523.

Again, he had much to say about the need for Washington and London to coordinate and crystallize their views whenever they had mutual interests in any spot on the globe—for example, India, Egypt, Iran—and then to publicly present a solid front to the third party in the dispute.

I gave my approval to part of his argument. . . . But I expressed the thought that if any other party in the dispute had the slightest semblance of justice on its side, it could now appeal to the United Nations . . . we could . . . be made to look like arbitrary imperialists if we tried to "gang up" publicly in supporting the principles in which we both believed. . . . I felt that the last thing the two strongest Western powers should do was to appear before the world as a combination of forces to compel adherence to their announced views. . . .[45]

The actual outcome of all these strenuous efforts by Churchill was so meager that it is soon told. On 11 May 1953, freed from constraint by Eden's serious illness, Churchill made the offer of a three-power summit conference the highlight of an important speech in the House of Commons. A preliminary meeting between himself, Eisenhower, and the French premier was arranged for June in Bermuda, but before that could happen Churchill had another stroke. The meeting was actually held in December. It led to a four-power foreign ministers' conference with Russia in January and February 1954, which reached complete deadlock on all European questions; but this was followed by the five-power Geneva conference on the Far East at which China was represented and in which Eden scored something of a triumph but Dulles found the results unacceptable.

Churchill and Eden had a conference with Eisenhower and Dulles in Washington in June 1954, of which Macmillan says, "Although the meeting in Washington was outwardly successful, it achieved little positive result." [46] On the way home by ship, Churchill maladroitly sent to Russia—without in any

---

[45] Eisenhower, *Mandate,* pp. 249–250. It will be noted how closely the ideas expressed tally with those of Sumner Welles and Crane Brinton, quoted above (pp. 150–151).

[46] Macmillan, *Tides of Fortune,* p. 533.

way informing the Americans in advance, and contrary to Eden's advice—an invitation for a summit conference between himself and Malenkov. The Russian reply indicated acceptance of the idea, but the proposed Churchill visit to Moscow, which had evoked indignation in Washington, never took place. Thus the great Churchill peacemaking effort petered out. The following April he resigned, and Eden's long-deferred succession as Prime Minister took place.

Eden had almost as much experience as Churchill in dealing with the United States, and much greater diplomatic skill, but his premiership was almost catastrophic for Anglo-American relations. A large part of the trouble was his very bad personal relationship with J. F. Dulles. It is by no means certain that any other British foreign secretary could have done any better. Eden's predecessor as Foreign Secretary, Herbert Morrison, considered that Dulles had welshed on a promise that he had made in connection with negotiating the Japanese peace treaty, and wrote, "I may be forgiven if I resolved there and then not fully to trust Dulles again." [47] It was not only the British who found Dulles an almost unbearable cross. Acheson considered contemptible Dulles's failure to protect his subordinates against unjust imputations on their loyalty; Dulles's opening of the Foreign Service to the investigations of "Cohn and Schine of malodorous memory" [48] ruined the careers of some good men, destroyed the morale of the Foreign Service, and impaired its efficacy as an instrument for honest reporting. But the State Department and Foreign Service meant very little to Dulles. He made minimal use of them as a policy-framing agency. His sense of his own self-sufficiency and rectitude was absolute. He behaved as though he thought all knowledge and all wisdom were to be found between his ears. He certainly believed that the only true moral compass of the world swung on its gimbals there. And, since in his own mind he could do no wrong, this freed

---

[47] Herman Finer, *Dulles over Suez: The Theory and Practice of his Diplomacy* (Chicago: Quadrangle Books, 1964), p. 84, quoting Morrison's autobiography.

[48] Acheson, *Present at the Creation*, p. 245.

him conveniently to employ behavior that he would have recognized readily in others as prevarication, inconsistency, and breach of faith. Such was the man to whom the easy-going Eisenhower left most decision-making in the foreign-policy field for the next five years, until Dulles's death.

In December 1952 Eden visited Eisenhower while he was still at SHAPE,[49] and took the highly unusual step of expressing the hope that, as President, Eisenhower would appoint someone other than Dulles as Secretary of State. "I made no reply except to say that I knew of no other American so well qualified as Foster to take over the duties of that particular office." [50]

The great clash between Dulles and Eden came over a question in the Middle East. In no other area of the world where both Britain and America had substantial interests did cooperation between the countries fail so badly. It is not coincidence that there is no other area where Russia has so spectacularly strengthened her position in the past twenty years. Twenty years ago, although earlier there had been Tsarist ambitions there, Russia had virtually no footing in the Middle East at all; today it bids fair to be the paramount power of the region. There was an almost total failure to coordinate British and American policies in the area. What this means is that America made no effort to coordinate her policies with those of the British; the British would have been glad enough to oblige.

The postwar period begins, however, with a modest success for the West; Russian occupation of Azerbaijan, the northernmost province of Iran, a wartime arrangement which the Russians seemed ready to make permanent, was terminated in 1946 as a result of American pressure, supported by Britain. The next question, and one which did ruffle the waters, was that of Palestine, held as a British Mandated Territory. Truman kept pressuring the British government to enlarge the permitted flow of Jewish immigrants into Palestine, while

49 Supreme Headquarters, Allied Powers, Europe: the military headquarters of NATO. Then in France, now in Belgium.

50 Eisenhower, *Mandate*, p. 142.

at the same time he kept evading any assumption of American responsibility, either political or economic, for the consequences of such a policy. When the British in disgust resigned the Mandate in 1948 and a sovereign Israel came into being, this particular question disappeared, to be succeeded by the questions raised by the existence of the Israeli state.

The period from 1951 to 1954, overlapping the presidencies of Truman and Eisenhower and the Labour and Conservative governments in England, saw a prolonged British-American hassle caused by the nationalization in 1951 of the Anglo-Iranian Oil Company's facilities by the Iranian administration of the fantastic Dr. Mosadeq. Since it was a British ox that had been gored and not an American, the U.S. government displayed the large-hearted tolerance and understanding it customarily did on such occasions, and kept urging the British to show moderation, patience, and avoid the use of force. The eventual resolution of the prolonged crisis in 1954, after Mosadeq had fallen, was a fairly acceptable compromise. It was particularly acceptable to the United States, because the international consortium which replaced Anglo-Iranian afforded a substantial place for American oil interests. However, in Eden's view this particular matter had turned out well. "At the end of July [1954], the British Government approved the final proposals, which were indeed a remarkable improvement on what might have been expected three years before, when we were out of Abadan with only an indefinite prospect of ever returning there." [51]

On any question concerning Egypt, the American anti-imperialist syndrome led almost automatically to the United States's leaning to the anti-British side. Egypt had technically only been a British colony during the very limited period 1914–1922, but Britain had in fact been the imperial power dominating Egypt since 1882, the British Government was the major shareholder in the Suez Canal Company, and in the early 1950s there were still British troops stationed in Egypt under the treaty of 1936.

[51] Anthony Eden, Earl of Avon, *Full Circle* (Boston: Houghton Mifflin Company, 1960), p. 242.

The U.S. government in the early 1950s put pressure on Britain to recognize King Farouk's claim to be King of the Sudan; the British Government did not believe that the claim of the Anglo-Egyptian condominium to become an independent country, rather than part of Egypt, should be prejudged. The Egyptian monarchy disappeared in the fall of 1952. Eventually, the Sudan opted not to join Egypt, and it became independent on its own on 1 January 1956.

More serious, because it led on to and alone made possible the Egyptian seizure of the Suez Canal, was the fact that Eden allowed himself to be prodded by very heavy American pressure into concluding an agreement with Egypt (19 October 1954) by which British troops were withdrawn from Egypt and the Suez base vacated. Eden was overoptimistic, and perhaps weak, in agreeing to this without achieving much more satisfactory terms.

The agreement contained no provision securing Israeli ships the use of the Canal (which Britain had feebly permitted Egypt to deny them since early 1949), although unrestricted use by ships of *all* nations was guaranteed in the Constantinople Convention of 1888, the basic document on its status. Britain in giving up its base gave up the only lever that it might have used to bring about improved Arab-Israeli relations, with no *quid pro quo* but a vague velleity: "The hope was rather that Anglo-American co-operation, strengthened by the agreements, could work more effectively for improved relations between Israel and the Arab states." "I did not then foresee the extent of Egyptian expansionist aims over other Arab states, nor the growing menace which Egyptian words and acts . . . would later bring upon Israel." [52] Eden might well regret this afterwards; Churchill, who as Prime Minister bore the ultimate responsibility, certainly did. He told his doctor, Lord Moran, in 1958, "I made a great mistake giving in to them when we left the Canal. I feel responsible." [53]

In 1954 and 1955 Britain and the United States were still

---

[52] *Ibid.*, pp. 289, 290.
[53] Lord Moran, *Winston Churchill: The Struggle for Survival, 1940–1965* (London: Constable and Company, 1966), entry for 7 March 1958.

looking for some way to create a Middle East defense organization parallel to NATO. Here, too, Eden ran into a case of U.S. equivocation. When the Baghdad Pact saw the light of day in 1955, Dulles (the inventor of the "Northern Tier" concept which it embodied) refused to join. As Eden saw it, "Having played a leading part to inspire the project, the United States Government held back while Britain joined it, alone of the Western powers. Worse still, they tried to take credit for this attitude in capitals like Cairo, which were hostile to the pact. . . ." [54]

The Suez imbroglio of 1956 exhibited once more all these factors already demonstrated—growing Egyptian ambitions, the enervating British desire always to placate America, the ambiguities and hostilities of Dulles—and brought them to boil in a crisis situation.[55] The crisis was brought on by Dulles, by his pettish rescinding, on 19 July 1956, of the offer to arrange the financing of the proposed Aswan High Dam. The offer had been made at his initiative in December; the dam was to have been financed, partly in loans and partly straight grants, through the World Bank. The money basically was to have been provided by the United States and Britain, in proportions of about three to one. Dulles's refusal of the financing may have been occasioned by Nasser's recognition of Communist China in May 1956, and by his close relations with Russia, though this was not new—the Egyptian-Czechoslovak arms deal had been announced the preceding September.[56] Dulles was indifferent to the fact that there was a hostage to fortune in the shape of the Suez Canal, a valuable piece of Western property now denuded of safeguarding

[54] Eden, *Full Circle*, p. 375.

[55] The main objective here, of course, is to make some comments on Anglo-American relations during the Suez imbroglio, not to give a complete account of it. The best general survey is Hugh Thomas, *Suez* (New York: Harper and Row, 1969). Finer, *Dulles over Suez*, is immensely long and detailed, and at the same time fascinating and appalling in its revelations. It is not so much pro-Eden as anti-Dulles. Reviewers disliked its rhetorical tone, but found it difficult to impugn its facts. Eisenhower's and Eden's own accounts are, of course, indispensable for a complete view. Macmillan's memoirs for this period have not yet appeared.

[56] Finer, *Dulles over Suez*, spends pp. 39–53 discussing all the possible reasons for Dulles's decision.

British troops. What mattered was that it was British, not American—therefore there was no point in paying "black-mail" to save it.[57]

Nasser proclaimed the nationalization of the Canal on 26 July. The rest of the summer and autumn passed in a tedious series of almost entirely bogus diplomatic moves in which Dulles managed to involve Eden without once making it clear exactly where the United States stood—whether it would support Britain if in the end the British took military action, or whether at least it would remain aloof; whether Britain could count upon support from the United States in putting pressure on Egypt short of war, or not. There are good judges who think that the best course for Eden, and the only one that would have achieved success, would have been to move British troops back in *immediately*. Had British troops "been in a position to act at a few days' notice, they could have occupied the Canal Zone with little more than transitory protests from the United States, the United Nations, and the Common-wealth." [58] But after a few years of peace, the British armed forces were naturally in no position to do anything of the kind. They were not ready to act until September, and then there were delays for another couple of months. What was needed was a military action executed with elegance and despatch, in the manner of the U.S. landings in Lebanon in 1958, or the Russian occupation of Czechoslovakia in 1968, and that seemed to be quite beyond Britain—even in November.

Where British public opinion stood in this matter was subject of controversy in 1956, and to some extent still is. On the whole there seems to be good reason to believe that the British military action, when it eventually came, was supported by rather more than half of the British public,[59] though the

57 Dulles said before the Foreign Relations Committee, "We would never have gone through with the plans for the Aswan Dam as a way of getting insurance for the non-seizure of the Suez Canal Company." Finer, p. 53. This is as if Wellington had said, "Publish and be damned," when a blackmailer was threatening to publish something about somebody else, not him.

58 Raymond Dawson and Richard Rosecrance, "Theory and Reality in the Anglo-American Alliance," *World Politics*, October 1966, p. 38.

59 Colin Cross mentions a factor which helps to explain this, and is probably true enough, but which has seldom found its way into print elsewhere:

opposite point of view had more access to the communications media.[60] The American public was not deeply concerned at all.

The British action was not motivated by any desire to strike out on an independent line from the United States—many British people may have wished this, but Eden's government certainly did not—but rather by the fact that "the unreliability—even sterility—of American leadership, at least with reference to British problems in the Middle East, had apparently reached a point of intolerability." [61]

It was not only Dulles that the British had to contend with. Their supposed great and good friend, Eisenhower, well and truly sabotaged any chance of putting pressure on Egypt to achieve a compromise settlement when he announced at a press conference on 4 September that the United States rejected completely and unconditionally any use of force. This occurred during a crucial mission to Cairo by Sir Robert Menzies, Prime Minister of Australia, and the impact of Eisenhower's dictum is best described and commented on in Sir Robert's words:

> This, of course, was, though well and honestly meant by the President, all the encouragement Nasser needed. By expressly and unconditionally excluding force, Presi-

---

"The British . . . regarded the Egyptians as lazy and corrupt, ungrateful for schemes for their benefit. The Egyptians became actual objects of hatred among many of the British soldiers . . . in a manner which happened nowhere else in the British Empire." *The Fall of the British Empire,* p. 105.

[60] It is known that the *Manchester Guardian* suffered a severe loss of readership because of its all-out opposition to Eden's policy. Yet most of these readers who quit reading the paper must have been fairly liberal in opinion or they would not have been reading it in the first place.

[61] Ross Berkes, "The Anglo-American Alliance," *Current History,* May 1964, p. 280. This is a very well-informed, lucid, and useful article. On the ambiguity of U.S. attitudes, notice the letter of 8 September 1956 from Eisenhower to Eden, which is usually cited because it enjoined moderation on the British. It does; but it also includes the sentence, "I assure you we are not blind to the fact that eventually there may be no escape from the use of force." Eisenhower, *Waging Peace 1956–1961* (Garden City, N.Y.: Doubleday and Company, Inc., 1965), p. 670. According to Thomas (*Suez,* p. 72), Eisenhower's original draft of the letter contained a sentence, deleted by Dulles, which reminded Eden that Britain had taken many years to deal with Napoleon. Eisenhower had apparently overlooked that Napoleon was not disposed of by peaceful means.

dent Eisenhower, who, after all, had played a notable part in the use of force as the *ultima ratio* in a great world conflict, gave the final power into the hands of Nasser. . . .

As I said in a message to Canberra, "it is all very well for people to denounce the use of force, but in a negotiation of this kind, it is good sense to keep the other man guessing."

For if force was unconditionally excluded, what had Nasser to do except sit tight, reject the Dulles proposals, reject any watered-down proposals that might be made, and continue the process until he had, in the homely phrase, "written his own ticket"?

I cannot regard it as an element in statesmanship to relieve one's opponent of anxiety. In great matters, nations do not commonly commit themselves in advance, in absolute terms, to anything . . . at a time when silence would have been golden, the President of the United States, by speaking, relieved us of whatever chance—and a very slim chance it was—we had of success.[62]

The Israeli-French-British invasion of Egypt, when it finally occurred, was certainly no military masterpiece on the British side, the chief defect being the preposterous fact that the punch was "telegraphed" for five days before it arrived (1 to 6 November), while the armada was sailing from Malta to Egypt. In a purely military sense, this did not matter. Resistance was negligible. Only twenty-one British soldiers were killed in the whole operation. What mattered was the opportunity for political opposition to crystallize.

Britain encountered the nightmarish situation of being condemned and opposed by both the Soviet Union and the United States. It was the financial pressure on sterling, and particularly the short-selling of sterling on a massive scale by the American authorities in a quite deliberate effort to break the pound, that was decisive, and led to the British acceptance of a cease-fire on 6 November. It was the British, too, who caved in; the French and the Israelis were both more resolute and indifferent to the pressures and threats. Perhaps it would be truer to say it was Eden who caved in, being both meta-

62 Sir Robert Gordon Menzies, *Afternoon Light: Some Memories of Men and Events* (New York: Coward-McCann, Inc., 1968), p. 165–66.

phorically and literally a man of weak stomach. Though hardly James Bond, he left on 23 November to recuperate at Ian Fleming's house in Jamaica. On 9 January 1957 he resigned as Prime Minister, being succeeded by Harold Macmillan.

Scholarly comment on Suez, as the years passed, has veered away from the violent denunciations of Eden that were common in intellectual circles at the time. The British-French-Israeli action now tends to be seen as a desperate endeavor to protect what was seen as a vital interest, an action to which they were driven by the failure of a great ally to lend support in the attempt to reach a settlement by other means. It was the type of action entirely common in an earlier day, and by no means unique in the present epoch.[63] Eden's own summing-up of the matter says:

> The course of the Suez Canal crisis was decided by the American attitude toward it. If the United States Government had approached this issue in the spirit of an ally, they would have done everything in their power, short of the use of force, to support the nations whose economic security depended upon the freedom of passage through the Suez Canal. They would have closely planned their policies with their allies and held stoutly to the decisions arrived at. . . . It is now clear that this was never the attitude of the United States Government. Rather did they try to gain time, coast along over difficulties as they arose and improvise policies, each following on the failure of its immediate predecessor.[64]

This is indeed not very different from, and not quite as harsh as, the judgment passed by Professor Stanley Hoffman of Harvard in his recent magisterial work on American for-

[63] Eden (*Full Circle*, p. 634) mentions one appropriate example: "We could not help contrasting the American attitude now with our own attitude during the Guatemala campaign [1954]. In that country the United States had encouraged the overthrow of a Communist-influenced government, which it considered a menace to the peace of Central America. We had understood her action there and had done what we could not to hamper her in the Security Council. The United States was now behaving in a precisely contrary manner toward us. . . ."

[64] Eden, *Full Circle*, p. 512.

eign policy. Speaking of the "curse" of short-term improvization as a feature of U.S. foreign policy, he says:

> Throughout the summer and early fall of 1956, as a show-
> down on the issue of the Suez Canal approached, Secretary
> Dulles did not alter his dilatory tactics. Strong pressure on
> Egypt . . . might have had results. . . . A statecraft devoted
> to the prevention of any use of force in the resolution of
> the crisis should have striven for serious alternatives to the
> use of force, instead of which Dulles' reluctance to resort
> even to mild forms of coercion seemed to condemn Britain
> and France to a choice between a desperado use of force
> and a humiliating resignation to a *fait accompli.* When
> they chose the former, the United States used the big stick
> at last—*but against Britain, France, and Israel*—and it left
> deep marks.[65]

Debate on Suez, like the classic debate about the Gallipoli
campaign launched by Churchill in the First World War, can
function at two levels. It is possible to argue that the whole
concept was wrong. It is also possible to argue more plausibly
that even if the general concept was right, or excusable, it
was still wrong to undertake it in the circumstances and in
the manner in which it was actually done. Some points belonging to the latter species of criticism have already been
mentioned. Clearly the technical preparation, both military
and economic, was inadequate. Clearly Eden managed to get
off balance in the famous arguments about "collusion"—manifestly, if one is going to do anything with allies, there certainly had better be "collusion"—i.e., advance cooperative
planning; there was some, but perhaps there was not enough.
Finally, it is clearly better not to embark upon something
like the Suez expedition at all, unless one has the stamina
to see it through to the end.

The great reason why the British policy in the Suez matter
is blamed is that it was a failure. Failure always stands self-
condemned, just as success always carries with it some kind

[65] Stanley Hoffman, *Gulliver's Troubles: or the Setting of American Foreign
Policy* (New York: McGraw-Hill Book Company for the Council on Foreign
Relations, 1968), p. 166.

of justification. To adapt a line from Herman Hupfeld's song (once famous as Rudy Vallee's signature tune, and later revived memorably in the film *Casablanca*), "The world will always welcome winners, As time goes by."

But if British policy was a failure, it should not escape notice that American policy was a failure too. To reduce British influence in the Middle East, in order to exalt that of the Egyptian dictator and, more important, of Russia—this was the singular triumph of Dulles and Eisenhower. The bitter fruits have been seen in every subsequent year. The process began early. In 1958 the one genuinely pro-Western and enlightened Arab government of the Middle East, the Nuri-es-Said regime in Iraq, fell, and the monarchy there was destroyed. The full price for American policy in 1956 has yet to be paid by the West. It will be high.

In terms of Anglo-American relations, however, the damage was less grave than anyone at the time supposed possible. Washington was willing to let bygones be bygones. On the British side, Eden's temporary declaration of independence came to be looked on as an aberration. The proposition that Britain *must* stay on good terms with the United States was restored to its place of primacy. Dulles was the only American statesman in two generations who had succeeded in exasperating a British Government into a genuinely independent policy, and it did not last. (The damage done to Franco-American relations was more profound, and more enduring.)

Harold Macmillan, who became Prime Minister in January 1957, was thought of as a stopgap by everyone—except, one suspects, himself. He was to have the longest tenure of the premiership of any man in the postwar period, almost seven years, including the remainder of Eisenhower's time and all but one month of Kennedy's. Relations between the very able Macmillan, a man whose calm and apparently lethargic manner concealed his skillful use and enjoyment of power, and Eisenhower, were excellent from the beginning. Macmillan and Eisenhower, after all, had cooperated more or less amiably for many months on an equal footing during the African campaign. Eisenhower obviously found Macmillan easier to get on with than he did either Churchill or Eden.

They had a pleasant meeting at Bermuda in March 1957. The U.S. administration began to work toward a revision of the Atomic Energy Act in Britain's favor, and this was accomplished in the revised Act of 1958. Under cover of a broad interchange of research information with NATO countries, the new law was really designed to assist Britain's national nuclear program. The legislation laid down the condition that "substantial progress" must already have been made before an allied country could participate in the exchange; an ingenious device whereby only Britain was able to benefit. In this way Britain substantially obtained what it had sought in vain in the period 1946–1950. Military cooperation between the two countries to the exclusion of others was also enhanced in various ways.

The restored good relations between Britain and the United States were symbolized in a way very convenient to Macmillan in the celebrated television broadcast of 31 August 1959, in which he and Eisenhower were seen having a long, friendly chat, dressed in evening clothes, in Downing Street. Two months after this the Conservative party won its third successive victory in a general election. Macmillan also took up again the Churchillian notion of fostering a summit conference —no doubt out of a genuine concern for world peace, but also because it was good politics for him at home, and tended to conceal the decline in Britain's importance. He visited Moscow in February 1959—the first British Prime Minister to do so since the war. "President Eisenhower did not much like it, but wished me good luck." [66] He got as far, eventually, as bringing Khrushchev and Eisenhower together in Paris in May 1960, but the U-2 incident fortuitously occurred and the conference broke up.

With Kennedy, Macmillan's relations were even more friendly and felicitous. Despite the difference in age—Macmillan was twenty-two years older than Kennedy—they had much in common. Both men were profoundly historically-

[66] Macmillan, *Winds of Change*, p. 26.

minded, with a great care and concern for literature and the proper use of language. Their political attitudes were not far apart. Both men instinctively distrusted doctrinaire Left and doctrinaire Right, preferring (in the title of Macmillan's early book) *The Middle Way*. They were also distantly related by marriage, being both connected to the enormously wealthy ducal house of the Cavendishes, Dukes of Devonshire; [67] and Macmillan's mother, like Churchill's, was an American. It is not surprising that, as Sorensen says in his book on Kennedy, Macmillan was the Western leader whom Kennedy liked best, and whom he met oftenest. [68] In Kennedy's too brief thousand days in the presidency, so tragically cut short, the two men met seven times in all, four times in 1961 alone. When Britain made the historic decision in July 1961 to attempt to enter the European Economic Community, it was with Kennedy's full knowledge and approval.

The happy relations of this brief, golden time—which now seems as distant as Tir Nan Og, as legendary as the days of the High Kings of Tara—were cemented by another peculiarly fortunate personal relationship, that between Kennedy and the British ambassador in Washington, David Ormsby-Gore, later Lord Harlech. Ormsby-Gore was British ambassador in Washington from October 1961 to April 1965. He and Kennedy were old friends. Ormsby-Gore was also a remote relative by marriage. [69] It was Kennedy who asked for his appointment to the Washington post. [70]

Kennedy said of Ormsby-Gore, "I trust David as I would my own Cabinet," [71] and he consulted with him with great

---

[67] Macmillan's wife, Lady Dorothy, was the third daughter of the 9th Duke of Devonshire, and aunt of the Marquess of Hartington (eldest son of the 10th Duke), who was married to President Kennedy's sister Kathleen, and who was killed in action with the Coldstream Guards on 10 September 1944. American marriages were not uncommon in the Cavendish family. Macmillan's brother-in-law Lord Charles Cavendish (second son of the 9th Duke) married Adele Astaire, sister and first dancing partner of Fred Astaire.

[68] Theodore C. Sorenson, *Kennedy* (New York: Harper and Row, 1965), p. 558.

[69] Ormsby-Gore's sister Katharine married Macmillan's only son.

[70] Anthony Sampson, *Macmillan* (New York: Simon and Schuster, 1967), p. 210.

[71] Sorenson, *Kennedy*, p. 559.

frequency. This was a parallel to the earlier Franks-Acheson friendship, but this time the British ambassador was the friend not merely of the Secretary of State, but of the President; moreover it was a friendship going back twenty-four years to the time when both had been young men in London. Consultation between Kennedy and Ormsby-Gore was particularly close during the Cuban missile crisis of October 1962. It was Ormsby-Gore, according to Robert Kennedy's memoir of the crisis, who suggested in conversation with the President a modification of American policy that, by allowing the Russians more time to make up their minds, assisted in the resolution of the crisis.[72] Still, this kind of personal liaison with the President was not the same thing as British power having a real effect on the situation. The British press, and to some extent the British people, were disturbed that here was a first-rate crisis whose consequences might well involve Britain, but over whose course Britain had no real influence at all.

The most important meeting between Kennedy and Macmillan was that held at Nassau in the Bahamas in December 1962. The issue here was that of advanced strategic weapons. When Britain in 1957 announced the forthcoming end of conscription (it ended in 1960, making Britain unique among major Western countries in not having compulsory military service) this was coupled with the decision as a kind of presumed counterweight to develop an intermediate-range missile, *Blue Streak*. However, the missile game was one that Britain could really not afford to play, and in 1960 *Blue Streak* was canceled on the ground of prohibitive cost. British reliance on American technology (but also, significantly, American readiness to assist) was underlined by the alternative adopted— the prolongation of the useful life of Britain's V-bomber force by equipping it with the projected U.S. air-to-ground missile, *Skybolt*. Then *Skybolt,* too, was canceled. Kennedy at Nassau felt that there was an obligation to provide an alternative, and the result was the truly remarkable offer, which Macmillan accepted, to sell Polaris missiles to Britain. U.S. Polaris sub-

[72] Robert F. Kennedy, *Thirteen Days: A Memoir of the Cuban Missile Crisis* (New York: Norton and Company, 1969), p. 66–67.

marines were already stationed, by special arrangement with Britain in 1960, at the Holy Loch on the Clyde estuary.

Macmillan had another great achievement to his credit, in a sense of an opposite kind to his Nassau deal. This was the major share he played as an active middleman in bringing about the Partial Nuclear Test-Ban Treaty of 1963. Kennedy handsomely acknowledged this in the letter which he wrote to Macmillan shortly before the latter's resignation due to illness, and his own death. "This morning, as I signed the instrument of ratification of the Nuclear Test Ban Treaty, I could not but reflect on the extent to which your steadiness of commitment and determined perseverance made this treaty possible. Thanks to your never flagging interest, we were ready with our views when the Soviet decided they were ready to negotiate. . . ." [73]

The Test-Ban Treaty was not only Macmillan's last major initiative, it was the last major foreign-policy initiative of the period of Conservative government in Britain. It is hardly too much to say that it is the last event of any real importance in Anglo-American relations, down to the present. In general it is the curious fact that in the seventh decade of the twentieth century international politics fell into a phase of stasis. One is often told that the present is an epoch of unprecedentedly rapid change. It would be equally, or more, plausible to say that in a large sense nothing of any real importance in international politics has occurred for the past ten years. The great questions of 1960—questions such as: Will Britain join the Common Market? Will Communist regimes take over the whole of Indochina? Will Israel survive, and if so within what frontiers? Will NATO survive? Will Communist China ever rejoin the community of nations?—these are still, oddly enough, the great questions of 1970. Most existing problems have become a little worse, but not to the point of serious international explosion. Nor, clearly, have they been solved.

The period 1962–1964 was a phase of transition in Anglo-

[73] Sampson, *Macmillan,* p. 219.

American affairs, in several senses. Kennedy was replaced by Johnson, who entirely lacked Kennedy's special feeling for England and special contacts with eminent Englishmen, and he by Nixon, of whom almost the same might be said. In England, there came about an inward-turning mood, an amalgam of frustration and frivolity. From 1957 to 1962, Macmillan had had extraordinarily good luck. After that, apart from the Nassau agreement and the Test-Ban Treaty, he and his successor, Sir Alec Douglas-Home, had hardly any luck at all. Domestic scandals concerning spying and sex proliferated, Acheson's West Point speech in December 1962 touched a raw nerve, de Gaulle's veto in January 1963 of British entry to the European Economic Community set British policy all aback with, for the moment, no place to go; the result of all this, and of other factors such as bad trade figures, was a national mood of self-doubt and frustration, not common in Britain. It prepared the way for the Labour party's general election victory of the next year. It found memorable expression in the July 1963 number of *Encounter,* a symposium of articles from various angles on Britain's plight under the general title *Suicide of a Nation?* All this was ridiculously exaggerated, of course, like most intellectual fashions. Seven years later, not very much had changed, but Britain was as alive as ever, most people there were a little more prosperous, and the Tories were back in Downing Street.

There were changes, all the same. The British man-in-the-street, and his masters, Conservative or Labour, in Downing Street, were gradually becoming accustomed to the idea that Britain was going to play a more modest role in the world in future. The army and navy were both being run down to the point where good judges thought the government had slipped into the fallacy—normal to British governments in peacetime—of assuming blithely that Britain would never be involved in another war. The Royal Navy, long a very poor third to the U.S. Navy (very large, but with replacement of ships inadequately financed in these years) and the growing and almost brand-new Soviet Navy, was in danger of losing

even that place to France. The British army was being run
down to a meager level. The eminent military historian Correlli Barnett wrote in 1970:

> after the Labour government's reorganizations, the re-
> serves were weaker than they had been for a hundred
> years—far weaker than in 1914 or 1939. . . .

Like others, and they were many, who did not see nuclear
weapons as a panacea (for, after all, many wars had been
fought since 1945, and none of them with nuclear weapons)
Barnett saw this policy as no more than

> a novel version of all the ancient heresies by which British
> governments had for centuries deluded themselves that
> there was no need to organize in peacetime the kind of
> armed forces that British involvement in Europe since the
> days of Elizabeth I had repeatedly shown we needed.[74]

In January 1968 Wilson made the historic announcement
that by 1971 British military and naval establishments East
of Suez would be withdrawn. This was looked upon, justly,
as the end of an era in British history—"the end of an auld
sang," as an eminent Scot said when the Scottish parliament
adjourned for the last time in 1707. It was true, indeed, that
when Edward Heath came into office with a Conservative Government in June 1970, he announced that this ultimate resignation of Britain's world role would not be carried through.
Nevertheless, it was quite unlikely that Britain's military presence in Singapore or elsewhere round the Indian Ocean perim-
eter—once, in essence, a British lake—would, in the future,
be other than a token presence of very small numbers. Even
so, the announcement was a very welcome one in Washington.

In the United States, the great theme of the late 1960s is
the growing involvement in the Vietnam War, an unrewarding
and amorphous struggle on the mainland of Asia. British involvement here was minimal. Harold Wilson in general supported the United States's large-scale commitment to the war
in 1965, but no British military help was sent as it had been

[74] Correlli Barnett, *Britain and Her Army, 1509—1970* (London: Allen
Lane, 1970), pp. 493—94.

in Korea, and Wilson dissociated himself in 1966 from the U.S. bombing of military targets in North Vietnam. During Kosygin's visit to London in February 1967 Wilson made a vigorous attempt to play the Churchill-Macmillan role of honest broker between the two world giants, but despite some momentary hope of success it came to nothing.

For the United States the Vietnam War had various unfortunate effects. It created serious divisions of opinion in American society. Also, it distracted American attention from areas which were, in fact, more vital. After the failure of the complicated MLF project for the sharing of nuclear arms with NATO allies, an abortive negotiation that occurred in the late Kennedy and early Johnson days, the United States virtually ceased to have a European policy. It followed, as a corollary, that it had no particular policy toward Britain. Perhaps more serious was the fact that it had no particular policy in the Middle East beyond expressions of the hope that everyone would start behaving reasonably in a part of the world where almost no one had ever done so; a part of the world, however, where—unlike Indochina—the stakes were real and the risk enormous.

In the United States, as in Britain, the later 1960s saw a turning inward, but obviously such a development in the case of the United States was fraught with more serious consequences for America's allies than was the attitude of Britain. In the United States, indeed, many groups in society exhibited an almost frantic isolationism. This mood held possibilities that European opinion had feared, unnecessarily, in 1945. In 1970, there was an ominous chance that the fears might be more justified.

American prestige was also damaged by the reawakening of the suspicion, never very deep asleep in European breasts, that American society is essentially unstable and that therefore the United States cannot be looked to for long-term leadership. But it was equally possible that this judgment exaggerated the importance of temporary and local phenomena.

Chapter Seven

ENVOI:
What Future Has the Past?

It Appears possible that in the fairly near future the British application to join the European Economic Community may succeed. De Gaulle has gone, and negotiations recommenced in the summer of 1970. If such a development happens, it would certainly imply some modification in the pattern of Anglo-American relations. It is customary to go beyond this, and to say that the time has come for a final decision in Britain between the New World orientation and the European, between maintaining a special relationship with the United States, and becoming a genuine and full partner in a European union.

This choice, if it had to be made and if it were made in this way, would indeed mark a very definite climacteric in the national life and policy of Britain. An endeavor to keep various options open, to demonstrate a certain "swithering" (to use a good Scots word) [1] between what might be called "oceanic" and "Continental" policies, has been characteristic British behavior since at any rate the close of the Middle Ages. In the post-1945 world it has been customary to phrase this by saying that Britain stands in the common area of three concentric circles—Europe, the Commonwealth, and the

[1] "Swithering" (to hesitate between possible choices) means what most English people *think* "havering" means. "Havering" actually means to talk nonsense.

special Anglo-American grouping, and that British policy must accommodate to this triple connection. This way of envisaging the problem is now passé; it has become tedious through repetition, and it served too much down to 1961 as an excuse for the avoidance of thought and of clarity in policy-formation. Besides, the Commonwealth has ceased to be a factor of any importance in the scales. The other two broad alternatives, however, remain.

It is possible that in the next few years some such deliberate choice will have to be made. However, it is easy to exaggerate how hard-and-fast such a choice will have to be. One may speak of it as a crossroads, but metaphors mislead. It may be a matter of selecting a major and a minor emphasis rather than choosing a road. Life seldom fits into the neat patterns of theory, and it is unlikely that Britain can or will be forced to make a clear and final choice between special links with the New World and the obvious, and perhaps pending, Continental relationship with Europe. The Common Market is not now, and may perhaps never become, a body for creating a common foreign policy. Membership in it would not keep Britain from continuing to try to align her policy as closely as possible with that of the United States. Would membership in EEC keep British students and scholars from spending some of their years in American universities, or from reading American books? It would and could do nothing to undermine that special closeness which is in the Anglo-American heritage.

It is also quite possible that the EEC negotiations will fail. If they do so, all is not lost for Britain. The Common Market has in recent years been developing a number of individual trading relationships by treaty with particular countries. Such an arrangement with Britain would be a possibility.

Failure of EEC negotiations for Britain might also be the occasion to attempt to breathe life into the project for a North Atlantic Free Trade Area (NAFTA)—an enlargement of EFTA which would include the United States.[2] This idea is

2 On NAFTA see Harry Johnson, ed., *New Trade Strategies for the World Economy* (London: Allen and Unwin, 1969).

beginning to generate some powerful support and would certainly have greater attractions for some British businessmen and economists than EEC.

These are matters of middle-range concern. Peering into the more distant future, still more remote long-term possibilities haunt the imagination. One is a federated Europe, with Britain a member. Another is a reunion of the British and American peoples, in effect an undoing of 1776. It is, perhaps, significant how very many people who have spent part of their life on either side of the Atlantic have been seized of this vision. The late C. S. Forester, the eminent English novelist and, in his later years, resident of Berkeley, California, in a long piece of semi-fiction, semi-essay, sketched how the constitutional problems of such a union were solved in the aftermath of some unidentified common disaster.[3] George W. Ball, the distinguished Undersecretary of State under both Presidents Kennedy and Johnson, went so far in 1965, "at a particularly discouraging point in Anglo-European relations," as to ask his staff to draw up a contingency plan for the reunion of the English-speaking peoples, although

> I never submitted it either to the Secretary of State or the President, since it would, I concluded, create more problems than it would solve. Yet the idea should not go unmentioned, for similar proposals have been suggested in both the British press and the American press, and until Britain joins Europe these possibilities will continue to hold attractions.[4]

The hostile and pejorative way to refer to projects of this kind is to say that they advocate Britain's becoming "the Fifty-First State." This is nonsense, of course; a federal system is built up of modules, and it can easily be extended to any extent

[3] This piece, about 12,000 words long, was written in the late 1950s. I read it at the author's invitation. It has never been published. It perhaps says something about Anglo-American relations that though in those years the *Saturday Evening Post* bought first serial rights for almost everything that Forester wrote, they would not touch this.

[4] George W. Ball, *The Discipline of Power: Essentials of a Modern World Structure* (Boston: Little, Brown, 1968), p. 110. The discussion of the possibility in Ball is of great interest.

that is appropriate, as the American Union in fact has been extended time and again as new states were added. If Anglo-American union were ever to come about, the equitable arrangement would be that the United Kingdom should constitute some thirteen additional states, and be represented by twenty-six Senators and an appropriate number of Congressmen.[5] As Stanley Baldwin said of such a vision in a speech at the Albert Hall in May 1935, "It may be a hundred years before that desirable end may be attained. It may never come to pass. But sometimes we may have our dreams."

A third possibility, which does not entirely exclude the one just discussed, is that of some form of political union embracing both Britain and the United States, and the democracies of Western Europe—or, for that matter, of Eastern Europe, if the Communist Empire there should ever dwindle. This was the project which was passionately and skillfully urged by Clarence Streit in a once-famous book published just before the outbreak of war in 1939, *Union Now.* The proposal was revived, essentially, in a book published in 1960 by Professor H. C. Allen, one of the most learned students of international relations in the North Atlantic area. He advocated what he called Atlantic Union:

> Those nations which lie on the seaboard of the North Atlantic all share in the Western heritage. Europe was the father of Western civilization, but the new worlds are equally its heirs. British Australasia is a vital bastion of the Atlantic peoples on the other side of the globe: America is blood and mind of the West. Britain, with her unique geographical position and her vital connections with distant corners of the earth, is best fitted to act as the link between the old world of Europe and the two new worlds across the seas. None of these four constituent parts of Western civilization can long continue now to thrive fully, except in intimate and integral association with the others. . . .[6]

[5] Other appropriate arrangements in proportion to population could be made for Ireland, for Canada, and indeed for Australia and New Zealand.

[6] H. C. Allen, *The Anglo-American Predicament: The British Commonwealth, The United States and European Unity* (London: Macmillan and Co., Ltd., 1960), pp. 233–34.

It is, of course, conceivable to have a closer Anglo-American union within a larger North Atlantic Union. Such projects may seem chimerical. They may seem, in Milton's words, to "sequester out of the world, into *Atlantic* and *Utopian* polities. . . ." But, as Professor Karl Deutsch has so ably demonstrated to us, political communities come into being when the precedent conditions are ripe for them, and conditions change; the one thing we know about history is that it is not static. The national sovereign state is not the final, supreme form of human political organization. Before 1939, the coming into existence of anything like the European Economic Community, with supra-national features and authority—even though these are still at an early stage of development—would have seemed quite impossible to most observers.

If we turn from these long-term possibilities to the more immediate future, considerations of an entirely different order are appropriate. For almost the first time in their mutual relations, Britain has something to offer which the United States wants—some continued British activity as a world power, a sharing in some small measure of responsibility with the United States. The advent of the Heath government affords a possibility that something may be made of this. There is also encouragement to be found in the recovery of economic health which Britain seemed to be achieving at long last as the century's seventh decade neared its end.[7] Britain's fundamental problem is economic; the path to gaining or maintaining political power and influence lies for her through economic strength—as it always has done.

When Prime Minister Wilson visited President Nixon in the spring of 1970—for the last time, as it was to prove— the press and the weekly journals were heavy with ponderous obituaries on the passing of the "special relationship." But these reports of death may be, as Mark Twain said when he

[7] Since one counts a century (of anything) from 1 to 100 and not from 0 to 99, the century began on 1 January 1901 and its seventh decade ends on 31 December 1970. This simple truth is ignored every ten years by every journalist and commentator who would rather get in a year ahead of the game than be correct.

read his own, exaggerated. Those who know most are the most cautious in expressing such an opinion. Messrs. Dawson and Rosecrance, in a profound article in *World Politics,* differed from the negative view sharply, saying, "That alliance is ordinarily set apart as a 'special relationship' as indeed it is, but it is still an alliance, the most durable and most influential of the nuclear age." [8] And a recent writer in *Foreign Affairs* has made a very relevant point: "Treaties of alliance are overvalued. . . . Where identity of interest exists between the parties, a treaty usually is not necessary; where it does not exist, often a treaty is not kept." [9] This is the essence of the matter. The Anglo-American partnership, which is unique, rests on a perceived common interest over a large, though not universal, range of questions, and that, in turn, is firmly based on history, tradition, and affinity. Without such grounds, treaties are but words; but such grounds exist, and will endure.

[8] Raymond Dawson and Richard Rosecrance, "Theory and Reality in the Anglo-American Alliance," *World Politics,* October 1966, pp. 21–22.

[9] David Fromkin, "Entangling Alliances," *Foreign Affairs,* July 1970, p. 689.

Index